ADVANCE PRAISE fo

"Cheng takes us through a systematic re-working of the classical doctrines of sin and grace, and lands us in a place where, surprisingly, these ideas can once again sing with life for Christian LGBTQ persons. It's a serious and splendid book."

—Serene Jones, President and Roosevelt Professor of Systematic Theology,
Union Theological Seminary in New York City

"This gifted theologian and teacher offers an accessible and compelling case for why LGBT persons (and others) need to take back the words 'sin' and 'grace.' Be forewarned: reading Cheng is likely to stretch your theological and moral imagination, but all to the good."

—Marvin M. Ellison, Willard S. Bass Professor of Christian Ethics,
Bangor Theological Seminary; author of
Making Love Just: Sexual Ethics for Perplexing Times and co-editor of
Sexuality and the Sacred: Sources for Theological Reflection, 2nd edition

"Patrick Cheng has given the Christian church and the theological academy a precious gift. Cheng's work ranks among the best scholarship of a new generation of theologians. I have experienced more amazing grace—and grown more mature theologically—because of this book."

—Tat-siong Benny Liew,
Vice President for Academic Affairs and Dean,
and Professor of New Testament,
Pacific School of Religion

"Cheng provides our hurting community with a healing theology; an accessible christology which celebrates an open and affirming Christianity desperately needed by most of our churches. This book is good news for all who are queer, as well as for those who are not!"

—Miguel A. De La Torre, Professor of Social Ethics and
Latino/a Studies, Iliff School of Theology;
2012 President of the Society of Christian Ethics

"'Christ is the treasure hidden in the scriptures,' wrote Irenaeus, the second century theologian. Christ *is* the treasure, and Cheng's work is a treasure map of LGBT advances in theology that helps us find, once again, that God loves all of us and wants us to be free."

—Rev. Dr. Susan Brooks Thistlethwaite, Professor of Theology and former president, Chicago Theological Seminary; blogger for the *Washington Post*; and prolific writer, author, and editor, including co-editor of *Lift Every Voice: Constructing Christian Theologies from the Underside*

"Patrick Cheng has produced a much-needed pastoral book for LGBTIQ and, in fact, all Christians. This is a remarkable theological and pastoral exploration that can help individual Christians and congregations to re-align their spiritual development."

—Rev. Dr. Robert E. Shore-Goss, Senior Pastor/Theologian, MCC in the Valley, North Hollywood; author of *Jesus Acted Up* and *Queering Christ*

"The act of reading Patrick Cheng's Christ-centered theology of sin and grace offers both healing pastoral care and political empowerment. Christians who have been wounded, alienated, or simply befuddled by the ongoing use of Christianity to further heterosexist hate and disenfranchisement have been waiting for this book."

—Traci C. West, Professor of Ethics and African American Studies, Drew University Theological School; author of *Disruptive Christian Ethics: When Racism and Women's Lives Matter*

From Sin to Amazing Grace

Discovering the Queer Christ

PATRICK S. CHENG

Seabury Books
NEW YORK

Cover design by Laurie Klein Westhafer

Typeset by Denise Hoff

Library of Congress Cataloging-in-Publication Data

Cheng, Patrick S.
From sin to amazing grace : discovering the queer Christ / Patrick S. Cheng.
p. cm.
Includes bibliographical references and index.
ISBN 978-1-59627-238-5 (pbk.) -- ISBN 978-1-59627-239-2 (ebook) 1. Sin. 2. Grace.
3. Jesus Christ--Persons and offices. 4. Homosexuality--Religious aspects--Christianity. I. Title.
BT715.C446 2012

230.086'64--dc23

2011048065

Seabury Books

445 Fifth Avenue

New York, New York 10016

www.churchpublishing.org

An imprint of Church Publishing Incorporated

5 4 3 2 1

To the grace-filled community
of the Episcopal Divinity School

Through many dangers, toils, and snares,
I have already come;
'Tis grace that brought me safe thus far,
And grace will lead me home.

—John Newton, "Amazing Grace" (1779)

Contents

Acknowledgments

I would like to thank the faculty, staff, students, trustees, and alumni/ae of the Episcopal Divinity School for their support and for providing an amazingly grace-filled environment for the writing of this book. In particular, I would like to express my appreciation for my faculty colleagues Angela Bauer-Levesque, Christopher Duraisingh, Miriam Gelfer, Bill Kondrath, Kwok Pui-lan, Joan Martin, Katherine Hancock Ragsdale, Ed Rodman, Susie Snyder, Fredrica Harris Thompsett, Larry Wills, and Gale Yee, as well as Aura Fluett, our superb reference librarian.

I also would like to thank my various colleagues in the academy and the church who have read, heard, and/or commented on previous versions of this work, including Rebecca Alpert, Ellen Armour, Tom Bohache, Kent Brintnall, James Cone, Miguel De La Torre, Kelly Brown Douglas, Christopher Duraisingh, Noach Dzmura, Marvin Ellison, Orlando Espín, Darlene Garner, Beverly Harrison, Carter Heyward, Candy Holmes, Mark Jordan, Kwok Pui-lan, Joan Martin, Kerri Mesner, Christopher Morse, Jim Mulcahy, Kate Ott, Christine Pae, Cameron Partridge, Axel Schwaigert, Bob Shore-Goss, Susie Snyder, Ken Stone, Linn Tonstad, Traci West, Heather White, Mel White, and Dave Woodyard. I especially would like to thank Susannah Cornwall, Megan Defranza, Thomas Eoyang, Ashley Harness, Jill Johnson, Catherine Owens, and Sue Spilecki for their detailed comments on various draft manuscripts.

This book also has benefitted from the valuable comments of the participants at my 2010 job talk at the Episcopal Divinity School; the staff and participants of the 2010 summer seminar on sexuality and religion at Emory University; the staff and participants of the 2010 Human Rights Campaign Summer Institute at Vanderbilt Divinity School; the participants in my workshop at the 2010 Metropolitan Community Churches General Conference in Acapulco, Mexico; the participants and attendees at the book panel for the second edition of *Sexuality and the Sacred* at the 2010 American Academy of Religion annual meeting; the students in the spring 2011 christology seminar taught by Cameron Partridge at the Harvard Divinity School; the students in my spring 2011 christology course and my June 2011 queer theology and pastoral care course at the Episcopal Divinity School; the attendees in my plenary talk at the 2011 People of African Descent conference in Washington, DC; the attendees at the 2011 Pride Evensong at the Church of Saint Luke in the Fields in New York City; and the students in the fall 2011 social ethics course and the fall 2011 theology course at Denison University.

I am grateful for the ongoing support of my colleagues in the Emerging Queer Asian Religion Scholars group: Mike Campos, Joe Goh, Elizabeth Leung, Hugo Córdova Quero, Miak Siew, and Lai Shan Yip. I am also grateful for the encouragement of various other friends and wise folk, including Faith Cantor, Kitt Cherry, Mary Beth Clack, Clayton Crawley, Louie Crew, Jon Eden, Diane Fisher, Sharon Groves, Mary Hunt, Michael Kelly, Kim Leary, Gina Masequesmay, Mary McKinney, Su Pak, Amy Revell, Joe Robinson, Sam Rodman, Roger Sneed, Chris Sosa, Geoffrey Tristram, Renee Ward, Mona West, Nancy Wilson, and the community of Christ Church Cambridge.

I would like to thank my wonderful editor at Seabury Books, Davis Perkins, and his talented editorial, production, and marketing team, including Mark Dazzo, Bill Falvey, Ryan Masteller, Deirdre Morrissey, Lillian Ort, and Laurie Westhafer. I am also grateful for the board of Church Publishing Incorporated and its chair, Ran Chase.

Last but certainly not least, I am grateful for the unwavering love and support of my husband and life partner of two decades, Michael Boothroyd; our puppy, Chartres; our extended families, including my mom Deanna, my brother Andy, my sister-in-law Abi, and my nephews Jordan and Noah; and my friends in cyberspace as well as in the real world. Of course, all editorial sins—in thought, word, or deed—remain mine alone.

—P.S.C.

Introduction

I first learned that I was a sinner in junior high school. Struggling to understand my budding attraction to other boys, I turned to my local public library for help. Being a devout Roman Catholic, I found a reference book on Catholic doctrine, and I furtively turned to the entry on "homosexuality." There I learned—to my horror—that I was not only a sinner, but that I was intrinsically disordered.[1] I shut the book in shame, and my relationship with God was never again the same.

It took another fifteen years—and a good dose of God's amazing grace—before I was able to walk into a church out of love and not fear. In those intervening years, I had met and fallen in love with my now-husband, Michael. Through Michael, I had experienced the power of God's incarnational love in a way that no theology book or doctrine could ever convey. Because of the grace of this relationship—that is, a relationship that was a pure gift from God and not something that I had "earned" or "deserved"—my eyes and ears were opened once more to the Good News.

Given the traumatic experiences of so many lesbian, gay, bisexual, and transgender ("LBGT") people—including myself—with respect to the doctrines of sin and grace, why do we need an entire book on this topic? Wouldn't queer[2] people be better off by just ignoring this topic altogether? Haven't we had enough of hateful so-called preachers screaming that "God Hates Fags" and ranting that our country will be destroyed by God if we continue to accept so-called abominations such as same-sex marriage? Do we really need to describe ourselves as "wretches" whenever we sing the hymn "Amazing Grace"?[3]

---

[1] See *Catechism of the Catholic Church*, 2nd ed. (Washington, DC: United States Catholic Conference, 1997), § 2357, at 566 (describing same-sex acts as "acts of grave depravity" and "intrinsically disordered").

[2] In this book, I use the term "queer" as an umbrella term—like "LGBT"—to describe people who identify themselves as being outside the societal norm with respect to sexuality or gender identity. That is, I use "queer" as a shorthand notion for lesbian, gay, bisexual, transgender, intersex, queer, questioning, two-spirited, and same-gender-loving people, as well as our allies. For more about the various uses of the word "queer" in a theological context, see Patrick S. Cheng, *Radical Love: An Introduction to Queer Theology* (New York: Seabury Books, 2011), 2–8.

[3] See John Newton, "Amazing Grace" (1779) ("Amazing grace! How sweet the sound,/that saved a wretch like me!"). Some contemporary versions of the hymn have replaced the word "wretch" with "soul," or otherwise changed the opening verse.

I strongly believe that now, more than ever, it is critical for LGBT people to address the issues of sin and grace head-on. Instead of ignoring or running away from this issue, it is time that we reclaim these doctrines for ourselves, much in the same way that we've reclaimed the word "queer" in recent decades. This book is the result of many years of trying to reconcile my experiences as an out, proud, gay man on the one hand, and a systematic theologian, theology teacher, and ordained minister on the other.[4] Indeed, my life's vocation as a queer theologian has been largely an attempt to make sense of that day back in junior high school when my queerness and my Christian faith first collided in the local public library.

In Part I of this book, I argue that we must move from a *crime-based* model to a *Christ-centered* model of sin and grace. The traditional understanding of sin and grace in Western Christianity has centered on notions of crime and punishment. As inheritors of the theological legacy of Augustine of Hippo, we have come to understand sin as a crime. That is, sin is a violation of God's laws, whether biblical or natural, and thus it demands punishment. As the story goes, the original offense committed by our first parents Adam and Eve in the Garden of Eden—that is, their eating of the forbidden fruit—was such an egregious crime that all of subsequent humanity has been punished with death as well as the "infection" or "taint" of original sin. As a result of this primal fall, we are damaged and unable to do any good on our own accord. To remedy this sad state of affairs, God sent Jesus Christ to redeem humanity because only a being who is both human *and* divine could rectify (that is, "atone" or "pay the price" for) such an egregious wrong. Grace, then, is God's *acquittal* of our crime and our *rehabilitation* so that we will no longer sin again.

We need to move away from this traditional crime-based model and towards a *Christ-centered*, or christological, model of sin and grace. Instead of understanding sin as a crime that needs to be punished, we need to understand sin as *immaturity* or incomplete growth, much in the same way that children and adolescents—and even adults!—make mistakes in the course of growing up. Simply

---

[4] For an earlier, essay-length version of this work, see Patrick S. Cheng, "Rethinking Sin and Grace for LGBT People Today," in *Sexuality and the Sacred: Sources for Theological Reflection*, ed. Marvin M. Ellison and Kelly Brown Douglas, 2nd ed. (Louisville, KY: Westminster/John Knox Press, 2010), 105–18.

put, we mess up because we are human beings who have not yet arrived at our final state of maturity. This view of sin and grace is a Christ-centered model because our ultimate goal, or *telos*, is to be made divine in the image of Christ. Christ is not only the Alpha (that is, the source of our creation), but Christ is also the Omega (that is, the ultimate goal of our existence).[5] Grace, therefore, can be understood as *becoming divine*. This is not a new concept; it is grounded in the writings of the early church theologian Irenaeus of Lyons as well as the Eastern Orthodox doctrine of *theōsis*, or deification.

In other words, we are called to move from an Augustinian model—in which sin and grace are understood respectively as *crime* and *acquittal*—to an Irenaean model in which sin and grace are understood respectively as *immaturity* and *becoming divine*. That is, instead of relying primarily on vice lists and viewing the Bible as a book of rules, we are challenged to interpret the gospel in light of our relationship with Jesus Christ, particularly as understood through the lens of our own social contexts. As Paul wrote in his letter to the Galatians, it is time that we leave behind a "disciplinarian" or legalistic model of sin and grace, and embrace a more spiritually mature—and challenging—model of sin and grace in which we are constantly "clothed" with Christ.[6]

In Part II of this book, I draw upon the Christ-centered model of sin and grace by proposing seven models of Jesus Christ as described by various LGBT theologians. In the same way that various identity groups since the 1960s have written about Jesus Christ from their own social location and contexts (for example, African American theologians have written about the Black Christ), LGBT theologians have engaged in christological reflection and written about the Queer Christ. The seven models of the Queer Christ are:

(1) The Erotic Christ;

(2) The Out Christ;

(3) The Liberator Christ;

(4) The Transgressive Christ;

(5) The Self-Loving Christ;

---

[5] Rev. 22:13. That is, we were chosen in Christ "before the foundation of the world," and all things will be gathered up in Christ in the "fullness of time." Eph. 1:4, 10. (All references to the Bible in this book are from the New Revised Standard Version unless otherwise specified.)

[6] Gal. 3:24–25, 27.

(6) The Interconnected Christ; and

(7) The Hybrid Christ.

Drawing upon the Christ-centered model of sin and grace, I define sin as that which is opposed to each of these models of the Queer Christ, and grace as that which helps us to grow and be conformed to each of these models. Thus, I propose the following seven new deadly sins and seven new amazing graces[7] in the context of the seven models of the Queer Christ:

(1) Sin as exploitation, grace as mutuality;

(2) Sin as the closet, grace as coming out;

(3) Sin as apathy, grace as activism;

(4) Sin as conformity, grace as deviance;

(5) Sin as shame, grace as pride;

(6) Sin as isolation, grace as interdependence; and

(7) Sin as singularity, grace as hybridity.

Each chapter of this book ends with study questions as well as suggestions for further reading. As such, this book can be used in a number of contexts, ranging from undergraduate and graduate classes to parish and congregational adult education programs. This book also can be used by those people—whether or not religious—who are interested in responding thoughtfully to the legalistic view of sin as articulated by the religious right. In sum, I strongly believe that a Christ-centered model of sin and grace is a much more helpful way of thinking about such issues for LGBT Christians and allies—as well as any others who have been hurt by such doctrines in the past.

1. Intended Audience

This book is written from my perspective as an openly gay theologian, and I have written it primarily with my LGBT Christian siblings—as well as our straight and cisgender allies[8]—in

[7] For seven "sinful problems" and seven "virtuous possibilities" in the realm of sexual ethics, see James B. Nelson, "Where Are We?: Seven Sinful Problems and Seven Virtuous Possibilities," in Ellison and Douglas, *Sexuality and the Sacred*, 95–104.

[8] The term "cisgender" refers to non-transgender people in the same way that "straight" refers to non-LGBT people. For a helpful glossary of transgender terms, see Fenway Health, "Glossary of Gender and Transgender Terms" (January 2010), available at http://www.fenwayhealth.org/site/DocServer/Handout_7-C_Glossary_of_Gender_and_Transgender_Terms__fi.pdf?docID=7081 (accessed on December 11, 2011).

mind. Specifically, I have written this book for those who, like me, have struggled deeply with the doctrines of sin and grace, and especially because such doctrines have often been used by the Christian right as a means of theological queer-bashing and not healing.

I believe, however, that this book has great relevance not just to LGBT people, but to *anyone* who has struggled with making sense of traditional doctrines of sin and grace. As feminist theologians and philosophers like Valerie Saiving, Mary Daly, Judith Plaskow, and Rosemary Ruether have pointed out, such doctrines historically have been shaped by men, and they have been used to subjugate and harm women, particularly to the extent that Eve (and, by implication, all women) has been blamed for the fall and original sin. Similarly, African Americans and other communities of color have been literally enslaved by the biblical narratives about the sin of Ham and curse of Canaan.

Thus, even though this book focuses on sin and grace from the experience of LGBT people, it is my hope and expectation that other people—whether in the classroom, congregation, or other communities—will find aspects of the book helpful in their own specific contexts. Although theology always arises out of a particular context, good theology can and must speak to universal issues and broader audiences. Historically speaking, Christian theology always has been shaped by the broader political, economic, and cultural contexts in which it is written. Indeed, we have become much more aware of the contextual nature of theology as a result of the rise of Latin American, black, feminist, and other liberation theologies in the late 1960s and early 1970s.

Perhaps those outside of the LGBT community might consider whether moving from a crime-based to a Christ-centered model of sin and grace is also helpful for their own specific communities and contexts. They may find it useful to discover similarities as well as differences with respect to the seven models of the Queer Christ, as well as the seven new deadly sins and seven new amazing graces that are described in this book. These models are not intended to limit, but rather to broaden the theological imagination. In other words, I hope that they can be a starting point, or window, into each of our own unique experiences.

2. Some Definitions

It is important to say a few words about the terminology used in the book. In general, I use the term "LGBT" as a shorthand for the lesbian, gay, bisexual, and transgender community as a whole. In general, lesbians are women who are primarily sexually attracted to other women. Gays are men who are primarily sexually attracted to other men, although sometimes the term "gay" is also used to include lesbians. Bisexuals are people who are sexually attracted to both sexes. And transgender people are individuals who identify with and/or express themselves in terms of a gender identity (for example, masculine gender) that is different than the biological sex that was assigned to them at birth (for example, female sex). Although these various terms can be helpful in terms of categorizing people, most gender and queer theorists believe that sexuality and gender identity categories are ultimately fluid—not fixed—concepts.[9]

Although I use the term "LGBT" as an umbrella term throughout this book, I want to make sure that I do not minimize or downplay the differences and diversity *within* the LGBT community by using a single term. Sexual orientation (that is, the "LGB") is a different issue than gender identity (that is, the "T"). The former category is about one's sexual attraction to women, men, or both sexes. The latter category is about how one identifies and/or expresses oneself within the gender continuum of masculine to feminine. Thus, a man can be gay (that is, he is sexually attracted to other men) but not transgender (that is, he identifies with his assigned birth sex of male). Or a person can be a trans woman (that is, she currently identifies with a gender identity of feminine that is different than her assigned birth sex of male) but not lesbian (that is, she is sexually attracted to other men). Furthermore, there is also a category of intersex, which denotes individuals who are born with reproductive or sexual anatomy—that is, chromosomes, hormone levels, genitals, and/or secondary sex characteristics—that "doesn't seem to fit the typical definitions

---

[9] For example, as queer theorists have argued, the categories of homosexuality and heterosexuality (that is, classifying people on the basis of the sex of their preferred sex partners) did not arise until the nineteenth century. That is, in ancient times, people were often classified on the basis of whether they were tops (that is penetrators) or bottoms (that is, penetrated), regardless of the sex of one's partner or partners. For a sex-positive refutation of the essentialist or "born that way" argument about homosexuality, see Janet R. Jakobsen and Ann Pellegrini, *Love the Sin: Sexual Regulation and the Limits of Religious Tolerance* (New York: New York University Press, 2003).

of female or male."[10] Notwithstanding these complexities, I do use the broad term "LGBT" to denote those individuals who do not fit within conventional societal norms of sexuality, gender identity, and/or biological sex.[11]

I also use the word "queer" in a number of different ways throughout this book. First, I use the word "queer" also as a shorthand—or, in some cases, as a synonym—for the umbrella term "LGBT." In some ways, however, "queer" is even more inclusive than "LGBT" because it also makes room for intersex, questioning, two-spirit, same-gender-loving, and other sexual or gender nonconforming individuals, as well as allies. Second, I use the word "queer" as a shorthand way of referring to practices that intentionally transgress or oppose the societal norm. For example, to "queer" something is to read it or interpret it in a non-normative or unexpected way, particularly with respect to issues of sexuality or gender identity. Thus, to "queer" religion is to lift up the voices or memories of marginalized people—including, but not limited to, LGBT people—who have been silenced by dominant religious traditions. Third, I use the word "queer" to describe the academic discipline of queer theory, which focuses on the deconstruction, or collapsing, of binaries such as male/female, masculine/feminine, and heterosexual/homosexual.[12] Sometimes "Q" is included in the LGBT acronym (that is, "LGBTQ") to include queer people.

Since the early 1990s, the LGBT community has reclaimed and embraced the word "queer." That is, the LGBT community has taken a word that was originally viewed as a highly offensive slur and transformed it into a positive description of the incredible diversity and transgressivity that is within the community. This has been the case not only with LGBT activist groups such as Queer Nation, which coined the slogan "We're Here, We're Queer, Get Used to It!," but also within the academy with respect to queer theory and queer studies. Even LGBT communities of faith

---

[10] See the Intersex Society of North America website, available at http://www.isna.org/faq/what_is_intersex (accessed on December 11, 2011). For an intersex theology, see Susannah Cornwall, *Sex and Uncertainty in the Body of Christ: Intersex Conditions and Christian Theology* (London: Equinox, 2010); Susannah Cornwall, "*Ratum et Consummatum*: Refiguring Non-Penetrative Sexual Activity Theologically, in Light of Intersex Conditions," *Theology and Sexuality* 16.1 (2010): 77–93. See also Megan Defranza, "Intersex and Imago: Sex, Gender, and Sexuality in Postmodern Theological Anthropology" (Ph.D. diss., Marquette University, 2011).

[11] For a helpful study guide on terminology relating to LGBT people, see Timothy Palmer and Debra W. Haffner, *A Time to Seek: Study Guide on Sexual and Gender Diversity*, available at http://www.religiousinstitute.org/sites/default/files/study_guides/timetoseekfinal.pdf (accessed on December 11, 2011).

[12] For a discussion of queer theory in the context of Christian theology, see Cheng, *Radical Love*, 35–38. For an introduction to queer theory and gender theory, see Riki Wilchins, *Queer Theory, Gender Theory: An Instant Primer* (Los Angeles: Alyson Books, 2004).

have embraced the word "queer." For example, the Metropolitan Community Church of New York hands out brightly colored stickers each year during the New York City Pride March that say "God Made Me Queer." Indeed, during the past decade there has been an incredible growth in the academic discipline of queer theology, which I have written about in my book *Radical Love*.[13]

3. What About Non-Christians?

Finally, a note about the Christian nature of this book. Because this book is a work of Christian theology, it uses unapologetically Christian language. As a self-identified Christian theologian, I "speak" or "talk" Christian. That is, I am committed to using the language, categories, and thought-forms of Christianity to describe my view of the divine and ultimate reality. This is not to take away from or denigrate the faith traditions of my LGBT siblings, however.

I have found that in many LGBT contexts—particularly in activist circles—there is a tendency to downplay or even silence Christian discourse. This is not surprising in light of how the religious right has often used such discourse as a weapon to attack LGBT people. Many of us still carry significant emotional and psychological wounds from these attacks.[14] As a Christian theologian, however, I am committed to writing authentically from my own social location and religious background.

That being said, I have been strongly influenced by other religious traditions in my life. For example, my beloved maternal grandparents—who lived with my parents, my younger brother, and me during my childhood—were not Christians; they were formed religiously in a Chinese Buddhist, Confucian, and Daoist context. My brother Andy is a convert to Judaism, which occurred several years after his marriage to Abi, my Jewish sister-in-law. I have worked closely with my LGBT Jewish friends from groups

[13] For a genealogy of queer theology, see Cheng, *Radical Love*, 25–42. For other overviews of queer theology, see Susannah Cornwall, *Controversies in Queer Theology* (London: SCM Press, 2011); Robert E. Shore-Goss, "Gay and Lesbian Theologies," in *Liberation Theologies in the United States: An Introduction*, ed. Stacey M. Floyd-Thomas and Anthony B. Pinn (New York: New York University Press, 2010), 181–208; and Elizabeth Stuart, *Gay and Lesbian Theologies: Repetitions with Critical Difference* (Aldershot, UK: Ashgate, 2003).

[14] Susannah Cornwall has a helpful discussion in her book *Controversies in Queer Theology* about the ambivalence that many LGBT people have with respect to Christianity. In one of the chapters of that book, Cornwall explicitly poses the question "Should Queer Christian People Stay Christians?" See Cornwall, *Controversies in Queer Theology*, 191–223.

such as Nehirim on theological issues over the years.[15] And I have written elsewhere about reclaiming East Asian spiritual practices and traditions in my own life.[16] Thus, I do not believe that institutional Christianity is the exclusive path to ultimate reality. Although my theology is highly christocentric, it is neither intended to be exclusivist nor a manifestation of Christian triumphalism.

Whenever I write about a Christ-centered view of sin and grace—or about the various models of the Queer Christ—I use the term "Christ" in a much broader sense than the classical second person of the Trinity as described in the historic creeds of Christianity. That is, I use the term "Christ" to describe *any* situation or encounter in which the divine intersects with the human.[17] Do I believe that the divine and human came together in a unique way in the person of Jesus of Nazareth over two thousand years ago? Yes. However, I also believe that we encounter the living Christ whenever the divine is made incarnate, whenever the Word is made flesh, and whenever we experience God-with-us. This encounter can occur in a place of worship, but it can also occur in the bedroom, dance floor, cyberspace, or sex club.[18] For it is in these encounters that Christ is truly cosmic—the Alpha (that is, beginning) and Omega (that is, end) of human existence.

Study Questions

1. What are your earliest memories, if any, of being called a sinner? How did that make you feel? Did that change your relationship with the church or other faith community?
2. How do you respond to the idea of the Queer Christ? Is it shocking? Familiar? Confusing?
3. How might a book on sin and grace from the perspective of LGBT people speak to someone who doesn't necessarily identify herself or himself as LGBT?

---

[15] For more information about Nehirim, see http://www.nehirim.org (accessed on December 11, 2011).

[16] See Patrick S. Cheng, "Reclaiming Our Traditions, Rituals, and Spaces: Spirituality and the Queer Asian Pacific American Experience," *Spiritus* 6, no. 2 (Fall 2006): 234–40.

[17] Indeed, this is consistent with the "christological universalism" of Karl Barth. That is, if Christ is truly the light of the world, then Christ can be "recognized anywhere," whether in "the secular sphere or the religious sphere." See Colin E. Gunton, *The Barth Lectures* (London: T&T Clark, 2007), 203–04.

[18] See, e.g., Paul J. Gorrell, "Rite to Party: Circuit Parties and Religious Experience," in *Gay Religion*, ed. Scott Thumma and Edward R. Gray (Walnut Creek, CA: AltaMira Press, 2005), 313–26; Robert E. Goss, *Queering Christ: Beyond Jesus Acted Up* (Cleveland, OH: Pilgrim Press, 2002), 56–71 ("Finding God in the Heart-Genital Connection").

4. How comfortable are you with the various terms used to describe LGBT people? How do you understand the difference between sexual orientation, gender identity, and biological sex?
5. What are some different ways in which the word "queer" can be used? How have you used—or experienced—the word "queer" in the past? The present?
6. What has been your experience with non-Christian faith traditions? How might you understand the term "Christ" expansively so as to include non-Christian perspectives and experiences?

For Further Study

Definitions

- Cheng, *Radical Love*, 2-8
- Fenway Health, "Glossary of Gender and Transgender Terms"
- Palmer and Haffner, *A Time to Seek*
- Wilchins, *Queer Theory, Gender Theory*

Queer Christ

- Bohache, *Christology from the Margins*, 209-61
- Cheng, *Radical Love*, 78-86
- Goss, *Queering Christ*

Queer Theology

- Cheng, *Radical Love*
- Cornwall, *Controversies in Queer Theology*
- Shore-Goss, "Gay and Lesbian Theologies"
- Stuart, *Gay and Lesbian Theologies*

Part I

From Sin to Amazing Grace

Chapter 1

Why a Book on Sin and Grace?

Before I started my doctoral studies in systematic theology, I served as the Assistant Pastor for Congregational Life at the Metropolitan Community Church of New York (MCCNY) in New York City. MCCNY was an amazing congregation. The liturgy was moving, the music was uplifting, and the preaching was powerful. The church was committed to serving the least among us;[1] it ran a food pantry as well as outreach programs to a variety of marginalized communities, including transgender folk and homeless LGBT youth. MCCNY was committed to social justice issues, it used gender-inclusive language in its liturgies, and it was one of the most diverse congregations I have ever seen in terms of race, ethnicity, and culture.

One of the things that puzzled me about MCCNY, however, was that sin or grace was rarely discussed from the pulpit. Yes, there was a condemnation of the evils of homophobia within religious and secular institutions. And yes, there was a condemnation of structural evils such as racism, sexism, poverty, and violence. However, there was little to no discussion about individual sins that separated us from God, our neighbors, or our true selves. Nor was there much discussion of the amazing grace that made us whole. As I deepened my theological studies, I found it more and more challenging not to have a language to critique the ways in which we *all* missed the mark—the senior pastor and myself

[1] Matt. 25:31–46.

included—and not just with respect to our sexualities and gender identities, but also with respect to the other aspects of our lives.

1. LGBT Aversion to Sin and Grace

Given the reluctance of LGBT faith communities such as MCCNY to use the language of sin and grace, why do we need an entire book on sin and grace from the perspective of LGBT people? It would seem that such a book is the last thing that the LGBT community needs. In general, sin and grace are highly unpopular subjects for contemporary Western society as a whole. In 1973, the psychiatrist Karl Menninger wrote about the general disappearance of sin-talk in American culture in his popular book *Whatever Became of Sin*?[2] Two decades later, in 1993, the Yale Divinity School theologian David Kelsey wrote an article in *Theology Today* asking a similar question: "Whatever Happened to the Doctrine of Sin?"[3] Little has changed almost another twenty years later. If anything, our culture has become even more secularized and allergic to sin-talk, as well as to its companion topic, grace.

Many LGBT people have a strong aversion to talking about sin and grace. This is not surprising because so many of us have been wounded deeply by these doctrines. Many of us have left the faith communities of our childhood because of the abusive ways in which these doctrines have been used against us. Some of us have even tried to kill ourselves—and, in some cases, succeeded—because of the belief that we are unredeemable sinners and that we are forever excluded from God's saving grace.

At best, I have found that LGBT Christians try not to think too much about the issues of sin and grace. Some of us convince ourselves that same-sex and gender-variant acts are not sinful based upon contemporary biblical scholarship, and we move on. Or we convince ourselves that the doctrine of sin has outlived its usefulness and therefore join "progressive" or LGBT-friendly denominations or communities that downplay or avoid the topic. Or we think about sin in terms of structural issues (such as racism,

---

[2] Karl Menninger, *Whatever Became of Sin?* (New York: Bantam Books, 1973). Menninger argued that sin has disappeared from contemporary discourse because the fundamental authority over "social offenses" has been shifted from the church to the state. That is, we have effectively converted sin into crime, thus rendering the category of sin "increasingly pointless from a practical standpoint." Menninger, *Whatever Became of Sin?*, 29.

[3] David H. Kelsey, "Whatever Happened to the Doctrine of Sin?," *Theology Today* 50, no. 2 (July 1993): 169–78.

sexism, or homophobia) but not individual sin. And, of course, many LGBT people simply leave the church altogether because of the suffering that we have experienced—and encountered—from the church's sin-talk. Once we have dispensed with the notion of sin, however, there is little need for the doctrine of God's grace.

Similarly, I have been surprised at the silence with respect to the doctrines of sin and grace in the LGBT theological academy. Although there have been numerous LGBT theological works written in the last few decades, very few of these works address the doctrines of sin and grace head-on.[4] Indeed, even though I have read literally hundreds of books and journal articles about queer Christianity and theology, I have found few sustained queer reflections on such doctrines.

This silence is understandable because, as I mentioned earlier, many LGBT people have been deeply wounded by sin-talk from homophobic religious leaders and communities. Furthermore, what kind of sadistic God would give LGBT people the amazing fruits of the Spirit—such as love, joy, peace, and patience—through their same-sex friendships and relationships,[5] and nevertheless still condemn us as sinners? Where is the grace in that? How can that ever be understood as Good News? For many LGBT Christians it is simply easier to remain silent about sin and grace.

2. Breaking the Silence on Sin and Grace

Notwithstanding the above silence with respect to sin and grace within the LGBT community, I am becoming increasingly convinced that we, as LGBT people of faith, must address the doctrine of sin—and its companion doctrine of grace—head on. We can no longer avoid or ignore the subject. In fact, the silence within the LGBT Christian community about sin and grace ultimately is not helpful and may in the long run even be harmful to us. By this I do not mean continuing the endless biblical arguments over a handful of LGBT "texts of terror" about what does or does not constitute allegedly sinful same-sex or gender-variant

[4] For an overview of the doctrine of sin in queer theology, see Cheng, *Radical Love*, 70–78. For a recent essay on queer sin from a Lutheran perspective, see Mary E. Lowe, "Sin from a Queer, Lutheran Perspective," in *Transformative Lutheran Theologies: Feminist, Womanist, and Mujerista Perspectives*, ed. Mary J. Streufert (Minneapolis, MN: Fortress Press, 2010), 71–86. For a recent book that uses original sin as the starting point for theological reflection on same-sex marriage, see Geoffrey Rees, *The Romance of Innocent Sexuality* (Eugene, OR: Cascade Books, 2011).

[5] As Paul writes in his Letter to the Galatians, "there is no law against such things" (Gal. 5:22–23).

behavior.[6] Rather, we must engage thoughtfully the larger doctrinal questions of sin, traditionally classified as hamartiology (which is derived from *hamartia*, the Greek word for sin).

Why, then, is talking about sin and grace so important for the LGBT community? I believe there are at least four reasons as to why we must break the silence about sin and grace. First, sin-talk remains at the heart of the oppression and suffering of LGBT people today. Second, sin-talk is the primary reason why LGBT people of faith are denied full participation in the life of the Church. Third, ignoring the doctrines of sin and grace deprives us of the theological tools to describe the true state of the world. Fourth, LGBT Christians need a more fully developed theology of sin and grace in order to better dialogue with the broader Christian community. Let us examine each of these four points in turn.

First of all, sin-talk remains at the heart of the oppression and suffering—emotional, spiritual, psychological, and physical—that LGBT people experience today. Despite recent political advances in the United States such as the repeal of "Don't Ask, Don't Tell" and the legalization of same-sex marriages in states such as New York, the religious right continues to describe same-sex and gender-variant behavior as "sinful" and uses this sin-talk to justify the denial of equal protection under the laws for LGBT people. In some cases, this can result in brutal hate crimes and other forms of violence against our community.[7]

Sin is not just a matter of abstract debate for LGBT people. Sin-talk has justified the persecution, imprisonment, torture, and even execution of LGBT people by governments around the world.[8] Sin-talk has resulted in suicides by young people and adults who are condemned by their families, communities, and churches for their sexualities and gender identities.[9] Sin-talk is also at the heart of discredited attempts at changing sexual and gender identities

---

[6] The term "texts of terror" is taken from Phyllis Trible, *Texts of Terror: Literary-Feminist Readings of Biblical Narratives* (Philadelphia, PA: Fortress Press, 1984). In the LGBT context, it refers to the handful of biblical passages that are used to justify prohibitions against same-sex and gender-variant behavior, including Gen. 19, Lev. 18:22, Lev. 20:13, Rom. 1:26–27, 1 Cor. 6:9, 1 Tim. 1:10. In addition to these texts, there are other passages such as Deut. 22:5 and Deut. 23:1 that are used to condemn gender-variant behavior.

[7] For the stories of several LGBT people who were murdered as a result of religious intolerance, see Stephen V. Sprinkle, *Unfinished Lives: Reviving the Memories of LGBTQ Hate Crimes Victims* (Eugene, OR: Resource Publications, 2011). For example, one murderer claimed that God had commissioned him to "hunt down and kill gays, 'just like it says in Leviticus'" and because "[s]exual perverts deserve to die, period." Sprinkle, *Unfinished Lives*, 39.

[8] The LGBT section of the Human Rights Watch website documents such abuses from around the world. See http://www.hrw.org/lgbt (accessed on December 11, 2011).

[9] See Patrick S. Cheng, "Faith, Hope, and Love: Ending LGBT Teen Suicide," *Huffington Post* (October 6, 2010), available at http://www.huffingtonpost.com/rev-patrick-s-cheng-phd/faith-hope-and-love-endin_b_749160.html (accessed on December 11, 2011).

through "ex-gay" or reparative therapy that purports to "pray away the gay."[10] Grace, in this context, is characterized as the so-called "gift" of abstaining from same-sex or gender-variant acts, which in the end is not only unrealistic, but harmful, for many self-actualized LGBT people.

Second, sin-talk is the primary reason why LGBT people of faith are denied full participation in the life of the Church, including the denial of sacraments and rites such as same-sex marriage and ordination. We are taught very early on that same-sex and gender-variant acts are sinful, and that we will be condemned to eternal punishment if we fail to repent and abstain from such acts. Sin-talk forces religious leaders into the closet even though they themselves may be engaged in same-sex or gender-variant acts.[11] Ignoring or dismissing this sin-talk will not make it go away. We must move beyond narrow biblical arguments and challenge, from a larger theological perspective, what the religious right is saying when it uses sin-talk. It is time for LGBT people to take back the words "sin" and "grace" in the same way that we have taken back the word "queer"!

Third, ignoring the doctrines of sin and grace deprives us of the theological tools to describe—and critique—the true state of the world. As the theologian Reinhold Niebuhr was so fond of stating, the doctrine of sin is the only empirically verifiable doctrine in the Christian faith.[12] How can we adequately describe and critique this world of ours that is filled with violence, terrorism, economic inequity, and sexual exploitation without sin-talk? And, on the other hand, how can we express our deepest hopes of reconciliation and healing without grace-talk? For example, Barbara Brown Taylor, an Episcopal priest and writer, has argued that the language of sin is not something to be avoided. Rather, sin-talk is precisely what allows us to move to grace-talk.[13]

As an out, gay man who has been a member of various LGBT communities for over twenty-five years, I have experienced a great deal of love and amazing grace from my queer siblings around the world. However, I also have witnessed a lot of brokenness and ugliness within the LGBT world—including within LGBT religious

---

[10] For an exposé of the ex-gay movement, see Wayne R. Besen, *Anything But Straight: Unmasking the Scandals and Lies Behind the Ex-Gay Myth* (Binghamton, NY: Harrington Park Press, 2003).

[11] For an online list of such individuals, see http://gayhomophobe.com (accessed on December 11, 2011).

[12] See Andrew S. Finstuen, *Original Sin and Everyday Protestants: The Theology of Reinhold Niebuhr, Billy Graham, and Paul Tillich in an Age of Anxiety* (Chapel Hill, NC: The University of North Carolina Press, 2009), 69.

[13] See Barbara Brown Taylor, *Speaking of Sin: The Lost Language of Salvation* (Lanham, MD: Cowley Publications, 2000).

communities—whether it is the ways in which we fail to treat others with loving-kindness when we are on the hunt for sexual conquests, or when we ourselves attain a certain amount of power and success, or when we encounter those who do not measure up to a certain standard of beauty, wealth, or social standing.[14] Here, again, the doctrines of sin and grace may be helpful ways to describe and critique this broken world.

Fourth, those of us who are LGBT Christians need a more fully developed theology of sin and grace in order to better dialogue with the broader Christian community. As the Marquette University sociologist Dawne Moon notes in her book *God, Sex, and Politics*, a basic problem with Christians who support LGBT people is the inability to talk about sin. Specifically, Moon notes that pro-LGBT Christians often are unable to challenge "head-on" the argument that same-sex acts are sinful; they often "dodge the question by responding 'What is sin, anyway?'"[15] This inability to engage directly with the doctrines of sin and grace can be problematic, particularly when a central theme of the gospels is that of reconciliation, and Jesus Christ is described repeatedly as eating with tax collectors and sinners.[16] As a result, many anti-LGBT Christians have the impression—and wrongly so—that pro-LGBT Christians do not have any concept of sin and, as such, have no need for salvation or Jesus Christ. I believe that a queer theology of sin and grace can advance the broader theological conversation by bridging the gap between pro-LGBT and anti-LGBT Christians.

For me, the key question—theologically speaking—is how can we rethink the classical tradition of sin without ignoring it altogether? That is, how can we avoid throwing the baby out with the bathwater? How can we challenge simplistic—and, in some cases, non-biblical—notions of sin that are used by the religious right to condemn us? How can we be empowered by the doctrine of sin as a way of critiquing the evil and the demonic within our very midst without further wounding people who have been wounded all of their lives? How can we have a dialogue with the broader

---

[14] For a description of the racism that exists in gay male cyberculture, see Patrick S. Cheng, "'I Am Yellow and Beautiful': Reflections on Queer Asian Spirituality and Gay Male Cyberculture," *Journal of Technology, Theology, and Religion* 2, no. 3 (June 2011): 1–21.

[15] Dawne Moon, *God, Sex, and Politics: Homosexuality and Everyday Theologies* (Chicago: University of Chicago Press, 2004), 89.

[16] Matt. 9:11, Mark 2:16, Luke 5:30. See George Carey, *Sinners: Jesus and His Earliest Followers* (Waco, TX: Baylor University Press, 2009).

Christian theological tradition about sin and yet not perpetuate the suffering and shame that sin-talk has inflicted upon our communities?

3. Reimagining Sin and Grace

The challenge of rethinking sin and grace for LGBT people is not a new one. In fact, LGBT theologians have engaged in the process of reimagining sin and grace for over half a century. In 1960, Robert Wood, an openly gay United Church of Christ minister, argued in his groundbreaking book *Christ and the Homosexual* that the real issue with the gay Christian is not so much that he[17] is a sinner, but rather that he becomes a "slave of homosexuality" and fails to deal with it rationally. In the closing chapter of his book, Wood writes directly to his homosexual reader. He says, in all capital letters, "The sin is not in being a homosexual, but in failing to adjust oneself to the added responsibility of being so."[18] According to Wood, grace takes the form of being saved from "a sense of hopelessness before God" and moving to the knowledge that "under certain conditions an expression of homosexuality can be moral."[19]

Some thirty years later, Robert Williams, the first openly gay man who was ordained to the Episcopal priesthood, also reimagined what sin and grace might mean for gays and lesbians. In his 1992 book *Just As I Am*, Williams argued that sin for gay men and lesbians should be understood as the rejection of oneself, or the desire "to be straight." For example, every classified ad that solicits a "straight acting and appearing" partner is a manifestation of that sin. Similarly, according to Williams, the desire of many LGBT people to be "assimilated into the mainstream" and the desire to be "just like you, except what we do in bed" is a "grievous sin."[20] Grace, by contrast, is the acceptance of oneself, lesbian or gay, as created by God.

In 1997, Elizabeth Stuart, the openly lesbian theologian who is currently the senior pro-vice-chancellor and professor of theology at the University of Winchester in the United Kingdom, reimagined sin for LGBT people in her book *Religion Is a Queer Thing*. In a

---

[17] Wood's book focuses primarily on gay men.
[18] Robert W. Wood, *Christ and the Homosexual (Some Observations)* (New York: Vantage Press, 1960), 208.
[19] Wood, *Christ and the Homosexual*, 211.
[20] Robert Williams, *Just as I Am: A Practical Guide to Being Out, Proud and Christian* (New York: HarperPerennial, 1992), 151.

chapter about salvation, Stuart argued that LGBT people needed to focus less on equating sin with sexuality and more on being liberated from "sinful" oppressive structures such as racism, sexism, and heterosexism. According to Stuart, salvation for LGBT people is not so much being saved from personal sins, but rather being saved from structural sins or biases against people of differing sexual orientations that "have been built into the structures of society."[21]

LGBT scholars also have reimagined sin and grace from a religious studies perspective. In their 2003 book *Love the Sin*, queer scholars Janet Jakobsen and Ann Pellegrini examine and challenge the ways in which sin-talk has been used in American public policy debates with respect to homosexuality. Not only do they critique the use of sin discourse by the Christian right, but they also criticize the ways in which LGBT-rights advocates have used the essentialist or "born this way" argument to argue that homosexuality is an innate characteristic and therefore should not be punished. For Jakobsen and Pellegrini, it doesn't matter how someone becomes LGBT. Even if sexuality and gender identity *were* a choice, they argue, such acts should not be punished. For Jakobsen and Pellegrini, the paramount ethical value is sexual freedom and recognizing that sexuality can be a "site for the production of values," including the "rich varieties of gay and lesbian community formation."[22]

In recent years, a number of theologians have used queer theory to reimagine sin and grace. For example, the Oberlin College feminist theologian Margaret Kamitsuka has challenged the binary classification of "male" and "female" forms of sin—as expressed in the work of Søren Kierkegaard and others—in her 2007 book *Feminist Theology and the Challenge of Difference*. Kamitsuka relies upon the work of queer theorist Michel Foucault on power relations, and she critiques sex binarism by arguing that sin can be understood in Foucauldian terms as either "undue cooperation with a disciplinary power" or "underdeveloped cooperation with disciplinary power."[23]

Similarly, the Augsburg College queer theologian Mary Lowe

---

[21] Elizabeth Stuart, "Salvation," in *Religion Is a Queer Thing: A Guide to the Christian Faith for Lesbian, Gay, Bisexual and Transgendered People*, ed. Elizabeth Stuart, Andy Braunston, Malcolm Edwards, John McMahon, and Tim Morrison (Cleveland, OH: Pilgrim Press, 1997), 89.

[22] Jakobsen and Pellegrini, *Love the Sin*, 17. See also Laurel C. Schneider, "What If It Is a Choice?: Some Implications of the Homosexuality Debates for Theology," in Ellison and Douglas, *Sexuality and the Sacred*, 197–204. For an alternative view, see Jay Michaelson, *God vs. Gay?: The Religious Case for Equality* (Boston: Beacon Press, 2011), 30–40 (arguing for LGBT equality based upon the "naturalness" of homosexuality).

[23] Margaret D. Kamitsuka, *Feminist Theology and the Challenge of Difference* (New York: Oxford University Press, 2007), 72; see also Margaret D. Kamitsuka, "Toward a Feminist Postmodern and Postcolonial Interpretation of Sin," *Journal of Religion* 84, no. 2 (April 2004): 179–211.

has argued in her 2010 article "Sin from a Queer, Lutheran Perspective" that sin can be understood in terms of the Foucauldian notion of discourse. That is, Lowe contends that a Foucauldian understanding of sin exposes the "sinful discourses of racism and homophobia" and "explains why it can be so hard to be converted from active or passive participation in sinful structures."[24] Lowe uses Luther's concept of *simul justus et peccator*—that is, as Christians we are paradoxically both righteous and sinful—to explain how individuals can be both freed and bound by sinful discourses.

Like Kamitsuka and Lowe, I have drawn from queer theory in reimagining sin and grace for LGBT people. For example, I have argued in my 2011 book *Radical Love* that sin can be understood as sexual and gender essentialism, or the "reinforcing of the boundaries that keep categories separate and distinct from each other."[25] By contrast, grace can be understood as radical love, or a "love so extreme that it dissolves all kinds of boundaries."[26] I also have proposed elsewhere that sin can be understood in christological—as opposed to legalistic—terms for LGBT people, which is the argument that is developed more fully in this book.[27]

Notwithstanding these efforts by theologians and scholars over the last fifty years to reimagine sin and grace for LGBT people, there has been little *sustained* reflection on the doctrines of sin and grace. That is, to date LGBT theologians have not proposed radically new ways of thinking about sin and grace in the same way as feminist, womanist, and other women of color theologians have done since the 1950s. Those theologians have effectuated a Copernican shift in theological discourse about sin and grace, as evidenced by the work of Valerie Saiving (defining sin for women as "underdevelopment or negation of the self"),[28] Judith Plaskow (critiquing Niebuhr and Tillich's notions of sin and grace),[29] Mary Daly (defining sin as women's "complicity in self-destruction"),[30] Rosemary Ruether (defining sin as sexism),[31] Susan Thistlethwaite (defining sin as the desire of white women to "uncritically

---

[24] Mary E. Lowe, "Sin from a Queer, Lutheran Perspective," in *Transformative Lutheran Theologies: Feminist, Womanist, and Mujerista Perspectives*, ed. Mary J. Streufert (Minneapolis, MN: Fortress Press, 2010), 77.

[25] Cheng, *Radical Love*, 74.

[26] Cheng, *Radical Love*, 71.

[27] See Cheng, "Rethinking Sin and Grace."

[28] Valerie Saiving Goldstein, "The Human Situation: A Feminine View," *Journal of Religion* 40, no. 2 (April 1960): 109.

[29] Judith Plaskow, *Sex, Sin and Grace: Women's Experience and the Theologies of Reinhold Niebuhr and Paul Tillich* (Washington, DC: University Press of America, 1980).

[30] Mary Daly, *Beyond God the Father: Toward a Philosophy of Women's Liberation* (Boston: Beacon Press, 1973), 51.

[31] Rosemary Radford Ruether, *Sexism and God-Talk: Toward a Feminist Theology* (Boston: Beacon Press, 1983), 173–83.

bond with black women without respecting the boundaries of difference"),[32] Delores Williams (defining sin as the defilement of black women's bodies),[33] Serene Jones (using feminist theory to rethink classical notions of sin and grace),[34] and Kwok Pui-lan (doing the same with postcolonial feminist theory).[35] It is time for LGBT theologians to create a Copernican shift of our own.

4. Moving from Crime to Christ

In this book, I propose that we shift from a *crime-based* model of sin and grace—that is, a model in which sin is understood as a crime against God, and grace is seen as acquittal and rehabilitation by God—to a *Christ-centered* model of sin and grace. In the Christ-centered model of sin and grace, sin is understood as immaturity, whereas grace is seen as deification (that is, becoming like God in the person of Christ and through the Holy Spirit).[36]

Over the last few decades, many LGBT theologians have written about the Queer Christ.[37] That is, they have responded to Jesus' question of "who do you say that I am?,"[38] in the same way in which theologians from other identity groups have written about the Black Christ, the Feminist Christ, the Asian Christ, and other contextual Christs. Thus, the primary implication of a move to a Christ-centered model of sin and grace for LGBT people is to place the Queer Christ at the center of thinking about sin and grace. In other words, both sin and grace are defined in terms of the Queer Christ. By shifting our focus from a crime-based model to a Christ-based model, we ourselves move from a place of sin to God's amazing grace. That is, instead of being driven by fear and guilt, we seek to model our lives on the Queer Christ, which is the end to which our lives are ultimately directed.

---

[32] Susan Brooks Thistlethwaite, *Sex, Race, and God: Christian Feminism in Black and White* (New York: Crossroad, 1989), 86. For some recent reflections on the fall and the wired world, see Susan Brooks Thistlethwaite, *Dreaming of Eden: American Religion and Politics in a Wired World* (New York: Palgrave Macmillan, 2010), 199–220.

[33] Delores S. Williams, "Sin, Nature, and Black Women's Bodies," in *Ecofeminism and the Sacred*, ed. Carol J. Adams (New York: Continuum, 1993), 29.

[34] Serene Jones, *Feminist Theory and Christian Theology: Cartographies of Grace* (Minneapolis, MN: Fortress Press, 2000), 94–125.

[35] Kwok Pui-lan, *Postcolonial Imagination and Feminist Theology* (Louisville, KY: Westminster John Knox Press, 2005), 145–46.

[36] In arguing for a move from a crime-based model to a Christ-based model, I am not suggesting that these two models are mutually exclusive or binary opposites. Nor am I suggesting that these two models are the only ways of thinking about sin and grace. For example, sin and grace can be understood within the context of sacrifice, which has a "cultic logic of its own, not a logic borrowed from law courts." Mike Higton, *Christian Doctrine* (London: SCM Press, 2008), 276. Rather, my argument is rooted in a critique of the dominant role that the crime-based model has played—and continues to play—in Western Christian discourse about sin and grace.

[37] For an overview of queer christologies, see Cheng, *Radical Love*, 78–86.

[38] Mark 8:29.

Study Questions

1. How do you feel about the terms "sin" and "grace"? Are these terms that you use in your daily life?
2. Why do you think LGBT people and others have avoided language about sin and grace?
3. Name four reasons why it is important for LGBT people—and others—to break the silence about sin and grace. Do you find these reasons convincing? Why or why not?
4. How have LGBT theologians and their allies addressed issues of sin and grace since the 1960s? Why do you think there has been relatively little sustained reflection on these doctrines to date?
5. How do you feel about moving from a crime-centered model of sin and grace to a Christ-centered model? Does it change significantly the way you think about sin and grace?
6. Examine the table of contents of this book. What chapters in Part II of the book about the Queer Christ seem the most interesting to you? The least interesting?

For Further Study

Breaking the Silence

- Sprinkle, *Unfinished Lives*
- Taylor, *Speaking of Sin*

Reimagining Sin and Grace

- Cheng, *Radical Love*, 70–78
- Cheng, "Rethinking Sin and Grace for LGBT People Today"
- Jakobsen and Pellegrini, *Love the Sin*
- Kamitsuka, *Feminist Theology and the Challenge of Difference*
- Lowe, "Sin from a Queer, Lutheran Perspective"
- Rees, *The Romance of Innocent Sexuality*
- Stuart, "Salvation"
- Williams, *Just as I Am*, 149–68
- Wood, *Christ and the Homosexual*

Queer Theory

- Cheng, *Radical Love*, 6–8
- Wilchins, *Queer Theory, Gender Theory*
- Wilcox, "Queer Theology and the Study of Religion"

Sin, Grace, and Feminist Theologies

- Daly, *Beyond God the Father*, 51
- Jones, *Feminist Theory and Christian Theology*, 94–125
- Kwok, *Postcolonial Imagination and Feminist Theology*, 145–46
- Plaskow, *Sex, Sin, and Grace*
- Ruether, *Sexism and God-Talk*, 173–83
- Saiving, "The Human Situation"
- Thistlethwaite, *Sex, Race, and God*, 77–91
- Williams, "Sin, Nature, and Black Women's Bodies"

Chapter 2

A Primer on Sin and Grace

As a queer theologian, I subscribe to several news feeds by LGBT activists who monitor the religious right and its homophobic activities. One thing that I've noticed in following the heated "culture wars" debates is that often the complex doctrines of sin and grace are oversimplified and distorted *by both sides*—that is, by both the anti-LGBT *and* the pro-LGBT people—especially in the context of sexuality and gender identity issues. That is, both sides tend to view sin as the violation of a divine law that is almost always limited to sexuality issues and that is promulgated by God through the Bible, which contains an official list of what is or is not sinful. Grace, on the other hand, is understood as a gift of strength or courage that helps people to turn away from sin and refrain from violating such divine laws in the future. Both the religious right *and* the secular left seem to accept these definitions of sin and grace without question.

In this chapter, I would like to present a more nuanced view of sin and grace. Specifically, I would like to present a brief primer on sin and grace that describes how these doctrines have been understood in the broader Christian theological tradition. For example, most sinful acts have very little to do with issues of sexuality or gender identity. Furthermore, sin has been understood traditionally not just as an act, but also as a condition. In fact, there are many ways of thinking about sin—even within the Bible itself—and particularly in the realm of contemporary theology. Although I may not agree with all of the theological positions that are discussed in the primer, I do think it is important to ensure that we are all on the same page with respect to what the theological tradition has said about sin and grace. Only after we have understood the basics of such doctrines can we turn to rethinking them with respect to the LGBT context.[1]

1. Sin

Sin, most simply defined, is *separation* from God. In the same way that we might be separated from a loved one—either emotionally or physically—after an argument or fight, sin can be understood as separation, or alienation, from God. For example, sometimes my husband, Michael, and I are separated emotionally because of an argument or misunderstanding between the two of us. Other times we are separated physically because of work-related travel. In both cases, however, I feel the pain of separation and loss until we are reunited. This painful feeling of separation can be a window into what it means to be in a state of sin.

As a young boy, I loved the church and wanted nothing more than to be a priest. While other neighborhood children were playing cops and robbers, I was playing communion in my mother's kitchen with Wonder Bread wafers and grape juice wine. During my teenage years, I came to the realization that I was gay and discovered that my church rejected me because of my sexuality. This led to intense anger and sadness on my part and my falling away from the church, Christianity, and even organized religion. Even though I now recognize that God was always there and had not abandoned me, I spent many years wandering in the secular wilderness before returning to the faith. By turning my back on God—primarily because I could not reconcile being both Christian and gay—I had voluntarily separated myself from God. I was experiencing the reality of sin as separation from God.

In this chapter, I will discuss three main topics about sin. First, I will discuss *actual sins*, or the individual acts that we commit that separate us from God. Second, I will discuss *original sin*, or a state of inherited sin that keeps us separated from God. Third, I will discuss the *rethinking of sin* that has occurred in the context of contemporary theology.

---

[1] For a brief overview of how the doctrines of sin and grace have evolved within the Christian theological tradition, see Louis Berkhof, *The History of Christian Doctrines* (Carlisle, PA: Banner of Truth Trust, 1937), 125–61; Bernhard Lohse, *A Short History of Christian Doctrine: From the First Century to the Present*, rev. American ed. (Philadelphia, PA: Fortress Press, 1985), 100–31.

a. Actual Sins: More Than Just Sex

When most of us hear the word "sin," what usually comes to mind are *actual sins*. Actual sins are the individual acts that we commit that separate us from God, such as stealing, lying, or murder. Moreover, what often first comes to mind in any discussion about actual sins are sexual sins, which traditionally have been understood as including same-sex or gender-variant acts. The strong association between sin and sex often tends to overshadow the many different kinds of actual sins.

In fact, actual sins involve much more than just sexual acts. This may seem like an obvious point, but it is surprising how often in the popular imagination sin is limited to sexual acts—and, in particular, non-procreative sexual acts. Even though the Bible contains more than 31,000 verses, Christian communities have spent countless hours in recent decades arguing about the meaning of only six or so verses (that is, 0.02% of the Bible) that purportedly relate to LGBT people.

Take, for example, the approximately two-dozen "vice and virtue" lists in the Bible. Much of what we would consider sinful in these lists relate to non-sexual acts such as stealing, lying, idolatry, and exploiting the poor such as widows and orphans.[2] The same holds true for other traditional lists of sins. Most of the Ten Commandments—for example, the prohibitions against polytheism, taking the Lord's name in vain, failing to keep the Sabbath, dishonoring one's parents, killing, stealing, bearing false witness, and coveting a neighbor's goods—are focused on non-sexual sins.[3] Similarly, all but one of the seven deadly sins—for example, the sins of sloth, envy, gluttony, greed, anger, and pride—are non-sexual in nature.[4]

In sum, even though sex is often the first thing that comes to mind when we hear the word "sin," traditional lists of actual sins such as the Ten Commandments and the seven deadly sins demonstrate that sin is in fact much more than just sex. One of the reasons why sin has been so intertwined with sex in the popular imagination is the doctrine of original sin, or inherited sin, to which we turn next.

---

[2] For a comprehensive listing of these vice and virtue lists, see William J. Webb, *Slaves, Women and Homosexuals: Exploring the Hermeneutics of Cultural Analysis* (Downers Grove, IL: InterVarsity Press, 2001), 192–94.

[3] See, e.g., *Catechism of the Catholic Church*, § 2331–2400, 560–76.

[4] The one exception, of course, is lust. For a contemporary discussion of the seven deadly sins, see Aviad Kleinberg, *Seven Deadly Sins: A Very Partial List* (Cambridge, MA: Belknap Press, 2008).

b. Original Sin: Not Just an Act, But Also a Condition

We have seen how sin consists of individual acts that separate us from God. However, sin is not just limited to such acts. According to the theological tradition, sin is also a condition. This condition is called *original sin*, and it was most powerfully articulated in the early fifth century by the great North African theologian Augustine of Hippo. According to the doctrine of original sin, we have *all* inherited the sinful state of our first parents, Adam and Eve. That is, original sin is a condition that is passed on from generation to generation through the sexual act. It is as if we are all "infected" with original sin. Although actual sins may arise as a result of original sin, original sin is itself a *condition* and not an act.[5]

According to Augustine, we are all punished with original sin as a result of Adam and Eve's disobedience in the Garden of Eden. According to the third chapter of the Book of Genesis, Adam and Eve disobeyed God by eating from the Tree of Knowledge of Good and Evil. Eve was tricked by the serpent into eating the fruit; the serpent told Eve that if she ate the fruit she would become "like God, knowing good and evil."[6] Eve then shared the fruit with Adam. As a result of this disobedience, God inflicted various punishments upon Adam and Eve, including death, and expelled them from the Garden of Eden.[7]

It was not just Adam and Eve who were affected by God's punishment, however. Augustine argued that the sinful state of Adam and Eve had been passed on to all subsequent generations through sexual intercourse. This was a result of Augustine's (mis)reading of the fifth chapter of Romans. In Romans 5:12, Paul writes that "just as sin came into the world through one man, and death came through sin, and so death spread to all *because all have sinned*."[8] Augustine, however, relied upon a faulty Latin translation of the original Greek in which the phrase "*because* all have sinned"—*eph hō* in the Greek—was translated as "*in whom* all have sinned." As a result of this mistranslation, Augustine argued that we have all sinned "in" Adam. That is, we have all sinned "in" Adam because his sin was passed down to all subsequent generations

---

[5] For an overview of how original sin developed in the early church, see Elaine Pagels, *Adam, Eve, and the Serpent: Sex and Politics in Early Christianity* (New York: Vintage Books, 1988).

[6] Gen. 3:5.

[7] Gen. 3.

[8] Rom. 5:12 (emphasis added).

through sexual intercourse. (This explains why Jesus Christ was born without sin; because he was born of a virgin, he was not "tainted" with human semen.)

Augustine writes in *Against Julian* that even infants are "under the power of the Devil" because they are born as a result of their parents' "concupiscence"—that is, sexual desire. For Augustine, the sexual organs are evil because "lust has greater power to move them than reason."[9] That is, just as Adam and Eve disobeyed God by eating of the forbidden fruit, the (male) sex organ disobeys human reason. Sometimes it works when we don't want it to work; and sometimes it doesn't work when we do want it to work. In fact, Augustine believed that before the fall Adam and Eve could procreate without any lust (that is, by "tranquil action"), just as one wills any other organ of the body to move![10]

It is important to understand that Augustine's argument for original sin was in the larger context of his theological argument with the British monk Pelagius and his disciples. Pelagius argued that we human beings are capable of attaining salvation through our own acts. That is, we have the ability to follow God's commands and thus be saved. Augustine, who was concerned that such a stance would undermine the sovereignty of God, responded that there was no way that human beings could save ourselves. This is because we are *all* tainted with original sin from our first parents.

Augustine ultimately won the argument with Pelagius, who was denounced as a heretic. As a result of Augustine's original sin argument, however, Christianity inherited an extremely negative view of human sexuality. The only saving grace of sex, Augustine argued, was procreation in the context of marriage. That is why so many Christians to this day are opposed to non-procreative sex—for example, same-sex acts—because non-procreative sex removes the sole rationale that makes sex "good." Furthermore, Augustine's original sin argument justified the practice of infant baptism, which was required to wash away the guilt of original sin (but not the effects of original sin such as concupiscence).

According to the traditional doctrine of original sin, we are all infected with original sin. As such, we are curved inwards towards ourselves—that is, *incurvatus in se*—as opposed to being

---

[9] Augustine of Hippo, *Against Julian* 4.4.34, in *St. Augustine on Marriage and Sexuality*, ed. Elizabeth Clark (Washington, DC: Catholic University Press of America, 1996), 91.

[10] Augustine, *Against Julian* 4.5.35, in Clark, *St. Augustine on Marriage and Sexuality*, 91–92.

oriented outwards to God and neighbor.[11] This means that we have a predisposition to committing actual sins. However, just because we are all infected with original sin, it does not mean that we no longer have free will. We still have the ability to decide whether or not to commit a certain act. (Unfortunately, the taint of original sin results in our inevitably wanting to make the wrong choice.) As such, we are still responsible for our sinful acts.[12]

Many people have found Augustine's theology of original sin difficult to understand, particularly in light of our post-Enlightenment scientific understanding about sexuality and reproduction. However, one possible way of understanding original sin from a contemporary perspective is through Charles Darwin's theory of evolution. As we have seen, original sin can be understood as an intrinsic state of selfishness, or *incurvatus in se*. What if this state of selfishness is linked to a genetic tendency towards the survival of the fittest, and this tendency is passed on from generation to generation through the reproductive act? Under this view, original sin can be understood in terms of evolution and natural selection. Although I do not necessarily subscribe to this view, I do think it raises some interesting questions about original sin and science.[13]

Our fascination with original sin continues today. Since the mid-1990s, a number of scholarly works have been written on original sin. Such works include Henri Blocher's *Original Sin*,[14] Andrew Finstuen's *Original Sin and Everyday Protestants*,[15] Alan Jacobs' *Original Sin*,[16] Ian McFarland's *In Adam's Fall*,[17] Marguerite Shuster's *The Fall and Sin*,[18] and Tatha Wiley's *Original Sin*.[19] These works demonstrate the ongoing interest and enduring fascination that theologians and religion scholars have with the doctrine of original sin.

---

[11] For a discussion of *incurvatus in se*, see Matt Jenson, *The Gravity of Sin: Augustine, Luther, and Barth on* Homo Incurvatus in Se (London: T&T Clark, 2006).

[12] Much of the theological debate between Protestants and Roman Catholics about original sin relates to the nature and extent of what was lost in the fall. In general, Roman Catholic theology tends to have a more optimistic view of human nature and the ability of human beings to cooperate with God's grace.

[13] In her book on original sin and violence, Marjorie Hewitt Suchocki cites a number of scientific studies about animal and human behavior, and notes the "strong implication" that aggressive instincts "derive from our own evolutionary history." Marjorie Hewitt Suchocki, *The Fall to Violence: Original Sin in Relational Theology* (New York: Continuum, 1994), 93.

[14] Henri Blocher, *Original Sin: Illuminating the Riddle* (Downer's Grove, IL: InterVarsity Press, 1997).

[15] Finstuen, *Original Sin and Everyday Protestants*.

[16] Alan Jacobs, *Original Sin: A Cultural History* (New York: HarperOne, 2008).

[17] Ian A. McFarland, *In Adam's Fall: A Meditation on the Christian Doctrine of Original Sin* (Malden, MA: Wiley-Blackwell, 2010).

[18] Marguerite Shuster, *The Fall and Sin: What We Have Become as Sinners* (Grand Rapids, MI: William B. Eerdmans Publishing, 2004).

[19] Tatha Wiley, *Original Sin: Origins, Developments, Contemporary Meanings* (New York: Paulist Press, 2002).

One last point about original sin and LGBT people. Many LGBT people have rejected the doctrine of original sin because often a comparison is made between original sin on the one hand and sexual orientation or gender identity on the other. That is, some anti-LGBT people have argued that, like the "disordered" condition of original sin, LGBT people have a "disordered" orientation towards same-sex or gender-variant acts. In other words, all of these conditions are "disordered" and contrary to the will of God.

I would respond that, under this line of argument, *heterosexuality* can be just as much of a "disorder" as homosexuality. That is, heterosexuality can easily turn into an idol, and "family values" can become a substitute for God.[20] For example, organizations like the Family Research Council, the American Family Association, and the National Organization for Marriage are so fixated on the primacy of heterosexual intercourse that they seem to lose sight of the gospel imperative to take care of the "least among us" in terms of welcoming the stranger,[21] who I would argue is often the LGBT person today. These organizations also lose sight of the fact that, according to scripture, ultimately our physical bodies will be transformed in our eschatological state, and gender—and marriage, for that matter!—will cease to have any meaning in the end.[22] Thus, heterosexuality also has the potential for diverting us from our true eschatological end, which is God.[23]

c. Rethinking Sin: Many Forms, Both Ancient and New

Finally, there have been many different ways of thinking about sin throughout the history of Christianity. Many people think there is only one "official" definition of sin and, accordingly, only one "official" listing of sins. This is simply not true. As a number of recent books on the history of sin have demonstrated—including Gary Anderson's *Sin*,[24] John Portman's *A History of Sin*,[25] David

---

[20] As Geoffrey Rees writes, a fixation on procreation as a "substitute satisfaction for the promise of resurrection" can be critiqued as idolatry. That is, the "idolatrous celebration of the mortal self through mortal generation" is a "form of idolatry" to which both opposite-sex and same-sex couples are liable. Rees, *The Romance of Innocent Sexuality*, 122.

[21] Matt. 25:31–46. See Patrick S. Cheng, "The Values Voter Summit and the Idolatry of 'Family Values,'" *Huffington Post* (October 13, 2011), available at http://www.huffingtonpost.com/rev-patrick-s-cheng-phd/values-voter-summit_b_1003623.html (accessed on December 11, 2011).

[22] 1 Cor. 15:51–54; Mark 12:25.

[23] For an interesting evangelical argument on how heterosexuality can divert us from our ultimate end, see Jenell Williams Paris, *The End of Sexual Identity: Why Sex Is Too Important to Define Who We Are* (Downers Grove, IL: IVP Books, 2011), 37–54 ("The Trouble with Heterosexuality").

[24] Anderson, *Sin*.

[25] John Portman, *A History of Sin: Its Evolution to Today and Beyond* (Lanham, MD: Rowman and Littlefield Publishers, 2007).

Smith's *With Willful Intent*,[26] and Oliver Thomson's *A History of Sin*[27]—the concept of sin has evolved significantly throughout the two millennia of Christian history.

For example, even within the Bible itself there are multiple definitions of sin. For example, the Hebrew Bible alone has over fifty words for sin. Each of the three main Hebrew words for sin has a different meaning and nuance: *hata'* (missing the mark); *pesha`* (rebellion); and *`awon* (moral guilt).[28] Similarly, there are multiple words for sin in the New Testament. In addition to *hamartia* (missing the mark), such words include *paraptōma* (trespass), *parabasis* (transgression), *parakoē* (disobedience), *adikia* (unrighteousness), *asebeia* (impiety), *kakia* (wickedness), *ponēros* (wickedness), and *opheiletēs* (debtor).[29] So even the Bible lacks a uniform definition—let alone a uniform listing—of sin.[30]

Similarly, over the years there have been many different taxonomies, or ways of listing and organizing, sin. The seven deadly sins—pride, envy, anger, sloth, greed, gluttony, and lust—that Gregory the Great compiled in his *Morals on the Book of Job* is one of the best-known taxonomies of sin.[31] Thomas Aquinas, on the other hand, organized his discussion of sins in the *Summa Theologiae* around the three theological virtues of faith, hope, and love, as well as the four cardinal virtues of prudence, justice, fortitude, and temperance.[32] As we have seen earlier, the current catechism of the Roman Catholic Church organizes its discussion of sins around the Ten Commandments. Finally, Dorothee Sölle, the German liberation theologian and former professor at Union Theological Seminary in New York, used the categories of orthodox, liberal, and liberation theologies as her organizing principle for thinking about sin.[33]

There also have been many different ways of thinking about sin in contemporary theology. Reinhold Niebuhr, the great

---

[26] David L. Smith, *With Willful Intent: A Theology of Sin* (Wheaton, IL: BridgePoint Books, 1993).

[27] Oliver Thomson, *A History of Sin* (Edinburgh: Canongate Press, 1993).

[28] See Robin C. Cover, "Sin, Sinners (OT)," in *Anchor Yale Bible Dictionary*, ed. David Noel Freedman (New Haven, CT: Yale University Press, 2008). 6:31–40.

[29] See E.P. Sanders, "Sin, Sinners (NT)," in *Anchor Yale Bible Dictionary*, 6:40–47. For other discussions of the biblical terms for sin, see Millard J. Erickson, *Christian Theology*, 2nd ed. (Grand Rapids, MI: Baker Books, 1983), 583–95; Smith, *With Willful Intent*, 153–310.

[30] For a helpful overview of the many different models of sin in the Bible, see Mark E. Biddle, *Missing the Mark: Sin and Its Consequences in Biblical Theology* (Nashville, TN: Abingdon Press, 2005).

[31] For a discussion of the seven deadly sins, see Kleinberg, *Seven Deadly Sins*.

[32] See Thomas Aquinas, *Summa Theologiae*, Ia IIae, QQ. 1–170.

[33] See Dorothee Sölle, *Thinking About God: An Introduction to Theology* (Harrisburg, PA: Trinity Press International, 1990), 54–67.

twentieth-century theologian who also taught at Union Theological Seminary, reinterpreted Augustine's doctrine of original sin for his contemporary context in *The Nature and Destiny of Man*. For Niebuhr, human beings are both finite (as creatures) and self-transcendent (as spiritual beings). Because of our self-transcendence, we are able to see our own finitude and the frailty of our existence. This results in anxiety on our part, and as a result we turn to the pride of power with respect to social, economic, and political matters to create a false sense of security. As Niebuhr's former student Langdon Gilkey described it, sin according to Niebuhr is the "anxious attempt to hide our finitude and to make ourselves the center of all life, to take the place of God."[34]

Since Niebuhr, contemporary theologians have articulated many different models for thinking about sin. For example, traditionally sin has been understood as arising out of pride or overreaching. However, since the 1950s, feminist theologians such as Valerie Saiving have argued that sin for women is actually a matter of hiding or not reaching high enough.[35] Liberation theologians such as James Cone and Gustavo Gutiérrez have argued since the late 1960s that sin is a matter of racial, political, or economic oppression.[36] Womanist theologians such as Delores Williams have argued that sin is the defilement of black women's bodies.[37]

In recent years, contemporary theologians have proposed many different ways of thinking about sin. For example, Gary Anderson, a biblical scholar at the University of Notre Dame, has written a history of sin in which he argues that *debt* has been the primary historical metaphor for sin.[38] Marjorie Hewitt Suchocki, a process theologian who taught at the Claremont School of Theology, has argued that the underlying root of sin is a *tendency towards violence*.[39] Linda Mercadante, a theologian at the Methodist Theological School in Ohio, has argued that sin can be understood as *addiction*.[40] Cornelius Plantinga, a former president of Calvin

---

[34] Langdon Gilkey, *On Niebuhr: A Theological Study* (Chicago: University of Chicago Press, 2001), 103.

[35] See Goldstein, "The Human Situation," 100–12.

[36] See James H. Cone, *A Black Theology of Liberation*, 20th anniversary ed. (Maryknoll, NY: Orbis Books, 1990), 103–09; Gustavo Gutiérrez, *A Theology of Liberation: History, Politics, and Salvation*, trans. and ed. Caridad Inda and John Eagleson, 15th anniversary ed. (Maryknoll, NY: Orbis Books, 1988), 100–05.

[37] See Williams, "Sin, Nature, and Black Women's Bodies," 24–29.

[38] See Gary A. Anderson, *Sin: A History* (New Haven, CT: Yale University Press, 2009).

[39] See Suchocki, *The Fall to Violence*.

[40] See Linda A. Mercadante, *Victims and Sinners: Spiritual Roots of Addiction and Recovery* (Louisville, KY: Westminster John Knox Press, 1996).

Theological Seminary, has compiled a comprehensive breviary of sin that includes many metaphors for sin, including *vandalism of shalom*, *spiritual corruption*, *parasite*, *masquerade*, and *folly*.[41]

The point of this discussion is that there are many different ways of thinking about sin, both biblically and theologically. Sin is not just about sex. Nor is it just an act. Nor is it a monolithic, fixed concept. Rather, sin should be understood as a separation from God that manifests itself in many forms and in many different contexts.

2. Grace

Grace, simply defined, is an amazing gift from God that helps us to be *reunited* with God after a period of separation. For LGBT people, an analogy to grace might be the joy felt at reconciling with one's friend, lover, or family member after an emotional or physical separation. For example, I often experience a deep sense of joy—not to mention peace and relief—after reconciling with Michael after an argument or even after returning from a long work-related trip. I have noticed, over the course of our twenty-year relationship, that sometimes reconciliation takes longer, or is harder to achieve, than at other times. In the same way, grace is not something that we can conjure up on our own timetable. It is a pure gift from God.

In terms of grace working in my own life, I had left the Roman Catholic Church and led a secular life after coming out of the closet. I graduated from college with a degree in English Literature, went to Harvard Law School, was elected to the law review, and then clerked for a federal appellate judge in Los Angeles. I did all the "right" things as a young lawyer, including working for two Wall Street law firms. Although I was making a six-figure salary in my mid-twenties and had all the external marks of success, I felt extremely empty inside and unsatisfied. A turning point for me was waking up one morning and telling Michael that I no longer knew what my values were or what I stood for.

I recall two instances of grace breaking through in my life around that time. First, I had heard about a church trial in which Walter Righter, a bishop of the Episcopal Church, was acquitted

---

[41] See Cornelius Plantinga, *Not the Way It's Supposed to Be: A Breviary of Sin* (Grand Rapids, MI: William B. Eerdmans Publishing, 1995).

(that is, not found guilty) of heresy for ordaining an openly gay man. That led me to learn more about the Episcopal Church and wander into the Church of Saint Luke in the Fields in Greenwich Village, where I ultimately fell back in love with God and the Christian faith. Second, I saw a flier posted on a street corner for a summer intensive course in biblical Hebrew at Union Theological Seminary. For some unknown reason, I felt a deep desire to take the class, even though I knew virtually nothing about biblical languages. Little did I know that the class would be the start of a decade-long journey to earning my Ph.D. in systematic theology at Union.

Although I ultimately followed my heart in terms of pursuing my love for theology, my vocational journey as a theologian has not always been easy. In particular, I was raised in an immigrant Asian American family in which success was not defined in spiritual terms. It was difficult to explain to my parents and other family members why I was pursuing theology even though I already had a law degree and a good job. My father also became very sick—and ultimately died of cancer—during the course of my doctoral program. It was a challenge to finish my field exams, to write and defend my dissertation, and to make a significant career change, all while working full time as a lawyer. (By this time, I had left law firm practice and was working as a lawyer for an agency of the Episcopal Church.) As the elder son in a Chinese American family, I also had to wrestle with feelings of filial responsibility that urged me to stay in a more financially lucrative career. Thanks to God's grace, however, I was able to stay the course.

As I write this book, I am happily teaching at an Episcopal seminary and writing about queer theology—something that I never in my wildest imagination could have predicted happening two decades ago when I graduated from college. This unexpected reunion with God after many years of estrangement and separation has been an example of the amazing grace at work in my life.

For many people, grace is a fuzzy concept. Unlike sin—which often can take a very specific and concrete form—grace can be a difficult concept to understand. Over the last few decades there have been a number of helpful academic works on the doctrine of grace, including Roger Haight's *The Experience and Language of*

Grace;[42] James Carpenter's *Nature and Grace*;[43] Stephen Duffy's *The Dynamics of Grace*;[44] John Hardon's *History and Theology of Grace*;[45] Neil Ormerod's *Creation, Grace, and Redemption*,[46] and Paul Zahl's *Grace in Practice*.[47] This section will try to distill the basics of grace by focusing on three specific aspects of grace. First, grace is a free gift from God that reunites us with God. Second, grace requires our cooperation, which can be costly to us. And third, grace is amazing, unexpected, and surprising. Let us examine each of these aspects in turn.

a. Grace as God's Gift

First, grace is a free gift from God that *reunites* us with God. There is no shortage of God's grace in the world. Indeed, God's superabundant grace can be described as an outpouring of love that is obscenely promiscuous! God's grace is grounded in God's infinite love, and, as such, there is a never-ending flow of grace into creation. However, grace is not something that we can earn through our hard work alone. Nor is grace something that can be willed into existence by us while we are separated from God. Although we might be able to initiate reconciliation with our loved ones when we are separated from them, it is an entirely different matter with God. Reconciliation with God is not something that we can accomplish on our own; we need God's grace in order to be reunited with God.

From a traditional theological perspective, grace is unearned because we are all held captive by original sin. Recall that Augustine of Hippo argued that we are all infected with original sin because of the disobedience of our primal parents, Adam and Eve. Because of this, we are unable to break out of the grip of original sin that holds us in bondage. Only God can give us the grace that is required to be reunited with God. As we have seen, Augustine developed his theology of original sin and grace as a result of his bitter dispute with Pelagius, a British monk who claimed that human beings did in fact have the ability to reach salvation through one's own moral discipline. Augustine refuted Pelagius by arguing that we are all under the bondage of original

[42] Roger Haight, *The Experience and Language of Grace* (New York: Paulist Press, 1979).
[43] James A. Carpenter, *Nature and Grace: Toward an Integral Perspective* (New York: Crossroad, 1988).
[44] Stephen J. Duffy, *The Dynamics of Grace* (Collegeville, MN: Liturgical Press, 1993).
[45] John Hardon, *History and Theology of Grace: The Catholic Teaching on Divine Grace* (Ave Maria, FL: Sapientia Press, 2002).
[46] Neil Ormerod, *Creation, Grace, and Redemption* (Maryknoll, NY: Orbis Books, 2007).
[47] Paul F.M. Zahl, *Grace in Practice: A Theology of Everyday Life* (Grand Rapids, MI: William B. Eerdmans Publishing, 2007).

sin and thus no one has the ability to reach salvation without God's grace.

A number of spiritual counselors and theologians have written about grace in a pastoral context. They have argued that, in certain pastoral contexts, there is nothing that we can do to heal ourselves. We must rely on the grace of God for healing, and not our own works. For example, Gerald May, a psychiatrist and spiritual counselor, has written in his book *Addiction and Grace* about the need to turn to grace in overcoming addictions, since doing so is "impossible by autonomous willpower alone."[48] Lewis Smedes, a professor at Fuller Theological Seminary, has written in his book *Shame and Grace* about the need for grace in healing feelings of shame or unworthiness. Smedes writes that the healing of shame begins with the "spiritual experience of grace."[49] Finally, Andrea Bieler, a professor at the Pacific School of Religion, and Hans-Martin Gutman, a professor at the University of Hamburg, have written about how grace can be embodied in the preaching moment.[50]

For our purposes, it will suffice to note that grace is a free gift from God. Although many complex theologies of grace have developed during the course of the history of Christianity, the key idea is that grace is not something that we can earn for ourselves. Rather, it is all God's doing. In the same way that we experience joy at being reunited with a loved one from whom we have been separated, we experience joy at being reunited with God.

b. Grace as Our Costly Cooperation

Even though grace is a free gift from God, it still demands that we be transformed by it. God's never-ending supply of grace is always there for the taking, but we still must decide to take it. In other words, grace requires us to cooperate with God.[51] This cooperation

---

[48] Gerald G. May, *Addiction and Grace: Love and Spirituality in the Healing of Addictions* (New York: HarperOne, 1988), 140. See also Mark R. McMinn, *Sin and Grace in Christian Counseling: An Integrative Paradigm* (Downers Grove, IL: IVP Academic, 2008).

[49] Lewis B. Smedes, *Shame and Grace: Healing the Shame We Don't Deserve* (New York: HarperSanFrancisco, 1993), 105.

[50] See Andrea Bieler and Hans-Martin Gutmann, *Embodying Grace: Proclaiming Justification in the Real World* (Minneapolis, MN: Fortress Press, 2010).

[51] A major theological dispute during the Protestant Reformation involved Arminianism, or the degree to which human beings can cooperate with God's grace in achieving salvation. For Calvinists, the fall completely obliterated the human ability to do any good. Thus, without God's grace we are helpless, which logically leads to a doctrine of predestination. According to Arminianism, however, human beings are able to cooperate with God. Similarly, Roman Catholic theology holds that the fall only removed the supernatural grace that was given by God to Adam and Eve. Under this view, human beings still have the natural ability after the fall to cooperate with God's grace to achieve salvation. Prior to Vatican II, the Roman Catholic Church had an elaborate framework of grace with technical terms such as *gratia habitualis sanctficans* (habitual sanctifying grace) and *gratia praeveniens* (prevenient grace). For a detailed description of this earlier framework, see Georg Kraus, "Grace," in *Handbook of Catholic Theology*, ed. Wolfgang Beinert and Francis Schüssler Fiorenza (New York: Herder and Herder, 1995), 302–10.

comes at a price, however. Grace demands that we follow Christ as disciples and be transformed. In other words, grace does not mean that we can accept it and then go back to our old lives of being separated from God, as if nothing had changed. Once we have truly experienced grace, our lives are transformed. We are no longer the people we once were. And this transformation comes at a cost.

For me, the in-breaking of grace that I experienced in discovering the Episcopal Church and pursuing a doctorate in systematic theology resulted in a radical transformation and upending of my life. As I mentioned above, I was raised in a first-generation Chinese American immigrant family that had very worldly ideas of what success might look like. Over the last decade, I have seen a gradual reorientation of my life towards God. It would have been the path of least resistance for me to stay as a lawyer for the rest of my life. However, I believe that God's grace has nudged me to take the more challenging path of dedicating my life to the pursuit of theology. Although in retrospect it seems like all of my transitions made all the sense in the world, both Michael and I actually experienced a great deal of uncertainty and anxiety about the future at each major point of transition in my life (for example, going to seminary full time, applying for doctoral studies, applying for teaching jobs, and so on). Grace is costly.

The concept of costly grace was articulated most clearly by Dietrich Bonhoeffer, a German pastor and theologian who was executed at the age of thirty-nine by the Nazi regime for plotting to assassinate Adolf Hitler. According to Bonhoeffer, even though grace is a free gift from God, it is ultimately not cheap. Those who receive God's grace are called to become disciples of Christ and be transformed. Bonhoeffer set forth his theology of grace in *The Cost of Discipleship*. He writes: "Cheap grace is the deadly enemy of our Church. . . . Cheap grace is grace without discipleship, grace without the cross, grace without Jesus Christ, living and incarnate."[52]

Eldin Villafañe, a professor at Gordon-Conwell Theological Seminary in South Hamilton, Massachusetts, has written about costly grace in his book *Beyond Cheap Grace*. Villafañe argues for a "radical discipleship" that rejects an attitude of "Please don't

---

[52] Dietrich Bonhoeffer, *The Cost of Discipleship* (New York: Touchstone, 1995), 43–45.

ask too much of me" or "Do not disturb" with respect to Christian discipleship.[53] Villafañe notes that we are constantly being bombarded with "media messages and images to a comfortable and self-satisfying life."[54] Similarly, Jon Walker in his book *Costly Grace* writes about the need to take risks beyond our "stash[ing] away our 401k's and plan for when we will do kingdom work in the future, never trusting God to provide."[55]

Ironically, many of the fundamentalist Christians who ask LGBT people to change our sexualities or gender identities have a selective theology of costly grace. That is, although they may transform their lives in some ways after accepting Jesus Christ as their savior (for example, in the area of sexual ethics), they do not transform their lives in other ways (for example, challenging the systemic sins of patriarchy, sexism, and homophobia). LGBT people, on the other hand, often experience costly grace when we leave the closet after receiving the grace of coming out; we risk our families, jobs, and sometimes even our physical safety in ways that many anti-LGBT people cannot understand.[56]

c. Grace as Surprise: Amazing and Unexpected

Third, grace is amazing. It is utterly unexpected, surprising, and astonishing. This idea is most famously expressed in the hymn "Amazing Grace" by John Newton with the opening lines: "Amazing grace! how sweet the sound,/that saved a wretch like me!/I once was lost, but now am found,/was blind, but now I see." Newton was a young slave trader who had converted to Christianity and eventually left the slave trade to became an ordained Anglican priest. It was not until the end of his life, however, that he became an abolitionist and spoke out against slavery.[57]

The implicit message of Newton's hymn is that if a slave trader can become an Anglican priest through the amazing power of God's grace, then all of us can be transformed. It should be noted that many people have difficulties with the word "wretch" in the first line of Newton's hymn and have replaced it with other

[53] Eldin Villafañe, *Beyond Cheap Grace: A Call to Radical Discipleship, Incarnation and Justice* (Grand Rapids, MI: William B. Eerdmans Publishing, 2006), 2.

[54] Villafañe, *Beyond Cheap Grace*, xii.

[55] Jon Walker, *Costly Grace: A Contemporary View of Dietrich Bonhoeffer's* The Cost of Discipleship (Abilene, TX: Leafwood Publishers, 2010), 29.

[56] For the stories of LGBT people who have been murdered because of homophobia and transphobia, see Sprinkle, *Unfinished Lives*.

[57] For a biography of John Newton's life, see Bernard Martin, *John Newton: A Biography* (Melbourne: William Heinemann, 1950).

words. For example, the phrase "that saved a wretch like me" has been changed to "that saved *and strengthened* me," "that saved a *soul* like me," or some other variation thereof.[58] On the one hand, I do appreciate and applaud these changes to the extent that they are needed to heal people on the margins (including LGBT people) who have been wounded by Christianity. Indeed, I was not ready to hear the word "wretch" when I first came back to church after many years away. However, I also can appreciate the word "wretch" to the extent that it shows how amazing and unexpected the transforming power of God's grace can be. There is also something that is radically equalizing about treating *all* of us—and not just some of us—as wretches. Ironically, it is only in hindsight—after we have experienced God's grace—that we are able to see how amazing, unexpected, surprising, and astonishing God's grace can be.

The Greek word for "amaze" or "astound"—*ekplēssō*—appears thirteen times in the New Testament and expresses the "astonished reaction of uncommitted onlookers to Jesus' teaching" or his healing power.[59] The word is used to describe Mary and Joseph's amazement to find their child sitting with the teachers in the Temple, and it is also used in the Acts of Apostles to describe the proconsul Sergius Paulus's reaction to Paul's teaching about Jesus Christ after he is temporarily blinded.[60] Indeed, we are reminded throughout the New Testament that God's grace is amazing precisely because of its connection with Jesus Christ. For Christians, Jesus Christ is the ultimate manifestation of God's grace.

For those of us who walk the Christian path, grace is not just an external "thing" that we receive from God for spiritual regeneration or growth (for example, a sacrament such as Baptism or the Holy Eucharist), but rather grace *is* Jesus Christ himself. Jesus Christ, as the Word made flesh, is the ultimate unmerited gift to us from God. Mary, as the Mother of the incarnate Word, is literally "full of grace" when she is with child with Jesus Christ.[61] For Christians, it is through the incarnation, life, crucifixion, and resurrection of Jesus Christ that God's grace is fully revealed.

[58] Shuster, *The Fall and Sin*, 100.

[59] Verlyn D. Verbrugge, ed., *New International Dictionary of New Testament Theology*, abridged ed. (Grand Rapids, MI: Zondervan, 2000), 175. See, e.g., Mark 1:22, 6:2; Luke 9:43.

[60] Luke 2:48; Acts 13:12.

[61] Luke 1:28. The angel Gabriel greets Mary as the "favored one"—*kecharitōmenē*—at the Annunciation, and this phrase is translated as "full of grace" in the Hail Mary prayer.

Thus, it is impossible for Christians to talk about grace without understanding its radically Christ-centered nature. And, as I have noted above, I believe that it is possible to understand "Christ" in expansive and/or symbolic terms (for example, as the intersection of the divine with the human, wherever that encounter may occur) so that it might speak to others in an interfaith or even a secular context.

A number of popular evangelical Christian books have been written about the amazing nature of God's grace, including Philip Yancey's *What's So Amazing About Grace?*[62] and Michael Horton's *Putting Amazing Back into Grace*.[63] While I am not usually a reader of such books, I do appreciate the fact that these books tell many powerful stories about how grace has worked in the lives of God's people. For example, Yancey dedicates an entire chapter in his book about his relationship with Mel White—one of his best friends and a trusted ghostwriter to many leading voices of the religious right—who came out of the closet on Christmas Eve in 1991. In a chapter entitled "Grace-Healed Eyes," Yancey wrote that his experience with White's coming out not only helped him to better understand the struggles faced by LGBT people—and especially LGBT Christians—but it also "strongly challenged my notion of how grace should affect my attitude toward 'different' people, even when those differences are serious and perhaps unresolvable."[64]

For me, the words to the hymn "Amazing Grace" describe the unexpected, surprising, and astonishing path of my vocational journey, from a tax lawyer to a queer Asian American activist, and from an English literature major to a systematic theologian. The adjective "amazing" accurately describes the ongoing effect of the reconciling grace that broke into my life with respect to both the Christian faith and my love for theology.[65]

---

[62] Philip Yancey, *What's So Amazing About Grace?* (Grand Rapids, MI: Zondervan, 1997).

[63] Michael Horton, *Putting Amazing Back into Grace: Embracing the Heart of the Gospel*, 2nd ed. (Grand Rapids, MI: Baker Books, 2002).

[64] Yancey, *What's So Amazing About Grace?*, 163. For more about Mel White's story, see Mel White, *Stranger at the Gate: To Be Gay and Christian in America* (New York: Plume, 1994).

[65] For a discussion about "grace as surprise" in the context of vocation, see L. William Countryman and M.R. Ritley, *Gifted By Otherness: Gay and Lesbian Christians in the Church* (Harrisburg, PA: Morehouse Publishing, 2001), 53–62.

Study Questions

1. How do you define sin? Does this differ from what you were taught about sin as a child? How does your religious or spiritual tradition, if any, define sin?
2. Why do you think there is such a strong association between sin and sexuality? What are some sins—other than sexual sins—that come to mind?
3. How would you describe original sin in your own words? How does original sin differ from actual sins?
4. How might heterosexuality be an idol? How might an excessive focus on "family values" take away from our relationship with God?
5. Which of the various biblical and theological definitions of sin that were discussed in this chapter appeal to you the most? The least?
6. How do you define grace? Does this differ from what you were taught about grace as a child? How does your religious or spiritual tradition, if any, define grace?
7. What does it mean to you that grace is a gift that cannot be earned? How might this understanding of grace help in the pastoral context of addiction or shame?
8. What are some examples of the cost of cooperating with God's grace? What does "radical discipleship" mean to you?
9. What are some ways in which God's amazing grace has worked in your life and the lives of those around you? How can Jesus Christ be thought of as grace itself?

For Further Study

Doctrines of Sin and Grace

- Berkhof, *The History of Christian Doctrines*, 125–61
- Lohse, *A Short History of Christian Doctrine*, 100–31
- Sölle, *Thinking About God*, 54–67, 77–94

Original Sin

- Blocher, *Original Sin*
- Finstuen, *Original Sin and Everyday Protestants*
- Jacobs, *Original Sin*
- McFarland, *In Adam's Fall*
- Shuster, *The Fall and Sin*
- Wiley, *Original Sin*

Histories of Sin

- Anderson, *Sin*
- Nelson, *What's Wrong with Sin?*
- Portman, *A History of Sin*
- Smith, *With Willful Intent*
- Thomson, *A History of Sin*

Biblical Sin

- Cover, "Sin, Sinners (OT)"
- Erickson, *Christian Theology*, 583–95
- Sanders, "Sin, Sinners (NT)"
- Smith, *With Willful Intent*, 153–310

Seven Deadly Sins

- DeYoung, *Glittering Vices*
- Kleinberg, *Seven Deadly Sins*

Contemporary Theologies on Sin

- Anderson, *Sin*
- Ellingsen, *Sin Bravely*
- Mercadante, *Victims and Sinners*
- Plantinga, *Not the Way It's Supposed to Be*
- Suchocki, *The Fall to Violence*

Overview of Grace

- Carpenter, *Nature and Grace*
- Duffy, *The Dynamics of Grace*
- Haight, *The Experience and Language of Grace*
- Hardon, *History and Theology of Grace*
- Ormerod, *Creation, Grace, and Redemption*
- Zahl, *Grace in Practice*

Grace and Pastoral Care

- Bieler and Gutman, *Embodying Grace*
- May, *Addiction and Grace*
- Smedes, *Shame and Grace*

Costly Grace

- Bonhoeffer, *The Cost of Discipleship*
- Sprinkle, *Unfinished Lives*
- Villafañe, *Beyond Cheap Grace*
- Walker, *Costly Grace*

Amazing Grace

- Countryman and Ritley, *Gifted By Otherness*, 53–62
- Horton, *Putting Amazing Back into Grace*
- Martin, *John Newton*
- Yancey, *What's So Amazing About Grace?*

Chapter 3

The Crime-Based Model of Sin and Grace

Before becoming a seminary professor, I worked as a lawyer for over fifteen years. Crime and punishment were often on my mind. While in law school, I took classes in criminal law and criminal procedure. After law school, I clerked for a federal appellate judge in Los Angeles, and we worked on many cases involving federal criminal law as well as appeals in cases involving the death penalty. I will never forget sitting in chambers during a night on which a convicted prisoner was scheduled to be executed, waiting for a last-minute stay of execution from the United States Supreme Court—a stay that never came. Never had the raw power of the criminal law to punish—and to take away another human being's life—been so powerfully demonstrated to me than on that night.

Traditional theological thinking about sin and grace is based upon a *crime-based* model. In other words, sin is seen as committing a crime against God. This criminal behavior is deserving of punishment, up to and including eternal death or damnation. Thanks to the grace of God, particularly through the sacrifice and crucifixion of Jesus Christ, we are acquitted of this crime. It is only because of this gift of grace that we are able to be rehabilitated from the crime (that is, to refrain from committing further crimes) against God.

Nowhere is this crime-based model of sin and grace more obvious than with respect to Christianity's treatment of same-sex and gender-variant acts. Throughout much of the history of the church, people who have committed such acts have been condemned as violating God's law and thus deserving of punishment. In fact, this transgression has been viewed as being so horrific that if it went unchecked—as in the case of the Sodom and Gomorrah narrative in Genesis 19—such acts would trigger God's collective punishment of not only the people committing such acts, but also their entire communities.

The crime-based model of sin and grace is ultimately inadequate and may even be dangerous for LGBT people. In this chapter, I begin with a description of the crime-based model of sin and grace. I describe how sin, grace, and atonement are treated within this model. I then turn to how same-sex and gender-variant acts have been viewed as crimes against God, and to the threat of God's collective punishment for such crimes. I conclude with several reasons why the crime-based model is problematic and why LGBT people need to search for a different model of sin and grace.

1. The Crime-Based Model

a. Sin as Crime

Theologically speaking, sin has traditionally been viewed as a *crime* against God. That is, sin is understood as a violation or transgression of God's divine law.[1] In the case of the criminal law, a crime is understood as an offense against the sovereign or state, and thus justice demands that the offender be punished (for example, imprisonment or execution). No amount of monetary compensation is adequate to "right the wrong" in the case of a crime because there is more than just a private victim involved.[2] Analogously, to the extent that sin is understood as a crime against God the sovereign, the punishment of the sinner is also required.

The crime-based model can be seen clearly in the traditional theology of original sin and interpretation of the third chapter of

---

[1] See, for example, Alan Richardson and John Bowden, eds., *The Westminster Dictionary of Christian Theology* (Philadelphia, PA: The Westminster Press, 1983), 539 (defining sin as "any word or deed or thought against the eternal law"); Erickson, *Christian Theology*, 595 (defining sin as the failure to "fulfill God's law"). I recognize that there have been other ways of understanding sin throughout the history of Christian theology (for example, the cultic or sacrificial model). However, I focus on the crime-based model here because of its prominence in the Western Christian tradition and its particularly pernicious effect on LGBT people.

[2] By contrast, tort law is designed to compensate the victim of a tort (for example, physical harm arising out of the negligence of the tortfeasor) and thus monetary damages are sufficient.

Genesis. That is, Adam and Eve are commanded by God not to eat of the fruit of the Tree of Knowledge of Good and Evil. Tricked by the serpent, Adam and Eve violate God's law by eating the fruit. Because of this crime, they are punished. They are expelled from the Garden of Eden and become subject to death. Furthermore, God subjects Adam to hard labor, and God subjects Eve to pain in childbirth.[3]

Not only are Adam and Eve punished, however, but all of their descendants—that is, us—are also punished for this crime. As we have seen earlier, the "infection" of original sin is passed on from generation to generation through concupiscence (that is, lust) and the sexual act. It is for this reason that the Christian tradition has insisted that sex be restricted to heterosexual marriage only; the inherent evil of the sexual act is rendered non-sinful only by the possibility of procreation within marriage.[4]

The rhetoric of sin as crime can be seen in the writings of many Christian theologians. For example, Augustine of Hippo wrote that, as a result of Adam's sin, "in Adam all die" and "all human beings are, as it were, one mass of sin owing a debt of punishment to that divine and highest justice."[5] Similarly, John Calvin wrote that "what God so severely punished must have been no light sin but a detestable crime" and that Adam "implicating us in his ruin, destroyed us with himself."[6]

One odd thing about the crime-based model of sin—at least from the perspective of someone who is legally trained—is that the essential jurisprudential notion of *mens rea*, that is, the criminal intent of the person committing the crime, does not appear to be satisfied by either Adam and Eve or their descendants. That is, to the extent that Adam and Eve were tricked by the serpent to eat of the fruit, they arguably did not intend to commit a criminal act. And even if they did have a criminal intent, it seems unjust to impute criminal intent upon their descendents (that is, all of us) who simply inherited this sin through biological transmission.

Theologians have traditionally responded to this point by

---

[3] See generally Gen. 3:16–19.

[4] Interestingly, the doctrine of original sin might actually lead to the surprising conclusion that procreative heterosexual sex is actually *more* sinful than same-sex acts, since the former has the potential of transmitting original sin to the next generation, whereas the latter does not. This is certainly consistent with Paul's admonition in 1 Cor. 7:38 that "he who refrains from marriage will do better."

[5] Augustine of Hippo, *To Simplicianus* 1.2, in *Augustine in His Own Words*, ed. William Harmless (Washington, DC: Catholic University of America Press, 2010), 386–87.

[6] John Calvin, *Institutes of the Christian Religion*, II.i.4, 6, in *Institutes of the Christian Religion*, ed. John T. McNeill (Louisville, KY: Westminster John Knox Press, 1960), 1:244, 248.

arguing that human beings actually still have free will—notwithstanding original sin—and thus are still culpable for actual sins. That is, human beings still are free to decide whether or not to commit a given act (for example, whether or not to pull the trigger on a gun), notwithstanding the fact that we are predisposed by original sin to make the wrong choice. However, as someone who is legally trained, I personally do not find this free-will argument to be very persuasive in terms of justifying the severity of punishment (that is, death) that results from Adam and Eve's sin.

b. Grace as Acquittal and Rehabilitation

If sin is understood as crime, then grace is *acquittal*, or being declared innocent, from that crime. Grace is the free and unmerited gift from God that declares the sinner "justified" or righteous before God. In the words of Augustine of Hippo, despite the fact that original sin creates within each of us a "criminal nature," God has saved us from the punishment that we deserve by grace. Grace, according to Augustine, is a gift "without which neither children nor adults can be saved" and is "given gratuitously and not for our merits, and for this reason is called 'grace.'"[7]

Why is Augustine so insistent that only God can acquit us from our original sin? That is, why is acquittal solely a matter of God's grace? Recall that Augustine's doctrine of original sin arose from his argument with the British monk Pelagius, who argued that human beings had the capacity to attain salvation through high moral standards and perfectionism. For Augustine, this approach detracted from the sovereignty of God, and thus Augustine insisted not only upon original sin as a condition that infected all of us, but also grace as something that can only come from God.[8]

Grace is not only a matter of acquittal, however. It is also a matter of *rehabilitation* from our old sinful ways. In other words, God gives us the gift of grace so that we can be "sanctified," or made holy, and turn away from our old lives of sin. While acquittal (that is, justification) is a discrete event, rehabilitation (that is, sanctification) is a life-long process. From a criminal law perspective, the concept of rehabilitation is an important part of the jurisprudence of punishment. That is, punishment can be justified

[7] Augustine of Hippo, *On Nature and Grace* 3.3, in Harmless, *Augustine in His Own Words*, 403.
[8] For a discussion of, and texts relating to, the Pelagian controversy, see Harmless, "Controversies (IV): Against the Pelagians," in *Augustine in His Own Words*, 373–436.

philosophically by a number of reasons such as retribution, deterrence, incapacitation, and rehabilitation. Due to the acquittal of our crime by God's grace (that is, our guilt has been wiped out), most of the traditional philosophical rationales for punishment are no longer applicable. However, we still need God's grace to rehabilitate us for the long term.[9]

c. Atonement as Penal Substitution

Finally, if sin is understood as crime, and grace is understood as acquittal and rehabilitation, then atonement can be understood as *penal substitution*. Atonement is the doctrine in Christian theology that describes how Jesus Christ's incarnation, crucifixion, and resurrection reconciles us (that is, leads to our "at-one-ment") in our estrangement or separation from God. In a crime-based model of sin and grace, atonement can be understood as an innocent third party (here, Jesus Christ) taking on the punishment (that is, penal substitution) that would otherwise be due to sinners (here, humanity).

Although there is no official doctrine of atonement—and, in fact, there are many different models[10]—the penal substitution model remains one of the most influential models of atonement and is consistent with the crime-based view of sin and grace. The penal substitution theory of atonement has its roots in the satisfaction theory of Anselm of Canterbury and his famous work *Why God Became Human*. In that work, Anselm sought to justify the incarnation. He argued that the incarnation was necessary because human beings had committed an infinitely great offense against God in the fall, and only a hybrid being in the form of a God-human (that is, Jesus Christ) could satisfy the infinite debt that was owed to God. No "regular" human being could ever pay such a price. Thus, the incarnation was necessary.[11]

Anselm's satisfaction model was transformed into the penal substitution model by John Calvin and other Reformation theologians. These theologians shifted the emphasis from satisfaction to punishment. That is, Jesus Christ not only satisfied an infinite

---

9 For a discussion of the philosophy of punishment and rehabilitation, see Jeffrie G. Murphy, *Punishment and Rehabilitation*, 3rd ed. (Belmont, CA: Wadsworth Publishing, 1995).

10 Some of these models include the ransom model of the early church, the satisfaction model of Anselm of Canterbury, and the moral influence model of Abelard. For an overview of ten different theories of atonement, see Peter Schmiechen, *Saving Power: Theories of Atonement and Forms of the Church* (Grand Rapids, MI: William B. Eerdmans Publishing, 2005).

11 See Anselm of Canterbury, "Why God Became Man," in *A Scholastic Miscellany: Anselm to Ockham*, ed. Eugene R. Fairweather (Louisville, KY: Westminster John Knox Press, 1956), 100–83.

debt that could only be paid by a God-human, but he also took on the punishment (here, death) that would have otherwise been inflicted on human beings. For example, Calvin argued in his *Institutes of the Christian Religion* that Christ "took upon himself and suffered the punishment that, from God's righteous judgment, threatened all sinners."[12]

Not surprisingly, the penal substitution theory of atonement is grounded in notions of crime and punishment. As we have seen, God in the person of Jesus Christ has taken on the punishment that would otherwise be meted out to us. The penal substitution theory is also grounded in notions of sacrifice and substitution (that is, a wrathful God can only be appeased if the life of another being is sacrificed in the sinner's place).

Despite the fact that the penal substitution theory of atonement has been roundly criticized by feminist theologians for encouraging child abuse and violence within the household,[13] and even though it is premised on the troubling jurisprudential notion of vicarious liability in the criminal law context (that is, a third party is held liable for the crimes of another party), it has remained an extremely influential theory of atonement. For our purposes, it is sufficient to note that the penal substitution theory of atonement reinforces the crime-based model of sin and atonement.[14]

2. The Crime-Based Model and LGBT People

For much of the history of Christianity, same-sex and gender-variant acts have been treated as crimes from the perspective of both the church and the state. With respect to the church, such acts have been treated as crimes against God that cry out for divine punishment. With respect to the state, such acts have been treated as crimes against society that demand secular punishment.

I believe what is behind this crime-based model is a deep-seated

[12] See Calvin, *Institutes of the Christian Religion*, II.xvi.2, in McNeill, *Institutes of the Christian Religion*, 1:505. For a discussion of the penal satisfaction theory of atonement, see Steve Jeffery, Michael Ovey, and Andrew Sach, *Pierced for Our Transgressions: Rediscovering the Glory of Penal Substitution* (Wheaton, IL: Crossway Books, 2007).

[13] See, for example, the essays in Joanne Carlson Brown and Carole R. Bohn, eds., *Christianity, Patriarchy, and Abuse: A Feminist Critique* (Cleveland, OH: Pilgrim Press, 1989).

[14] I have argued elsewhere that the Christ event can be understood not so much in terms of a substitutionary punishment in order to placate a wrathful God, but rather in terms of God's rejection of the universal scapegoating mechanism that results in the bullying and victimization of LGBT and other marginalized people. That is, Jesus Christ is the theological scapegoat *par excellence*, and it is through the resurrection that God rejects the scapegoating mechanism. It is through this condemnation of scapegoating that God gives us the gift, or grace, of reuniting us with God. See Cheng, *Radical Love*, 94–98.

fear of collective punishment—that is, group punishment—by God. Because of the church's interpretation of biblical narratives like Sodom and Gomorrah in Genesis 19 as God's collective punishment for same-sex acts, many Christians have felt the need to eradicate same-sex as well as gender-variant acts in their own communities so as to ward off the possibility of divine punishment.

In this section, I will trace the notion of collective punishment in biblical, theological, and historical narratives about same-sex and gender-variant acts. In recent years, there have been a number of biblical, ethical, and philosophical studies on the problem of collective responsibility, and I believe that this is a topic that is worth exploring in future scholarship.[15]

a. The Bible

The Bible has been one of the main sources reinforcing the crime-based model of sin and grace. Not only has the notion of collective punishment been used to condemn LGBT people, but it also has been used historically to subjugate people of color and women. For example, racial supremacists have historically justified the enslavement of black people as a result of the notion of God's collective punishment of people of African descent for Ham's sin against Noah.[16] Christian men have historically rationalized the second-class treatment of women as a result of the notion of God's collective punishment of women for Eve's role in the fall.[17]

Ironically, the Bible contains only half a dozen or so verses (out of over 31,000 verses) that purportedly condemn same-sex and gender-variant acts. It is not clear whether such prohibitions would actually apply to those people whom we identify as LGBT today. Many biblical scholars have argued that such prohibitions occurred in the context of rape and other non-consensual situations (for example, sex with slaves). Furthermore, these scholars have argued that these prohibitions reflected patriarchal anxieties about men (and not women) submitting to other men. Neither situation is applicable to the context of same-sex relationships today.

---

[15] See Joel S. Kaminsky, *Corporate Responsibility in the Hebrew Bible* (Sheffield, UK: Sheffield Academic Press, 1995); Larry May and Stacey Hoffman, eds., *Collective Responsibility: Five Decades of Debate in Theoretical and Applied Ethics* (Lanham, MD: Roman and Littlefield Publishers, 1991); Gregory F. Mellema, *Collective Responsibility* (Amsterdam, Netherlands: Rodopi, 1997).

[16] See Gen. 9:22-27, in which Noah curses Ham's son, Canaan, and designates Canaan as the "lowest of slaves" after Ham "saw the nakedness" of Noah.

[17] See Peter J. Gomes, *The Good Book: Reading the Bible with Mind and Heart* (New York: HarperSanFrancisco, 1996), 120-43; John Shelby Spong, *The Sins of Scripture: Exposing the Bible's Texts of Hate to Reveal the God of Love* (New York: HarperOne, 2005), 69-119.

Nevertheless, these half-dozen or so verses have been interpreted by many anti-LGBT Christians as prescribing various types of punishment for same-sex and gender-variant acts. For example, Leviticus 18:22 and 20:13 taken together prescribe the death penalty for any man who "with a male . . . lie[s] the lying down of a woman." Deuteronomy 22:5 prohibits women from wearing a "man's apparel" as well as men from putting on a "woman's garment." First Corinthians 6:9 states that, among many others, *malakoi* (literally "soft ones") and *arsenokoitai* (literally "man-bedder") will not inherit the Kingdom of God. First Timothy 1:10 describes as "lawless" the *arsenokoitai* (again, "man-bedder").

Many books have been written about why these verses should not apply to LGBT people today. For example, it has been argued that Leviticus actually refers to ritual laws and such prohibitions were culturally specific to the ancient Israelites. Similarly, it has been argued that the ban on cross-dressing in Deuteronomy was a reflection of ancient Israelite anxieties about not mixing together dissimilar things and maintaining the boundaries between the Israelites and their neighbors. Furthermore, it has been argued that the terms in First Corinthians and First Timothy do not refer to consensual or mutual sex acts, but rather relationships that exploit one of the parties. I will not explore these arguments in depth, but I do want to acknowledge that this remains a contested area of scholarship.[18]

I am interested, however, in focusing on two purportedly anti-LGBT passages: first, the story of Sodom and Gomorrah in Genesis 19; and second, the passage about same-sex and gender-variant acts in Romans 1. Both of these passages are interesting because they deal with the question of collective punishment. That is, they are both examples of divine punishment on entire communities (as opposed to individuals). It is my thesis that deep anxiety over the divine collective punishment is what has led to the persecution of people who engage in same-sex and gender-variant acts over the centuries.

In Genesis 19, two disguised angels visit the city of Sodom. Lot,

---

[18] See L. William Countryman, *Dirt, Greed, and Sex: Sexual Ethics in the New Testament and Their Implications for Today*, rev. ed. (Minneapolis, MN: Fortress Press, 2007); Tobias Stanislas Haller, *Reasonable and Holy: Engaging Same-Sexuality* (New York: Seabury Books, 2009); Daniel A. Helminiak, *What the Bible* Really *Says About Homosexuality*, millennium edition (Tajique, NM: Alamo Square Press, 2000); Michaelson, *God vs. Gay?*, 55–111 ("What the 'bad verses' really say about homosexuality"); Justin Tanis, *Trans-Gendered: Theology, Ministry, and Communities of Faith* (Cleveland, OH: Pilgrim Press, 2003), 55–84 ("Gender Variance and the Scriptures").

a recent arrival to the city, offers to house them overnight. The men of Sodom surround Lot's house and demand that Lot turn over the visitors so that they can "know" them. Lot offers up his daughters, but the men of Sodom refuse. They attempt to break into the house, but they are blinded by light, which saves the visitors from harm. The next morning, Lot and his family leave the city along with the disguised visitors. After they have left, God destroys Sodom along with Gomorrah and their other sister cities by sending down fire and brimstone. Lot's wife looks back and is turned into a pillar of salt. This story is a classic example of collective punishment, in which a larger number of people are punished for the sins or crimes of others.[19]

The notion of collective punishment in the narrative of Sodom and Gomorrah is echoed in the New Testament by the first chapter of Paul's letter to the Romans. In that letter, same-sex and gender-variant behavior is actually described as God's *punishment* for idolatry. Because the gentiles "exchanged the glory of the immortal God for images resembling a mortal human being or birds or four-footed animals or reptiles," God punished these individuals by giving them up to "degrading passions." That is, God inflicts same-sex and gender-variant behavior as a form of punishment on those who engaged in idol-worship and served the creature instead of the Creator. Because same-sex and gender-variant acts are described as the consequence of idolatry, there is a strong element of collective punishment in Romans as well.[20]

Many biblical scholars have debated whether the true crime of Sodom was inhospitality and whether the first chapter of Romans was merely a rhetorical trap by Paul to show the Jewish Christians that they were actually no better than the Gentile Christians. What scholars have *not* done in great detail, however, is to examine the notion of collective punishment and how that might have deeply impacted the treatment of same-sex and gender-variant acts in subsequent Christian theology and church history.

---

[19] Gen. 19.

[20] Rom. 1:21–32.

b. Theology

Throughout the history of Christianity, many theologians have condemned same-sex and gender-variant acts from a crime-based view of sin. Again, my thesis is that this condemnation may be the result of ancient anxieties about collective punishment—especially as described in the Sodom narrative in Genesis 19—and how permitting such acts could lead to divine punishment of the larger society. We still see this attitude today with televangelists such as Pat Robertson who warn that God will destroy the United States for supporting the rights of LGBT people.[21]

One of the earliest writers to make the connection between same-sex acts and collective punishment was Philo, a Hellenistic Jewish writer who was a contemporary of Jesus and Paul. Prior to Philo, most references to Sodom's sin involved the inhospitality of its inhabitants and their failure to help the poor and needy.[22] However, Philo, in his work *On Abraham*, blames the destruction of Sodom on its inhabitants who were engaged in same-sex acts and "corrupting in this way the whole race of man."[23] Other early texts that connected same-sex acts with collective punishment included the works of Clement of Alexandria, John Chrysostom, and the *Apostolic Constitutions*.[24]

The connection between same-sex acts and collective punishment was reinforced by the writings of the fourth-century theologian Augustine of Hippo. In *City of God*, Augustine explained that God destroyed Sodom as "punishment" because the inhabitants of Sodom had made same-sex acts so prevalent there that it was effectively sanctioned by human law. In fact, this punishment was simply a foretaste of the "divine judgment to come."[25] Similarly, Augustine argues in *Confessions* that any sexual act that is "contrary to nature" must be "everywhere and at all times"

---

[21] See Brian Tashman, "Robertson: God Will Destroy America for Marriage Equality" (June 27, 2011), available at http://www.rightwingwatch.org/content/robertson-god-will-destroy-america-marriage-equality (accessed on December 11, 2011).

[22] Ezek. 16:49 ("This was the guilt of your sister Sodom: she and her daughters had pride, excess of food, and prosperous ease, but did not aid the poor and needy.").

[23] Philo, *De Abrahamo* 26.135–36, in *The Works of Philo*, trans. C.D. Yonge, new updated ed. (Peabody, MA: Hendrickson Publishers, Inc., 1993), 422–23 (emphasis added).

[24] Clement of Alexandria noted in *The Instructor* that what happened to the inhabitants of Sodom was a "judgment of those who had done wrong," which included the "burning with insane love for boys." Clement of Alexandria, *Paedagogus* 4.9 (*ANF* 2:282). John Chrysostom noted that because the inhabitants of Sodom "burned in their lust one towards another" and were infertile, God made sure that the "very earth itself was burned up" and made "womb of the land ever barren and destitute of all fruits." John Chrysostom, *Homilies on the Statues to the People of Antioch* 19.7 (*NPNF1* 9:466–67). The *Apostolic Constitutions* taught that "[t]hou shalt not corrupt boys" because such "wickedness" is "contrary to nature" and arose from Sodom, which was "entirely consumed with fire sent by God." *Apostolic Constitutions* 7.2 (*ANF* 7:466).

[25] Augustine, *De civitate Dei* 16.30 (*NPNF1* 2:328).

punished, regardless of the "customs or compacts of any nation" because it is a matter of divine law.[26]

The medieval theologian Peter Damian wrote an entire treatise, the *Book of Gomorrah*, about the "criminal wickedness" of the "sin against nature."[27] Mark Jordan, an openly gay theologian and professor at Harvard Divinity School, has traced the creation and evolution of the term "sodomy" in the Middle Ages in his work *The Invention of Sodomy in Christian Theology*. Jordan examines not only the theological work of Peter Damian, but also that of Alan of Lille, Albert the Great, and Thomas Aquinas.[28]

This focus on same-sex acts and collective punishment continued into the Reformation. Martin Luther in his *Lectures on Genesis* criticized the "terrible sin" and "monstrous depravity" of the same-sex acts committed by the inhabitants of Sodom.[29] Similarly, John Calvin, in his *Commentary on Romans*, uses a criminal understanding of sin to describe the sinfulness of same-sex acts. Calvin notes that the "fearful crime" of unnatural lust is worse than bestiality because it "reverse[s] the whole order of nature" as ordained by God.[30]

In the twentieth century, Reinhold Niebuhr referred to the sin of "unnatural lust" in his discussion of sensuality in *The Nature and Destiny of Man*. Quoting from the first chapter of Romans, Niebuhr condemned same-sex acts as "vile passions" that are "against nature." For Niebuhr, like Paul and Augustine, unnatural lust is a consequence of the "more primal sin of rebellion against God."[31]

In sum, many theologians and writers, ranging from

---

[26] Augustine, *Confessiones* 3.8(15) (*NPNF1* 1:65). Augustine describes the "crime" of the inhabitants of Sodom as an offense against the "divine law," which prohibits men from "abus[ing] one another." According to Augustine, the very fellowship between God and humanity is violated whenever nature is "polluted by the perversity of lust."

[27] According to Damian, such acts "makes a citizen of the heavenly Jerusalem into an heir of infernal Babylon." Peter Damian, *Liber Gomorrhianus* 1, in *Book of Gomorrah: An Eleventh-Century Treatise Against Clerical Homosexual Practices*, trans. Pierre J. Payer (Waterloo, Ontario: Wilfrid Laurier University Press, 1982), 29. For Damian, the sin against nature "surpasses the enormity of all vices" in that it "tries to overturn the walls of the heavenly homeland and is busy repairing the renewed bulwarks of Sodom." Damian, *Liber Gomorrhianus* 16, in Payer, *Book of Gomorrah*, 63.

[28] See Mark Jordan, *The Invention of Sodomy in Christian Theology* (Chicago: University of Chicago Press, 1997).

[29] Luther argued that the "heinous conduct" of the people of Sodom was especially disgraceful because such acts were widespread, proclaimed in public, directed at strangers, and could have led to the collapse of civil government. Martin Luther, *Lectures on Genesis* 19.4–5 (*LW* 3:251–52, 255–56); see also Martin Luther, *Lectures on Romans* 1.24–25 (*LW* 25:165–66).

[30] John Calvin, *Commentary on Romans* 1.26, in *Calvin's Commentaries: The Epistles of Paul the Apostle to the Romans and to the Thessalonians*, ed. David W. Torrance and Thomas F. Torrance, trans. Ross Mackenzie (Grand Rapids, MI: William B. Eerdmans Publishing Company, 1995), 36. In his *Commentary on Genesis*, Calvin focuses on the lack of reason in the inhabitants of Sodom. He writes about the "blind and impetuous" lust of such individuals, and how they rushed to Lot's house like "brute animals." According to Calvin, the mixture of lust and the absence of shame results in a "vile barbarism" in which "many kinds of sin are mixed together." John Calvin, *Commentary on Genesis* 19.4, in *The Crossway Classic Commentaries: Genesis*, ed. Alister McGrath and J.I. Packer (Wheaton, IL: Crossway Books, 2001), 81.

[31] Reinhold Niebuhr, *The Nature and Destiny of Man: A Christian Interpretation* (New York: Charles Scribner's Sons, 1941), 1:230.

contemporaries of Jesus to those of the twentieth century, have cited the Sodom narrative as well as the first chapter of Romans—both of which deal expressly with collective punishment—to condemn same-sex and gender-variant acts.[32]

c. Church History

With respect to church history, the physical torture and execution of people who engaged in same-sex or gender-variant behavior was authorized by legislation that was often passed following times of natural disasters such as earthquakes and plagues. For example, the Christian emperor Justinian issued a decree in 538 C.E. that prescribed the death penalty for same-sex acts, which he blamed for natural disasters. Other disasters followed, including military conquest, bubonic plague, and earthquakes, and so another decree against same-sex acts was issued in 544 C.E.[33]

Byrne Fone, in *Homophobia: A History*, traces the presence of homophobia in the history of the Christian church through the ages. Fone argues that the anti-LGBT reading of the Sodom narrative was largely created by Philo, the Hellenized Jewish scholar, who was influenced by the anti-sexual attitudes of neoplatonism as well as the desire to preserve the distinction between the Jewish people and the gentiles.[34] Fone then traces anti-LGBT attitudes in Christian theology through the early church, the Middle Ages, and the reformation. These attitudes led to widespread persecution, torture, and execution of individuals who engaged in same-sex acts in the fourteenth through seventeenth centuries, including Florence, Seville, and Geneva.[35]

Scholars such as Bernadette Brooten and Judith Brown have also traced the impact of Christian homophobia with respect to same-sex and gender-variant acts among women.[36] Similarly, theologians such as Vanessa Sheridan and Virginia Mollenkott have described the ways in which the church has persecuted gender-variant

---

[32] For a concise summary of Christian homophobia from apostolic times through the mid-twentieth century, see Peter Coleman, *Gay Christians: A Moral Dilemma* (London: SCM Press, 1989), 89–124. Classic sources on same-sex and gender-variant acts in church history include Derrick Sherwin Bailey, *Homosexuality and the Western Christian Tradition* (London: Longmans, Green, and Company, 1955); and John Boswell, *Christianity, Social Tolerance, and Homosexuality: Gay People in Western Europe from the Beginning of the Christian Era to the Fourteenth Century* (Chicago: University of Chicago Press, 1980).

[33] See Byrne Fone, *Homophobia: A History* (New York: Picador USA, 2000), 115–16.

[34] See Fone, *Homophobia*, 89–92.

[35] See Fone, *Homophobia*, 192–214.

[36] See Bernadette J. Brooten, *Love Between Women: Early Christian Responses to Female Homoeroticism* (Chicago: University of Chicago Press, 1996); Judith C. Brown, *Immodest Acts: The Life of a Lesbian Nun in Renaissance Italy* (New York: Oxford University Press, 1986).

people (for example, the Council of Constantinople's prohibition of cross-dressing in 691 C.E. and the Medieval church's linking of cross-dressing with witchcraft), as well as affirming them (for example, in the form of transgender saints).[37]

In my view, what underlies homophobia is a fear of divine punishment, especially the kind of collective punishment that is implicated in the Sodom story. As we have seen, the Christian Roman emperor Justinian adopted the death penalty for same-sex acts after several disasters had occurred. I believe it is no coincidence that homophobia in Europe saw a sharp rise starting in the latter half of the twelfth century and lasting through the fourteenth century, as noted by John Boswell,[38] which was around the same time that the bubonic plague was spreading through Europe. Indeed, I believe that the fear of divine punishment has resulted in the purging of LGBT people and our same-sex and gender-variant ancestors—as well as other outsiders such as Jewish people and witches—throughout history. And this is why people continue to oppose rights for LGBT people today. Indeed, it is not surprising that the rhetoric of divine punishment lies at the heart of anti-LGBT religious speech by individuals such as Fred Phelps and Pat Robertson.[39]

As we have seen earlier, grace in the context of the crime-based model is acquittal and rehabilitation. In the LGBT context, this translates into ex-gay therapies that help "convert" LGBT people away from their sexualities and gender identities. That is, these therapies offer the "grace" of rehabilitation to those who wish to leave the "gay lifestyle." Although these therapies have been widely discredited by mainstream mental health professionals,[40] they continue to persist under a crime-based approach to same-sex and gender-variant acts.

I believe that the crime-based model of sin and grace has particular resonance for LGBT people because the Sodom and Gomorrah narrative has been interpreted historically as God's

---

[37] See Vanessa Sheridan, *Crossing Over: Liberating the Transgendered Christian* (Cleveland, OH: Pilgrim Press, 2001), 26–27; Virginia Ramey Mollenkott, *Omnigender: A Trans-Religious Approach* (Cleveland, OH: Pilgrim Press, 2001), 114–18 ("Transgender in Church History").

[38] See Boswell, *Christianity, Social Tolerance, and Homosexuality*, 334.

[39] In addition to divine punishment, there is also the issue of erotophobia, or the fear of sexuality and the erotic, which can be traced back to the early church. For a detailed discussion about sexual renunciation and the early church, see Peter Brown, *The Body and Society: Men, Women, and Sexual Renunciation in Early Christianity*, 20th anniversary ed. (New York: Columbia University Press, 2008).

[40] For a critique of ex-gay programs, see Besen, *Anything But Straight*. See also the Truth Wins Out website, available at http://www.truthwinsout.org (accessed on December 11, 2011).

collective punishment of same-sex acts. For example, the Sodom story historically has been used to justify the punishment—up to and including execution—of people engaging in same-sex and gender-variant acts, often following a natural disaster. We continue to see the rhetoric of divine punishment today from anti-LGBT Christians who predict that God will punish us whenever something positive for LGBT people—such as the legalization of same-sex marriage—occurs.

3. Problems with the Crime-Based Model

There are at least six problems with the crime-based model of sin and grace. First, such a model detracts from the central message of the New Testament of justification by grace. Second, such a model results in an obsession with defining "right" or "wrong" behavior. Third, such a model offends our notions of justice. Fourth, such a model does little to bring the Good News to LGBT people. Fifth, such a model is not the only way to think about sin from a biblical perspective. Sixth, it is not clear that the crime being punished in the Bible is the same thing that we are talking about today. Let us examine each problem in turn.

First, this model detracts from the central message of the New Testament, which is justification by grace alone. By characterizing sin as the violation of God's eternal laws, the focus inevitably shifts to specific acts that may or may not violate such laws. This in turn leads to an obsession with punishing groups that are thought to engage in sinful acts (for example, LGBT people), as opposed to a focus on God's unmerited grace, which is actually the only thing that can help human beings to overcome the bondage of original sin.

Second, the crime-based model results in an obsession with defining "right" or "wrong" behavior. Specifically, this takes the form of endless argumentation and prooftexting over what the Bible "actually" says about same-sex acts. While I strongly believe in the importance of biblical studies and exegesis with respect to LGBT issues, I also think that a narrow focus on what God prohibits or allows in scripture takes away from the larger framework of original sin and the theological significance of Jesus Christ in salvation history. That is, the Bible becomes simply a book of rules, as opposed to the revelation of God's relationship with—and love for—humanity as the Word made flesh.[41]

Third, the crime-based model of sin offends our notions of justice. As noted earlier, the traditional model of original sin is based upon a notion of collective punishment. That is, we are punished for the actions of our ancestors, even though we did not commit or even will those actions. Furthermore, under traditional Christian notions of atonement, an innocent third party (Jesus Christ) takes on the punishment that would otherwise be inflicted upon us, much as an object of sacrifice "stands in" for us with respect to divine wrath. Both of these notions are highly problematic in that there is a fundamental mismatch between a person who commits a crime and the person who is punished for such crime.

Fourth, the crime-based model of sin does little to help bring the Good News to LGBT people. First of all, labeling someone as a criminal is not exactly the most effective way of spreading the gospel, especially when the very thing that is being condemned (for example, our closest and most intimate relationships) is deeply rooted in love. Second, what kind of sadistic God would create people to be same-sex loving or gender variant and then say that they cannot engage in such acts without being punished for eternity? How is this Good News? Such a model is based upon fear and blackmail, and not love. *Metanoia*, or conversion, occurs only *after* one experiences the unconditional love of God. The eyes and ears of people will not be opened if they are told repeatedly how awful they are. That certainly was not Jesus' way.[42]

Fifth, the crime-based model of sin is not the only way to think about sin from a biblical perspective. As Mark Biddle has argued in his book *Missing the Mark: Sin and Its Consequences in Biblical Theology*, a crime-based approach to sin does not reflect the complexity of sin and the Bible. According to Biddle, such a model is "insufficient" and needs to be supplemented by other models of sin.[43] That is, sin is not so much about "disobedience

[41] In recent years, LGBT biblical scholars have published a number of LGBT-positive readings of scripture that are grounded in LGBT experience as opposed to the LGBT texts of terror. Some of these works include: Robert E. Goss and Mona West, eds., *Take Back the Word: A Queer Reading of the Bible* (Cleveland, OH: Pilgrim Press, 2000); Deryn Guest, Robert E. Goss, Mona West, and Thomas Bohache, eds., *The Queer Bible Commentary* (London: SCM Press, 2006); Teresa J. Hornsby and Ken Stone, eds., *Bible Trouble: Queer Reading at the Boundaries of Biblical Scholarship* (Atlanta: Society of Biblical Literature, 2011); Ken Stone, ed., *Queer Commentary and the Hebrew Bible* (Cleveland, OH: Pilgrim Press, 2001).

[42] See Carey, *Sinners*.

[43] Biddle, *Missing the Mark*, 1.

to some precept of the law," but rather the "violation of the basic relationship with God."[44]

Sixth, it is not clear that the crime being punished in the Bible is the same thing that we are talking about today. As noted above, ancient prohibitions against same-sex acts involved concerns about rape as well as patriarchal fears about men (as opposed to women) submitting to other men. Such acts are very different than the kinds of consensual and egalitarian relationships entered into by LGBT people today. Indeed, the very concept of a "homosexual" (that is, someone whose identity is defined by the biological sex of his sexual partners) was not coined until the nineteenth century, so biblical translations that refer to "homosexuals" are anachronistic at best and deceptive at worst. How can we risk punishing people—either in the religious or civil spheres—if we are not sure that we are even talking about the same thing? This is akin to executing a person who has been accused of a crime but is innocent of such crime because the crime was fundamentally ill-defined in the first place.

Given the shortcomings of a crime-based model, what would happen if we thought about sin and grace outside of the crime-based model? What if we moved to a model in which Jesus Christ, instead of crime, was at the center of our reflection on sin and grace? It is to this question that we now turn.

Study Questions

1. What experience, if any, do you have with the criminal justice system? How does punishment relate to your understanding of God and Christian theology?
2. Describe the crime-based model of sin and grace. How is sin understood under such a model?
3. How is grace understood under a crime-based model of sin and grace?
4. What is atonement? How is atonement understood in a crime-based model of sin and grace?

[44] Biddle, *Missing the Mark*, 44.

5. How have the Bible, theology, and church history been used to reinforce a crime-based model of sin and grace, particularly for LGBT people? How does the issue of collective punishment relate to this model?
6. Describe six problems with the crime-based model of sin and grace. Which of these problems do you find the most troublesome? The least troublesome?

For Further Study

Crime-Based Model

- Biddle, *Missing the Mark*

Atonement

- Cheng, *Radical Love*, 94–98
- Sach, *Pierced for Our Transgressions*
- Schmiechen, *Saving Power*

Collective Punishment

- Kaminsky, *Corporate Responsibility in the Hebrew Bible*
- May and Hoffman, *Collective Responsibility*
- Mellema, *Collective Responsibility*

Bible and LGBT People

- Countryman, *Dirt, Greed, and Sex*
- Goss and West, *Take Back the Word*
- Guest, Goss, West, and Bohache, *The Queer Bible Commentary*
- Haller, *Reasonable and Holy*
- Helminiak, *What the Bible* Really *Says About Homosexuality*
- Hornsby and Stone, *Bible Trouble*
- Michaelson, *God vs. Gay?*
- Stone, *Queer Commentary and the Hebrew Bible*
- Tanis, *Trans-Gendered*, 55–84

Theology and LGBT People

- Bailey, *Homosexuality and the Western Christian Tradition*
- Boswell, *Christianity, Social Tolerance, and Homosexuality*
- Coleman, *Gay Christians*, 89–124

Church History and LGBT People

- Boswell, *Christianity, Social Tolerance, and Homosexuality*
- Brooten, *Love Between Women*
- Brown, *Immodest Acts*
- Fone, *Homophobia*
- Mollenkott, *Omnigender*, 114–18
- Sheridan, *Crossing Over*, 26–27

Chapter 4

An Alternative: The Christ-Centered Model of Sin and Grace

Michael and I have been dads for two and a half years to Chartres, our Bichon Frise puppy. We've certainly learned a lot about Chartres—and ourselves—as we've watched her grow and mature since she was only a few months old. There are times when she really tries our patience, and I have a renewed appreciation for what my parents went through during my childhood and adolescence! This is not to equate raising a puppy to the challenges of raising a child, of course, but rather to note that pets often are a very important part of LGBT households, and especially those LGBT households without children.

My experience with Chartres has helped me to grow and to appreciate the amazing grace and beauty of all of God's creation. This process of maturation calls to mind 1 Corinthians 13 in which Paul talks about speaking, thinking, and reasoning like children when we are young, and putting an end to our childish ways only when we are adults.[1] The reality is that, like Chartres, we are all in a process of maturation; we all see through a mirror dimly until the day on which we are able to see Jesus Christ face to face.

This idea of maturation and the entire cosmos moving towards Jesus Christ suggests an alternative model of sin and grace. What if we moved from a crime-centered model of sin and grace to a Christ-centered, or christological, model? That is, what if Jesus Christ—understood as the *telos*, or end goal, of creation—is at the

[1] 1 Cor. 13:11–12.

center of our reflection about sin and grace? What if sin is understood less as a crime or a fall from an original state of perfection, but rather as *immaturity*, spiritual or otherwise? Similarly, what if grace were understood less as an acquittal or rehabilitation of criminals, but rather as *deification*, or the process of growing and maturing to become like God?

In this chapter, I argue for an alternative model that I call the *Christ-centered* model of sin and grace. This model is based upon the Eastern Orthodox notion of *theōsis,* or deification, which is defined as the process of becoming like God. That is, sin is not seen in terms of a crime deserving of punishment. Nor is sin seen as a fall from an original state of perfection. Rather, sin is seen as a function of our human *immaturity*. That is, we are still in the process of growth towards God, and we haven't yet arrived at the end. Sin can be thought of as the misdirected wanderings of immature human beings—starting with Adam and Eve—who turn away from humanity's final goal of deification by disobeying God. By contrast, grace is *deification*, or the process of growing towards God as manifested in Jesus Christ through the Holy Spirit.[2]

This is not some new-fangled "New Age" theology, but it is actually rooted in the ancient Christian tradition, starting with the early church theologians like Irenaeus, continuing to medieval theologians like Bonaventure, and including twentieth-century theologians like Karl Barth. In this model, Jesus Christ—and not crime—is at the center of our thinking about sin and grace. It is a Copernican revolution of sorts for thinking about sin and grace. This model allows LGBT people to use the christologies that speak to us—that is, christologies written by and from the perspective of LGBT people—as the starting point for defining sin and grace.

If we use the shorthand term "Queer Christ" to describe these LGBT-positive christologies, we can define sin and grace in terms of the Queer Christ. Specifically, sin for LGBT people is defined by whatever is opposed to the Queer Christ. By contrast, grace for LGBT people is defined by whatever is consistent with—or grows

---

[2] A number of theologians have written about the importance of the Holy Spirit in the context of christological reflection. Although the focus of this book is not on pneumatology, or the doctrine of the Holy Spirit, I do recognize the importance of Spirit-based christologies. See, for example, Wendy Farley, *Gathering Those Driven Away: A Theology of Incarnation* (Louisville, KY: Westminster John Knox, 2011), 115–32; Elizabeth A. Johnson, *She Who Is: The Mystery of God in Feminist Theological Discourse* (New York: Crossroad, 1992), 82–86, 139–40 (discussing the relationship between the Holy Spirit and Jesus Christ's birth, ministry, and resurrection); Eugene F. Rogers, "The Spirit Rests on the Son Paraphysically," in *The Lord and Giver of Life: Perspectives on Constructive Pneumatology*, ed. David H. Jensen (Louisville, KY: Westminster John Knox Press, 2008), 87–95. For an overview of queer pneumatology, see Cheng, *Radical Love*, 100–05.

towards—the Queer Christ. Thus, instead of focusing upon a crime-centered model of sin and grace, we now move to constructing a theology of sin and grace based upon the Queer Christ.

1. The Christ-Centered Model

a. Sin as Immaturity

Under the Christ-centered model, sin is understood not as a crime, but rather as *immaturity*. That is, like a child or adolescent who has yet to grow to full adulthood, we human beings are constantly in a process of growing toward our ultimate end, which is Jesus Christ, the Alpha and Omega of all things. Under this model, the Fall can be understood not so much as a criminal act and subsequent punishment, but rather as the actions of immature human beings—Adam and Eve—who were still in a process of maturation. Similarly, sin can be understood as the misdirected wanderings of immature human beings who continue to be formed in the image of Christ.

For example, in my own life I have experienced the sin of immaturity with respect to my spiritual growth and relationship to authority. When I was a child, I relied mostly upon external sources of authority (for example, my unquestioned following of church teachings or biblical prooftexting) for my understanding of God. As I have matured in my spiritual growth, I have started to trust my own internal compass as a reflection of God's will for my life. A few years ago, I participated in the Spiritual Exercises of St. Ignatius over the course of nearly a year through St. Francis Xavier Church, a Jesuit parish in New York City. Initially, I was extremely troubled at the thought of finding God's will within my own deepest desires, which is a key teaching of the Spiritual Exercises.[3] I now recognize the truth of that teaching; I am actually most separated from God when I rely exclusively upon external—and not internal—sources of authority. This often happens during times of fear and uncertainty, when I forget the importance of finding God within—and not just outside of—myself.

This Christ-centered approach to thinking about sin is

---

[3] There is the danger, of course, of self-deception with respect to God's will. This is why spiritual direction or discernment within a community context is particularly important as a safeguard. For a discussion of the relationship between spirituality, sexuality, and desire, see Philip Sheldrake, *Befriending Our Desires* (London: Darton, Longman and Todd, 2001).

consistent with an Eastern Orthodox reading of the Garden of Eden story in Genesis 3. According to this reading, Adam and Eve did not so much fall from an original state of perfection, but rather were in a process of growing—which continues with humanity today. The introduction of death into the world can be understood not so much as punishment, but rather as an end to the ongoing suffering of immature beings who, at the last day, will once again come face to face with God. As the theologian James Carpenter described it, the fall did not result in the loss of grace. Instead, it merely resulted in a "diminution of the effect of grace."[4] Adam and Eve are "never forsaken by God or deserted by grace."[5]

As a consequence of this alternative reading of the Garden of Eden story, human beings are not so much infected with original sin, but rather continue along the path of growth towards Jesus Christ as the ultimate fulfillment of the cosmos. Sin in this model, therefore, is remaining in a state of immaturity; it is turning away or refusing to recognize the grace of God's revelation in Jesus Christ. Under the Christ-centered model of sin and grace, the starting point is christology, as opposed to an independent or free-standing doctrine of sin.

b. Grace as Deification

If sin is defined as immaturity, then grace can be understood under the Christ-centered model as *deification*, or becoming divine.[6] As discussed earlier, the Eastern Orthodox doctrine of deification, or *theōsis*, is a much more optimistic view of the human condition than the crime-centered doctrine of original sin. Instead of fallen beings who are held in bondage under the original sin of our first parents, we human beings are seen as incomplete persons who are constantly growing in stature towards God in Jesus Christ through the Holy Spirit. Although we may wander away from God and lose our way from time to time—which results in sin and our separation from God—we will ultimately find our way back home.

---

[4] James A. Carpenter, *Nature and Grace: Toward an Integral Perspective* (New York: Crossroad, 1988), 30.

[5] Carpenter, *Nature and Grace*, 31.

[6] For some helpful introductions to deification, or the doctrine of *theōsis*, see Michael J. Christensen and Jeffrey A. Wittung, eds., *Partakers of the Divine Nature: The History and Development of Deification in the Christian Traditions* (Grand Rapids, MI: Baker Academic, 2007); Farley, *Gathering Those Driven Away*, 169–86; Stephen Finlan and Vladimir Kharlamov, eds., *Theōsis: Deification in Christian Theology*, vol. 1 (Eugene, OR: Pickwick Publications, 2006); Veli-Matti Kärkkäinen, *One with God: Salvation as Deification and Justification* (Collegeville, MI: Liturgical Press, 2004); Vladimir Kharlamov, ed., *Theōsis: Deification in Christian Theology*, vol. 2 (Eugene, OR: Pickwick Publications, 2011); Norman Russell, *The Doctrine of Deification in the Greek Patristic Tradition* (Oxford, UK: Oxford University Press, 2004); Norman Russell, *Fellow Workers with God: Orthodox Thinking on Theosis* (Crestwood, NY: St. Vladimir's Seminary Press, 2009).

The notion of grace as deification—that is, the process of becoming divine—is grounded in biblical texts such as Psalm 82:6 ("I say, 'You are gods, children of the Most High, all of you'")[7] and 2 Peter 1:4 ("[You] may become participants in the divine nature").[8] Deification is also grounded theologically in the chiastic[9] notion of the divine exchange in which God became human in Jesus Christ so that human beings could become divine. That is, human nature was fundamentally transformed in the incarnation and Christ event. God emptied Godself of divinity (that is, *kenōsis*) in the incarnation so that humanity could be filled with divinity. In the words of the third-century theologian Athanasius of Alexandria, God "became human [so] that we might become divine."[10]

As we have already seen, sin occurs whenever we—like Adam and Eve—remain spiritually immature by opposing or turning away from our ultimate end of deification (that is, becoming like Jesus Christ). Grace, by contrast, is whenever we grow into the fullness of our true nature by becoming like Jesus Christ. In that process of growth, we are transfigured, and we become "participants of the divine nature."[11] Daniel Keating, a professor of theology at Sacred Heart Major Seminary in Detroit, Michigan, has written about the intimate connection between grace and deification in his book *Deification and Grace*. According to Keating, the doctrine of deification affirms that "we become gods, not by nature, but by grace."[12]

Furthermore, grace is not just the process of growing towards maturity in Christ. The doctrine of *theōsis* also acknowledges that Jesus Christ—as the Word incarnate and the revelation of God—*is grace itself*. That is, Jesus Christ, as the ultimate fulfillment of the cosmos, is the greatest unmerited gift of all from God. In light of the centrality of Jesus Christ in the doctrine of *theōsis*, deification is a useful theological source for the Christ-centered model of sin and grace.

---

[7] Psa. 82:6.
[8] 2 Pet. 1:4.
[9] Here, the word "chiastic" refers to the symbolic crossing-over of the divine and the human. That is, the divine becomes human and, on the other hand, the human becomes divine.
[10] See Russell, *Fellow Workers with God*, 39 (quoting Athanasius, *On the Incarnation* 5.7).
[11] 2 Pet. 1:4.
[12] Daniel A. Keating, *Deification and Grace* (Ave Maria, FL: Sapientia Press, 2007), 92.

c. Atonement as Renewal

Atonement takes on a different meaning in light of the Christ-centered model of sin and grace. Instead of understanding atonement (that is, the "at-one-ment" between humanity and God) solely in terms of penal substitution, we can understand atonement as the *renewal* of the cosmos. Because we have lost our way, God has sent Jesus Christ—in whom all things were created and in whom all things "hold together"[13]—to "gather up all things"[14] and to renew creation.

In other words, Jesus Christ is like the address or final destination that we enter into a GPS system that helps us find our way back to God after we have lost our way. Creation is renewed through the Christ event, and Jesus Christ becomes the lodestar that leads us back home. The Christ event is not so much a penal transaction in which Jesus Christ pays the ultimate penalty for the crime committed by our first parents (which actually makes the incarnation strangely contingent on the fall). Rather, the Christ event is God's renewal of creation after Adam and Eve were separated from God through their immature wanderings. Furthermore, because all things will be gathered up in Christ in the fullness of time,[15] the incarnation was part of God's plan from the beginning, and it would have happened with or without the fall. Jesus Christ is both the Alpha and the Omega and, as such, Christ is the ultimate manifestation of grace and the end to which we are all directed.[16]

2. History of the Christ-Centered Model

Where did the Christ-centered model of sin and grace come from? In order to construct an alternative to the traditional crime-based model of sin and grace, we must first examine the theological roots of the Christ-centered model. We have seen that this model is grounded in the Eastern Orthodox Christian theological notion of *theōsis*. In this section, we will examine the work of three theologians who can serve as sources for a Christ-centered model of sin and grace: (a) Irenaeus of Lyons; (b) Bonaventure; and (c) Karl Barth.

[13] Col. 1:16–17.
[14] Eph. 1:10.
[15] Eph. 1:10.
[16] For an articulation of the renewal model of atonement theory, see Schmiechen, *Saving Power*, 169–221 ("The Renewal of Creation").

a. Irenaeus of Lyons

One source for a Christ-centered model of sin and grace is Irenaeus of Lyons, the second-century theologian who is best known for his refutation of gnostic heresies in *Against Heresies*. In that work, Irenaeus understood Jesus Christ to be the fullest expression of the image and likeness of God. Instead of viewing creation—including human flesh—as inherently evil (as the gnostics did), Irenaeus viewed creation as fundamentally good. Adam was not formed, as the gnostics had argued, by some evil creator deity. Rather, Adam was created by the same God of the New Testament and patterned, albeit imperfectly, after the image of the preexistent Christ. As Irenaeus put it, "the creator who formed the world is the *only God* and there is none besides him who received from himself the *model and figure* of things which have been made."[17]

In Irenaeus's view, Adam and Eve's disobedience was not so much a crime or a disastrous fall from an original state of perfection. Rather, Adam and Eve were immature creatures who had not yet fully attained the stature of Jesus Christ. In other words, Adam and Eve were patterned after Jesus Christ, but, like children or adolescents, they were not yet fully developed. According to Irenaeus, humanity matures over time: "God created humankind so that it would *grow and increase*. . . . humankind is *in the process of being created*."[18]

Mark Biddle, the Baptist Theological Seminary biblical scholar and author of *Missing the Mark*, notes that, in Irenaeus' view, the fall merely "interrupted" the process of maturation, so that humanity's state after the fall was in "arrested development." The sin of Adam and Eve was that they tasted of the fruit of the Tree of the Knowledge of Good and Evil "prematurely." That is, they were "not yet mature enough for the knowledge."[19]

Similarly, James Carpenter, a former professor at General Theological Seminary in New York City, noted that the negative effects of the fall are limited under an Eastern Orthodox understanding of the fall. That is, "Adam is injured by the fall but he does not fall flat on his face; he stumbles, falters badly, and loses

---

[17] Irenaeus, *Against Heresies* 2.16.3 (emphasis added), in Eric Osborn, *Irenaeus of Lyons* (Cambridge, UK: Cambridge University Press, 2001), 60. For a summary of Irenaeus's views on creation and the divine plan of salvation, see Denis Minns, *Irenaeus: An Introduction* (London: T&T Clark International, 2010), 31–45, 69–95. See also Osborn, *Irenaeus of Lyons*, 51–73, 95–140; M.C. Steenberg, *Irenaeus on Creation: The Cosmic Christ and the Saga of Redemption* (Leiden, Netherlands: Brill, 2008).

[18] Irenaeus, *Against Heresies* 4.11.1-2 (emphasis added), in Minns, *Irenaeus*, 84-85.

[19] Biddle, *Missing the Mark*, 5.

his direction."[20] As such, the theology of the East can be understood as a theology of the "grace of redemption."[21] For Carpenter, the theology of the Eastern church is "immensely appealing," particularly with respect to its "inclusiveness and generosity."[22]

In sum, the image and likeness of God is only revealed fully in the Christ event, which God had planned all along. Jesus Christ, according to Irenaeus, was the recapitulation, or restatement, of Adam. That is, the "goal of this process of maturation [by humanity] is Christ, the Alpha and the Omega."[23] Irenaeus understood Jesus Christ to be at the center of God's plan of salvation. Creation and salvation were bound together; God patterned humanity after the preexistent Christ, and Jesus Christ is the end to which creation is ultimately directed. According to Irenaeus, Jesus Christ "became what we are in order to make us what he is himself."[24] For this reason, Irenaeus is a helpful source for the Christ-centered model of sin and grace.

b. Bonaventure

A second source for the Christ-centered model of sin and grace is the thirteenth-century theologian Bonaventure. Bonaventure, like other medieval Franciscan theologians, is known for his highly christocentric theology. According to Bonaventure, Jesus Christ is the "foundation of all authentic doctrine, whether apostolic or prophetic according to both Laws, the Old and the New."[25] Furthermore, Jesus Christ is at the center of all knowledge: "[N]othing can render things perfectly knowable unless Christ is present, the Son of God, and the Teacher."[26]

As in the case of Irenaeus' theology, Jesus Christ is very much at the center of Bonaventure's theology. Specifically, Bonaventure understands Jesus Christ to be the final goal of creation and the cosmos. Zachary Hayes, a professor of systematic theology at the Catholic Theological Union, has written that, for Bonaventure, a "world transformed in Christ is what God's creative love intends from all eternity."[27] In other words, the incarnation occurred not

---

[20] Carpenter, *Nature and Grace*, 31.
[21] Carpenter, *Nature and Grace*, 34.
[22] Carpenter, *Nature and Grace*, 34.
[23] Biddle, *Missing the Mark*, 5.
[24] Irenaeus, *Against Heresies* 5, pref., in Russell, *Fellow Workers with God*, 38.
[25] Bonaventure, "Christ, The One Teacher of All," in *Bonaventure, Mystic of God's Word*, ed. Timothy J. Johnson (Hyde Park, NY: New City Press, 1999), 154–55.
[26] Bonaventure, "Christ," in Johnson, *Bonaventure*, 155.
[27] Zachary Hayes, *The Gift of Being: A Theology of Creation* (Collegeville, MN: Liturgical Press, 2001), 107.

so much because human beings sinned, but rather because the incarnation was part of God's larger plan to share the divine life with the created order.[28]

Christopher Cullen, a professor of philosophy at Fordham University, has written about the relationship between Jesus Christ, grace, and deification in Bonaventure's theology. According to Cullen, Bonaventure understands the goal of human existence as being "deiformed" or "God-formed" in order to restore the soul that has been damaged by sin.[29] This restoration or transformation occurs when we imitate the life of Jesus Christ, "even in the details of his life."[30] By imitating Christ, we receive the "grace and merit" that "flow into those who freely accept [Christ] in faith and love."[31]

Thus, as in the case of other Christ-centered theologies, sin for Bonaventure occurs when we refuse to follow—or turn away from —God's revelation in Jesus Christ. As Ilia Delio, a professor of ecclesiastical history at Washington Theological Union, has noted, sin for Bonaventure is a "turning from the good and a turning toward nothingness."[32] That is, even though God turns towards us in the incarnation, we turn away from God in our sin. By contrast, grace is the gift of freedom to turn towards God in Jesus Christ. A "total turning to Christ" is what constitutes grace for Bonaventure and what restores us.[33]

c. Karl Barth

A third source for a Christ-centered model of sin and grace is the great twentieth-century theologian Karl Barth. Jesus Christ is at the center of Barth's theology—so much so that it has been described as "christomonism" by his detractors[34]—and thus it is no surprise that Barth's theology of sin and grace is also highly christocentric. Specifically, Barth discusses sin and grace in volume IV of *Church Dogmatics*, which covers the doctrine of reconciliation.

According to Barth, sin has no independent existence as a

[28] Hayes cites the work of John Duns Scotus here as the "most explicit formulation" of the Franciscan tradition of cosmic christology. See Hayes, *The Gift of Being*, 107.

[29] See Christopher M. Cullen, *Bonaventure* (Oxford: Oxford University Press, 2006), 156.

[30] Cullen, *Bonaventure*, 148.

[31] Cullen, *Bonaventure*, 148.

[32] Ilia Delio, *The Humility of God: A Franciscan Perspective* (Cincinnati, OH: St. Anthony Messenger Press, 2005), 61.

[33] Ilia Delio, *Simply Bonaventure: An Introduction to His Life, Thought, and Writings* (Hyde Park, NY: New City Press, 2001), 79.

[34] See Karl Barth, "A Theological Dialogue," *Theology Today* 19, no. 2 (July 1962): 171–77, in which Barth talks about christomonism in response to a question posed to him at the 1962 Warfield Lectures at Princeton Theological Seminary: "Christomonism (that's an awful catchword!) was invented by an old friend of mine whose name I will not mention." Barth, "A Theological Dialogue," 172.

doctrine. That is, sin can only be understood in relationship to Jesus Christ. To maintain otherwise—for example, to articulate a free-standing hamartiology or doctrine of sin—would be a form of sin itself.[35] Thus, Barth begins with christology instead of the traditional dogmatic category of sin. Barth outlines three forms of sin, each of which is the result of opposing to what God has done for us in Jesus Christ.

First, sin can take the classical form of *pride* to the extent that human beings lift up ourselves in opposition to the humiliation of God who comes down from heaven in the person of Jesus Christ (that is, in the incarnation and crucifixion). However, pride is not the only manifestation of sin. Second, sin can also take the form of *sloth* to the extent that human beings keep ourselves down in opposition to the exaltation of the God who is raised up in Jesus Christ (that is, in the resurrection and ascension). This form of sin is similar to what feminist theologians like Valerie Saiving have written about in terms of sin for women as self-abnegation or hiding. Third, sin can take the form of *falsehood*, which opposes the truth of God in Jesus Christ.

Thus, all three forms of sin in Barth's work—pride, sloth, and falsehood—are defined in opposition to God's revelation in Jesus Christ. Pride is defined in opposition to the descending Christ; sloth is defined in opposition to the risen Christ; and falsehood is defined in opposition to the true Christ. Grace, on the other hand, takes the form of God's free act of reconciling humanity to Godself in Jesus Christ. Grace takes the three-fold form of God's humbling, exaltation, and truthfulness in Jesus Christ. In sum, Barth uses a Christ-centered model for determining sin and grace, and this model can be useful in our own attempts to rethink the crime-centered model of sin and grace.[36]

Some may question this use of Barth in light of his criticism of same-sex acts in his discussion of male-female complementarity in volume III/4 of *Church Dogmatics*.[37] It should be noted,

---

[35] See Karl Barth, *Church Dogmatics* IV/1 (Edinburgh: T&T Clark, 1956), 389.

[36] For a survey of Barth's doctrine of reconciliation, see Karl Barth, *Church Dogmatics* IV/1, 79–154. For a useful summary of Barth's three-fold description of sin, see Matt Jenson, *The Gravity of Sin: Augustine, Luther and Barth on* Homo Incurvatus in Se (London: T&T Clark, 2006), 130–87; see also Allen Jorgenson, "Karl Barth's Christological Treatment of Sin," *Scottish Journal of Theology* 54, no. 4 (2001): 439–62. For a discussion of grace and Karl Barth's theology and ethics, see G.C. Berkouwer, *The Triumph of Grace in the Theology of Karl Barth: An Introduction and Critical Appraisal* (Grand Rapids, MI: Wm. B. Eerdmans Publishing, 1956); Daniel L. Migliore, "Commanding Grace: Karl Barth's Theological Ethics," in *Commanding Grace: Studies in Karl Barth's Ethics*, ed. Daniel L. Migliore (Grand Rapids, MI: William B. Eerdmans Publishing, 2010), 1–25.

[37] Karl Barth, *Church Dogmatics* III/4 (Edinburgh: T&T Clark, 1961), 165–66.

however, that Barth changed his mind towards the end of his life. In a letter written in 1968, his assistant Eberhard Busch noted that Barth "is today not completely satisfied any more with his former, incidental comments and would certainly formulate them today somewhat differently." Busch wrote that Barth "could, in conversation with doctors and psychologists, come to a new judgment and exposition of the phenomenon."[38]

3. The Amazing Grace of the Queer Christ

So what do we do with a Christ-centered model of sin and grace? How might it change the thinking of LGBT Christians—or all Christians, for that matter—with respect to sin and grace? For me, the significance of the Christ-centered model is that it uses christology as the starting point for theological reflection about sin and grace. Rather than viewing sin as a criminal violation, or viewing grace as the acquittal or rehabilitation of sinners, a Christ-centered model of sin and grace begins with Jesus Christ.

This turn to christology is significant because this allows LGBT people to use *queer christologies* as the starting point for our own reflection about sin and grace. During the last few decades, many LGBT theologians have written about the LGBT or Queer Christ. These include Robert E. Shore-Goss, who wrote *Queering Christ: Beyond Jesus Acted Up*,[39] and Thomas Bohache, who wrote *Christology from the Margins*.[40] That is, these theologians have answered the question that Jesus poses to his disciples: "Who do you say that I am?"[41] The Queer Christ is simply an extension of contextual christologies that have arisen since the 1960s in which different groups have articulated their answers to the central christological question.[42] Queer christologies are a manifestation of God's amazing grace, and thus they are an appropriate starting point for LGBT reflection on sin and grace.

---

[38] Karl Barth, "Freedom for Community," in *Theology and Sexuality: Classic and Contemporary Readings*, ed. Eugene F. Rogers, Jr. (Oxford, UK: Blackwell Publishers, 2002), 115.

[39] Goss, *Queering Christ*.

[40] Thomas Bohache, *Christology from the Margins* (London: SCM Press, 2008). For an overview of queer christologies, see Cheng, *Radical Love*, 78–86.

[41] Mark 8:29.

[42] For an overview of contemporary christologies, including black and feminist christologies, see Veli-Matti Kärkkäinen, *Christology: A Global Introduction* (Grand Rapids, MI: Baker Academic, 2003). See also Robert J. Schreiter, ed., *Faces of Jesus in Africa* (Maryknoll, NY: Orbis Books, 1991) (African christologies); Harold J. Recinos and Hugo Magallanes, eds., *Jesus in the Hispanic Community: Images of Christ from Theology to Popular Religion* (Louisville, KY: Westminster John Knox Press, 2009) (Latino/a christologies); R.S. Sugirtharajah, *Asian Faces of Jesus* (Maryknoll, NY: Orbis Books, 1993) (Asian christologies).

In the second part of this book, I will propose seven models of the Queer Christ that are based upon queer christological reflections by LGBT theologians:

(1) The Erotic Christ;
(2) The Out Christ;
(3) The Liberator Christ;
(4) The Transgressive Christ;
(5) The Self-Loving Christ;
(6) The Interconnected Christ; and
(7) The Hybrid Christ.

As Sallie McFague writes in her influential book on theological models, these models are not intended to be mutually exclusive, nor are they intended to be the only ways of thinking about the Queer Christ.[43] Rather, they are analytical tools that can help us think about christology from an LGBT perspective.

Based upon these seven models of the Queer Christ, I propose seven new deadly queer sins:

(1) exploitation;
(2) the closet;
(3) apathy;
(4) conformity;
(5) shame;
(6) isolation; and
(7) singularity.

These sins arise out of the opposition of human beings against the Queer Christ as seen in the above seven models.

Conversely, I propose seven amazing queer graces of:

(1) mutuality;
(2) coming out;
(3) activism;
(4) deviance;
(5) pride;
(6) interdependence; and
(7) hybridity.

These graces arise out of what it means to follow the Queer Christ as seen in the above seven models. Let us now turn to Part II of the book and see what we discover in terms of the seven models of the Queer Christ.

---

[43] Sallie McFague, *Models of God: Theology for a Ecological, Nuclear Age* (Philadelphia, PA: Fortress Press, 1987), 31–40.

Study Questions

1. How have you experienced growth and maturation in your own life as well as the lives of others who are close to you? How might this shed some light on the maturation of the human race?
2. How can sin be understood in a Christ-centered model of sin and grace, as opposed to a crime-centered model? What are some ways in which you have experienced spiritual immaturity?
3. What is deification? How can the Eastern Orthodox doctrine of *theōsis* inform our thinking about sin and grace?
4. How might we think about atonement differently in a Christ-centered model of sin and grace?
5. How might the theologies of Irenaeus of Lyons, Bonaventure, and Karl Barth be helpful in terms of constructing a Christ-centered model of sin and grace?
6. What is queer christology? Which of the seven models of the Queer Christ speak most to you? What are the deadly sins and amazing graces that correspond to such models?

For Further Study

Deification or Theōsis

- Christensen and Wittung, *Partakers of the Divine Nature*
- Farley, *Gathering Those Driven Away*, 169–86
- Finlan and Kharlamov, *Theōsis*, vol. 1
- Kärkkäinen, *One with God*
- Keating, *Deification and Grace*
- Kharlamov, *Theōsis*, vol. 2
- Russell, *Fellow Workers with God*
- Russell, *The Doctrine of Deification in the Greek Patristic Tradition*

Irenaeus of Lyons

- Biddle, *Missing the Mark*, 5–7
- Carpenter, *Nature and Grace*, 18–36
- Minns, *Irenaeus*
- Osborn, *Irenaeus of Lyons*
- Steenberg, *Irenaeus on Creation*

Bonaventure

- Cullen, *Bonaventure*
- Delio, *Simply Bonaventure*
- Delio, *The Humility of God*
- Hayes, *The Gift of Being*
- Johnson, *Bonaventure*

Karl Barth

- Barth, *Church Dogmatics* III/4
- Barth, *Church Dogmatics* IV/1
- Barth, "Freedom for Community"
- Berkouwer, *The Triumph of Grace in the Theology of Karl Barth*
- Jenson, *The Gravity of Sin*, 130–87
- Jorgenson, "Karl Barth's Christological Treatment of Sin"
- Migliore, "Commanding Grace"

Queer Christologies

- Bohache, *Christology from the Margins*
- Cheng, *Radical Love*, 78–86
- Goss, *Queering Christ*

Part II

Discovering the Queer Christ

Chapter 5

Model One: The Erotic Christ

In Part I of this book, I proposed moving from a *crime-based* model to a *Christ-centered* model in thinking about sin and grace. I argued that the Christ-centered model—which is grounded both in the Eastern Orthodox tradition that draws upon the christocentric theology of Irenaeus of Lyons, as well as the Western tradition exemplified by the christocentric theologies of Bonaventure and Karl Barth—is a much more useful way of thinking about sin and grace for LGBT people.

In Part II of this book, I draw upon this Christ-centered approach to sin and grace, and propose *seven new deadly sins* and *seven new amazing graces*. I begin by articulating seven models of the Queer Christ, which are based upon the christological reflections of LGBT theologians. These seven models are:

(1) The Erotic Christ;
(2) The Out Christ;
(3) The Liberator Christ;
(4) The Transgressive Christ;
(5) The Self-Loving Christ;
(6) The Interconnected Christ; and
(7) The Hybrid Christ.

I then define sin and grace in relation to each model of the Queer Christ. I begin with the first of the seven models of the Queer Christ: The Erotic Christ.

1. The Erotic Christ

The first Christ-centered model of sin and grace is the *Erotic Christ*. For many people, the notion of the Erotic Christ is surprising and unexpected because Jesus Christ is usually thought about in non-erotic terms. Indeed, for many people, spirituality and sexuality exist in two mutually exclusive realms, and it would be sacrilegious to think about the Erotic Christ. One important contribution of LGBT theologians, however, has been to bring the two realms of sexuality and the sacred together, and a number of these theologians have written about the Erotic Christ in their christological reflections.[1]

What is the erotic? In her famous essay, "Uses of the Erotic," the black lesbian feminist writer Audre Lorde wrote that the erotic was not so much a matter of soft-core pornography, but rather a deep relationship with and yearning for the other. For Lorde, the erotic is the power that arises out of "sharing deeply" with another person. It is to recognize and honor our own desires. It is also to recognize and honor the other—whether as friend, lover, or family member—as an embodied person. The erotic is to "share our joy in the satisfying" of the other, rather than simply using other people as "objects of satisfaction."[2]

The Erotic Christ arises out of the reality that Jesus Christ, as the Word made flesh, is the very embodiment of God's deepest desires for us. In the words of the Nicene Creed, Jesus Christ came down from heaven not for God's own self-gratification, but rather "for us and for our salvation." In the gospels, Jesus repeatedly shows his love and desire for all those who come into contact with him, including physical touch. He uses touch as a way to cure people of disease and disabilities,[3] as well as to bring them back to life.[4] He washes the feet of his disciples,[5] and he even allows the Beloved Disciple to lie close to his breast at the last supper.[6]

Conversely, Jesus is touched physically by many of the people

---

1 Some anthologies that bring together sexuality and the sacred include Ellison and Douglas, *Sexuality and the Sacred*; Marvin M. Ellison and Sylvia Thorson-Smith, eds., *Body and Soul: Rethinking Sexuality as Justice-Love* (Cleveland, OH: Pilgrim Press, 2003); James B. Nelson and Sandra P. Longfellow, eds., *Sexuality and the Sacred: Sources for Theological Reflection* (Louisville, KY: Westminster/John Knox Press, 1994).

2 See Audre Lorde, "Uses of the Erotic: The Erotic as Power," in Ellison and Douglas, *Sexuality and the Sacred*, 75, 77.

3 Matt. 9:29 (touching the eyes of two blind men); Mark 7:31–37 (touching the ears and tongue of the deaf man with the speech impediment).

4 Mark 5:35–43 (Jairus' daughter); Luke 7:11–17 (the widow's son at Nain).

5 John 13:1–20.

6 John 13:23.

who come into contact with him. He is touched by the bleeding woman who hoped that his powers could heal her.[7] He is bathed in expensive ointment by the woman at Bethany.[8] He is kissed by Judas at the Garden of Gethsemane.[9] Following the crucifixion, Jesus' body is cleaned and prepared by others for burial.[10] After his resurrection, Jesus allows Thomas to place his finger in the mark of the nails and also to place his hand in his side.[11] All of these physical interactions are manifestations of God's love for us—and our reciprocal love for God—through the Erotic Christ.

Carter Heyward, the lesbian theologian and Episcopal priest, has written about the Erotic Christ in the context of the "radically mutual character" of Jesus Christ's life, death, and resurrection. For Heyward, the erotic is power in mutual relation, and her christology focuses on this theme. In her book *Saving Jesus from Those Who Are Right*, Heyward argues that the significance of Jesus Christ lies not only in the ways in which he touched others (both physically and otherwise), but also in the ways in which he was "healed, liberated, and transformed" by those who he encountered. This power in mutual relation is *not* something that exists solely within the Trinitarian relationship between God, Jesus Christ, or the Holy Spirit. Rather, this power is present in *all* of us who have ever "loved, held, yearned, lost."[12]

Kittredge Cherry, a lesbian minister with the Metropolitan Community Churches, also has written extensively about the Erotic Christ. Cherry has published a book, *Art That Dares*, in which she reproduces images of contemporary art that depict the Erotic Christ.[13] For example, some of these images include a queer interpretation of the Stations of the Cross by the New York City painter Douglas Blanchard in which a gay Jesus Christ is arrested, tortured, and executed. Other images include Becki Jayne Harrelson's "Judas Kiss," which depicts a nearly naked Jesus and Judas in a passionate embrace. Many of these images—and other works—can be found on Cherry's website and blog, "Jesus in Love."[14]

---

7 Mark 5:28–34.
8 Mark 14:3–6.
9 Matt. 26:49.
10 Matt. 27:59 (Joseph of Arimathea); John 19:40 (Nicodemus).
11 John 20:24–29.
12 Carter Heyward, *Saving Jesus from Those Who Are Right: Rethinking What It Means to Be Christian* (Minneapolis: Fortress Press, 1999), 74. See also Carter Heyward, *Touching Our Strength: The Erotic As Power and the Love of God* (New York: HarperSanFrancisco, 1989).
13 Kittredge Cherry, *Art That Dares: Gay Jesus, Woman Christ, and More* (Berkeley, CA: Androgyne Press, 2007).
14 See the "Jesus in Love" website, available at http://www.jesusinlove.org (accessed on December 11, 2011).

Gay male theologians—especially those who grew up Roman Catholic—also have written about the Erotic Christ, most commonly in terms of Jesus Christ being an object of erotic desire. For example, Donald Boisvert, a gay professor of religion at Concordia University, wrote a chapter on the Erotic Christ in his book *Sanctity and Male Desire*. In that chapter, Boisvert talks about his own "special enthrallment" from a young age with the corpus of the crucified Jesus Christ. For Boisvert, the "handsomely glorious body of Jesus [that] hung from the cross" creates a space in which he and other gay men could "enter into an act of erotic and spiritual intimacy with their lord."[15]

Similarly, the gay theologian and Metropolitan Community Church minister Robert Shore-Goss has written in an essay about how, as a young Jesuit novice, he fantasized in prayer about a "naked Jesus as a muscular, handsome, bearded man" and burying his face in Jesus' "hair-matted chest." As a Jesuit priest, Shore-Goss envisioned Jesus as a lover. Shore-Goss writes that he had "sexual intercourse with Jesus" many times while masturbating, and it was a natural progression for Shore-Goss to evolve as a "lover of Jesus" to "falling in love with a man." Later, when Shore-Goss had sex with his first lover, Frank, he experienced lovemaking as communion. He writes: "I saw Christ's face within Frank's face as I penetrated him in intercourse" and "[a]s I was penetrated, I felt penetrated by Frank and Christ."[16]

In sum, LGBT theologians have written about the Erotic Christ in terms of both power-as-relation as well as sexual desire. This arises out of the fact that Jesus Christ, as the Word made flesh, is the incarnational expression of God's deepest desires for us, particularly in a Christ-centered model of sin and grace. Building upon that model, we now turn to a discussion of what sin and grace would look like in the context of the Erotic Christ.

2. Sin as Exploitation

What is sin in light of the Erotic Christ? Recall that we defined sin as that which is opposed to God's revelation in Jesus Christ. If the Erotic Christ is God's deepest desire to be in relationship with us, then sin can be understood as the opposite of that desire,

---

[15] Donald L. Boisvert, *Sanctity and Male Desire: A Gay Reading of Saints* (Cleveland, OH: Pilgrim Press, 2004), 170–71.
[16] Goss, *Queering Christ*, 10, 18, 22.

or *exploitation*. Exploitation is the lack of mutuality or concern for the needs and desires, sexual or otherwise, of another person. That is, the other person is seen merely as an object and a means to an end. Exploitation is the antithesis of the "I-Thou" relationship described by Martin Buber.[17]

A key aspect of exploitation relates to consent. Consent is a key ethical norm for LGBT sexual relationships. True consent must be a mutual or two-way agreement. Exploitation is the refusal to honor the other's person ability to consent to a sexual act or relationship. The sin of exploitation occurs when the other person has not consented—or cannot consent—to a sexual relationship, whether this is due to age, mental disability, state of mind (for example, intoxication), or power (for example, between a supervisor and her or his direct report at work). The sin of exploitation can also occur in the context of an existing partnership when one partner wishes to engage in sexual activity outside of the partnership and the other partner has not consented to such activity. Of course, these issues are not limited to the LGBT community, but it is nevertheless important to acknowledge them in the context of the sin of exploitation.

Another aspect of exploitation relates to treating one's sexual partner as a mere object of gratification. Some people, particularly those who struggle with sex addiction and/or low self-esteem, engage in anonymous, unsafe, and/or drug-fueled hook-ups in which self-gratification is the primary if not only concern. The sex addict's partner or partners are reduced to objects for stimulation and are not seen as full human beings in themselves. In *Cruise Control*, Robert Weiss writes about how some men with multiple addictions (for example, sex and drug addictions) have not taken basic precautions to protect their partners from infection with HIV or other sexually transmitted diseases when they are high on crystal meth or other party drugs.[18] This is the sin of exploitation at work—using one's partner as an object and not as a fellow human being.

Yet another aspect of exploitation relates to sexual racism in the LGBT online community. As I have written elsewhere, gay men of color are often either completely fetishized on the one hand or

---

[17] See Martin Buber, *I and Thou* (Edinburgh: T&T Clark, 1937).

[18] See Robert Weiss, *Cruise Control: Understanding Sex Addiction in Gay Men* (Los Angeles, CA: Alyson Books, 2005), 86.

completely marginalized on the other.[19] With respect to fetishization, the gay Asian American community has coined the term "rice queen" to describe older white men who date and have sex exclusively with younger Asian men, many of whom may be less secure in terms of financial status and/or self-esteem. With respect to marginalization, gay Asian men frequently experience blatant rejection in online cruising and hook-up sites, to the point where the catchphrase of "No fats, fems, or Asians" on personal ads is a matter of common knowledge.[20]

Finally, it should be noted that the sin of exploitation does not have to be in the context of a sexual relationship. There are also many non-sexual contexts, such as an employer-employee relationship, in which LGBT people fail to treat each other with mutuality and respect. Indeed, exploitation can even occur in church-related contexts. Mary Hunt, a lesbian Roman Catholic theologian and co-founder of the Women's Alliance for Theology, Ethics, and Ritual (WATER), has written extensively about the "kyriarchy" or "structures of lordship" that underlie the Roman Catholic Church and that "oppress most people and privilege a few." She critiques the structure as "rigidly hierarchical" and elevating clerics "above the rest in their status or decision-making or sacramental power."[21] As the gay theologian Gary David Comstock put it, sin is the "violation of mutuality and reciprocity." That is, sin is an "exercise of power over others that compromises their living fully," whether it is in the context of systemic or interpersonal issues.[22]

[19] See Patrick S. Cheng, "'I Am Yellow and Beautiful': Reflections on Queer Asian Spirituality and Gay Male Cyberculture," *Journal of Technology, Theology, and Religion* 2, no. 3 (June 2011): 1–21.

[20] For anthologies of writings by LGBT Asian North Americans on these issues, see Song Cho, ed., *Rice: Explorations Into Gay Asian Culture and Politics* (Toronto, Canada: Queer Press, 1998); David L. Eng and Alice Y. Hom, *Q&A: Queer in Asian America* (Philadelphia, PA: Temple University Press, 1998); Russell Leong, ed., *Asian American Sexualities: Dimensions of the Gay and Lesbian Experience* (New York: Routledge, 1996); Sharon Lim-Hing, ed., *The Very Inside: An Anthology of Writing by Asian and Pacific Islander Lesbian and Bisexual Women* (Toronto, Canada: Sister Vision Press, 1994).

[21] Mary E. Hunt, "New Feminist Catholics: Community and Ministry," in *New Feminist Christianity: Many Voices, Many Views*, ed. Mary E. Hunt and Diann L. Neu (Woodstock, VT: Skylight Paths, 2010), 269–70, 282.

[22] Gary David Comstock, *Gay Theology Without Apology* (Cleveland, OH: Pilgrim Press, 1993), 130.

3. Grace as Mutuality

What is grace in the context of the Erotic Christ? Here, grace is *mutuality*, or the deep awareness of being-in-relationship with another person. As Audre Lorde describes it, mutuality can take the form of something as simple as "sharing deeply any pursuit with another person" such as dancing.[23] It is an awareness and honoring of the well-being of the other, sexually or otherwise. It is seeing the other as a "thou" and not an "it."

The grace of mutuality can take the form of friendship. Mary Hunt has proposed a theology of friendship based upon values of "attentiveness, generativity, community-building, and justice-seeking" in her book *Fierce Tenderness*.[24] Similarly, Elizabeth Stuart has written in her book *Just Good Friends* about how the "dynamics of sexuality and passion" should be experienced in *all* relationships and not just sexual relationships. That is, we should not view our "sexual" relationships as fundamentally distinct from our "normal" relationships. Both should be grounded in friendship and mutuality. That is, we are called to be "promiscuous with [our] love." For Stuart, friendships are the "relationships in which we become most fully what God intends us to be."[25]

Marvin Ellison, a gay Christian ethicist and professor at Bangor Theological Seminary, has written about the grace of mutuality that takes the form of erotic justice. For Ellison, "*sexual injustice, not sexuality, [is] the moral problem* in this culture." Progressive people of faith, according to Ellison, are called to exercise both "personal well-being" in their bodies, and "right-relatedness with others throughout the social order." Furthermore, Ellison notes that sexuality is a means of grace for many LGBT people. That is, grace occurs "through our body touching."[26] This echoes what Serene Jones, the president of Union Theological Seminary in New York City, has written about finding grace in the human body, or what she calls the "body's grace."[27]

One of the gifts of the LGBT community is the amazing diversity of sexual relationships and practices. Dave Nimmons, in his

---

[23] See Lorde, "Uses of the Erotic," 75.

[24] Mary E. Hunt, *Fierce Tenderness: A Feminist Theology of Friendship* (New York: Crossroad, 1991), 172.

[25] Elizabeth Stuart, *Just Good Friends: Towards a Lesbian and Gay Theology of Relationships* (London: Mowbray, 1995), 213, 220.

[26] Marvin M. Ellison, *Erotic Justice: A Liberating Ethic of Sexuality* (Louisville, KY: Westminster John Knox Press, 1996), 114–16 (emphasis in original).

[27] Serene Jones, *Trauma and Grace: Theology in a Ruptured World* (Louisville, KY: Westminster John Knox Press, 2009), 157–61.

book *The Soul Beneath the Skin: The Unseen Hearts and Habits of Gay Men*, writes about the "sexual Madagascar" that constitutes the gay male community.[28] In fact, Nimmons lists almost one hundred alternative gay male "socio-sexual innovations" in just a single page of his book.[29] What these practices have in common is a deep sense of relationality with other gay men. All of these ways of relating with other people can be understood as a manifestation of the grace of mutuality in light of the Erotic Christ.

The grace of mutuality is not limited to couples or dyads; it can take the form of many different relational configurations. For example, Dossie Easton and Janet W. Hardy have written about an ethical approach to the wide spectrum of sexual relationships, including polyamory and open relationships, in *The Ethical Slut*. Easton and Hardy articulate a number of ethical principles that, in their view, should govern such relationships, including consent, honesty, recognition of the ramifications of sexual choices, respect for the other(s), and ownership of feelings.[30] A number of Christian theologians and ethicists have also written about the possibility of finding grace in such relationships.[31]

In fact, the Bible contains numerous narratives about the grace of mutuality in many different kinds of relational configurations, including same-sex relationships. Nancy Wilson, a lesbian theologian and the current moderator of the Metropolitan Community Churches, has written about many same-sex relationships in the Bible, including Jesus and the Beloved Disciple, Jonathan and David, Ruth and Naomi, and the Roman centurian and his servant.[32] Virginia Mollenkott, a professor emerita at William Paterson University who has been active in transgender issues, has compiled a list of *forty* different relational configurations that are described the Bible![33] Indeed, the grace of mutuality is present in many forms in the Bible.

---

[28] The island of Madagascar in the Indian Ocean is known for its biodiversity, or diversity of life forms.

[29] David Nimmons, *The Soul Beneath the Skin: The Unseen Hearts and Habits of Gay Men* (New York: St. Martin's Griffin, 2002), 80.

[30] See Dossie Easton and Janet W. Hardy, *The Ethical Slut: A Practical Guide to Polyamory, Open Relationships and Other Adventures*, 2nd ed. (Berkeley, CA: Celestial Arts, 2009), 20–21.

[31] See W. Scott Haldeman, "A Queer Fidelity: Reinventing Christian Marriage," in Ellison and Douglas, *Sexuality and the Sacred*, 304–16 (proposing multiple models of fidelity in marriage); Kathy Rudy, *Sex and the Church: Gender, Homosexuality, and the Transformation of Christian Ethics* (Boston: Beacon Press, 1997) (proposing an ethic of hospitality); Laurel C. Schneider, "Promiscuous Incarnation," in *The Embrace of Eros: Bodies, Desires, and Sexuality in Christianity*, ed. Margaret D. Kamitsuka (Minneapolis, MN: Fortress Press, 2010), 231–46 (finding God's promiscuous love in the incarnation). Marvin Ellison devotes a chapter in his forthcoming book on this issue. See Marvin M. Ellison, *Making Love Just: An Ethical Guide for the Sexually Perplexed* (Minneapolis, MN: Fortress Press, forthcoming 2012).

[32] See Nancy Wilson, *Our Tribe: Queer Folks, God, Jesus, and the Bible* (New York: HarperSanFrancisco, 1995), 111–64 ("Outing the Bible: Our Gay and Lesbian Tribal Texts").

[33] See Virginia Ramey Mollenkott, *Sensuous Spirituality: Out from Fundamentalism* (New York: Crossroad, 1992), 194–97.

Finally, the grace of mutuality can be found in unexpected places such as BDSM (bondage and discipline, dominance and submission, and sadism and masochism) scenes and the leather community. Easton and Hardy, the authors of *The Ethical Slut*, have also written *Radical Ecstasy*, which is a book about the spiritual dimensions of BDSM practices.[34] One misconception of such practices is that they involve non-consensual or non-mutual acts of violence. This is actually not true; BDSM scenes are carefully negotiated beforehand by the parties, and the bottom[35] has an "out" at all times in the form of a safe word.

As Thomas V. Peterson has written in his essay "Gay Men's Spiritual Experience in the Leather Community," BDSM practices are not only highly relational, but they are also highly spiritual.[36] Jeff Mann, a Roman Catholic practitioner of BDSM, described a particularly hot sexual encounter in terms of having sex with his "Christ in the Candlelight," "tasting the Sacrificed God's bound body," and finding his religion that night. According to Mann, "[t]heophany had become not intellectual abstraction but physical and emotional experience" with the other.[37]

Tony Ayres, a gay man of Chinese descent from Australia, experienced the grace of the Erotic Christ during an anonymous sexual encounter in a Hong Kong sauna with another gay Asian man during a business trip. Prior to that sexual encounter, Ayres had consciously avoided having sex with other Asian men during his life. This is not unusual for many gay Asian men, who often see other gay Asian men as sexually unattractive or as "competition" for what is perceived to be a limited pool of gay white men who are attracted to Asian men. As Ayres described his experience, "I found myself giving way to it, being swept away by a desire which I had never experienced before. It was a desire which had nothing to do with politics. He did not want me because I was Chinese. I did not reject him because he was Chinese. We just wanted each other. It was simple." That sexual encounter, although anonymous,

---

[34] Dossie Easton and Janet W. Hardy, *Radical Ecstasy: SM Journeys to Transcendence* (Oakland, CA: Greenery Press, 2004).

[35] Easton and Hardy have defined a bottom in the BDSM context as "someone who has the ability to eroticize or otherwise enjoy some sensations or emotions—such as pain, helplessness, powerlessness and humiliation—that would be unpleasant in another context." Dossie Easton and Janet W. Hardy, *The New Bottoming Book* (Emeryville, CA: Greenery Press, 2001), 3.

[36] Thomas V. Peterson, "Gay Men's Spiritual Experience in the Leather Community," in Thumma and Gray, *Gay Religion*, 337–50.

[37] Jeff Mann, "Binding the God," in *Queer and Catholic*, ed. Amie M. Evans and Trebor Healey (New York: Routledge, 2008), 65–66.

represented the grace of the Erotic Christ. The encounter allowed Ayres to understand, for the first time in his life, "what desire was about," and it allowed him to be in mutual relationship with another gay Asian man. And in so doing, he experienced "the most exquisite feeling of liberation."[38]

In the end, the grace of mutuality in the context of the Erotic Christ is about connections: connections with each other; connections with the cosmos; and connections with God. As Carter Heyward puts it, the grace of the Erotic Christ takes the form of "justice-love" and sharing in "the earth and the resources vital to our survival and happiness as people and creatures."[39] The grace of mutuality is understanding that we are all connected deeply to each other and creation. It requires a commitment to changing how we see and interact with the world, whether socially, politically, or sexually. The grace of mutuality is a gift that allows us to feel an authentic connection with others and with God.

Study Questions

1. Who is the Erotic Christ? How does Audre Lorde define the "erotic," and how might that definition help us to understand the Erotic Christ?
2. Which depiction of the Erotic Christ in this chapter appeals to you the most? The least?
3. What is sin in light of the Erotic Christ? Why is consent such an important ethical norm for LGBT sexual relationships?
4. What is grace in light of the Erotic Christ? In what ways have you experienced the grace of mutuality in your relationships?
5. How might the diversity of sexual practices in the LGBT community, including polyamory and BDSM, reflect the grace of the Erotic Christ?

---

[38] Tony Ayres, "China Doll—The Experience of Being a Gay Chinese Australian," in *Multicultural Queer: Australian Narratives*, ed. Peter A. Jackson and Gerard Sullivan (Binghamton, NY: Harrington Park Press, 1999), 96–97.
[39] Heyward, *Saving Jesus from Those Who Are Right*, 71.

For Further Study

Sexuality and the Sacred

- Ellison and Douglas, *Sexuality and the Sacred*, 2nd ed.
- Ellison and Thorson-Smith, *Body and Soul*
- Lorde, "Uses of the Erotic"
- Nelson and Longfellow, *Sexuality and the Sacred*

The Erotic Christ

- Boisvert, *Sanctity and Male Desire*, 168–82
- Cherry, *Art That Dares*
- Goss, *Queering Christ*, 3–35
- Heyward, *Saving Jesus from Those Who Are Right*

Sin as Exploitation

- Cheng, "'I Am Yellow and Beautiful'"
- Comstock, *Gay Theology Without Apology*, 130–31
- Hunt, "New Feminist Catholics"
- Weiss, *Cruise Control*

Grace as Mutuality

- Ayres, "China Doll"
- Easton and Hardy, *Radical Ecstacy*
- Easton and Hardy, *The Ethical Slut*
- Ellison, *Erotic Justice*
- Ellison, *Making Love Just*
- Haldeman, "A Queer Fidelity"
- Hunt, *Fierce Tenderness*
- Jones, *Trauma and Grace*, 157–61
- Mann, "Binding the God"
- Mollenkott, *Sensuous Spirituality*
- Nimmons, *The Soul Beneath the Skin*
- Peterson, "Gay Men's Spiritual Experience in the Leather Community"
- Rudy, *Sex and the Church*
- Schneider, "Promiscuous Incarnation"
- Stuart, *Just Good Friends*
- Wilson, *Our Tribe*

Chapter 6

Model Two: The Out Christ

1. The Out Christ

The second Christ-centered model of sin and grace for LGBT people is the *Out Christ*. The Out Christ arises out of the understanding that God reveals Godself most fully in the person of Jesus Christ. In other words, God "comes out of the closet" in the person of Jesus Christ. As Christians, we believe that the true nature of God is revealed (for example, God's solidarity with the marginalized and oppressed) in the Christ event. That is, God comes out in the incarnation, ministry, crucifixion, and resurrection of Jesus Christ. Indeed, the notion of the Out Christ as the revelation of God is supported by Jesus Christ's description in the Fourth Gospel as the *logos*, or Word of God.[1]

Chris Glaser, a gay theologian and Metropolitan Community Church minister, has written about the Out Christ in his book *Coming Out as Sacrament*. In that book, Glaser describes Jesus Christ as nothing less than God's very own coming out to humanity: "The story of the New Testament is that God comes out of the closet of heaven and out of the religious system of time to reveal Godself in the person of Jesus the Christ."[2] In other words, for Glaser, the New Testament is all about God coming out in the person of Jesus Christ.

[1] For a discussion of the doctrine of revelation and queer theology, see Cheng, *Radical Love*, 44–49.

[2] Chris Glaser, *Coming Out As Sacrament* (Louisville, KY: Westminster John Knox Press, 1998), 85.

According to Glaser, it is in Jesus Christ that God reveals God's solidarity with the marginalized and oppressed of the world. For example, God comes out as an infant who is born in "a strange town and in a land and culture dominated by a foreign power, the Roman Empire." God also comes out in solidarity with the oppressed through the ministry of Jesus, who "defends women and eunuchs and those of mixed race (Samaritans) and responds to other races (the Roman centurion, the Syrophoenician woman)." In the crucifixion, God comes out by extending "an inclusive paradise to a crucified criminal." And finally, in the resurrection, God comes out as one who "lives despite human violence, a true survivor of human abuse and victimization."[3]

Another manifestation of the Out Christ in the gospels is Jesus Christ's ongoing struggle to reveal himself—that is, to "come out" about his divinity—to those around him. As the gay theologian Daniel Helminiak put it, "Jesus had the problem of 'coming out.'" Helminiak notes that Jesus "sensed deep and unique moments within himself, but he was not able to easily share them with others."[4] For example, in a number of passages in the gospels—such as the messianic secret passages in Mark—Jesus instructs others not to say anything about who he is. Self-revelation for Jesus was dangerous and, in fact, it ultimately led to his execution by the religious and political authorities of his day.

At other times, however, Jesus engages in self-disclosure about his true self. He wants to know what his disciples think about his identity by asking them, "Who do you say that I am?"[5] Jesus reveals himself quite dramatically to Peter, James, and John in the Transfiguration,[6] as well as to Thomas and others in his post-resurrection appearances. Indeed, the entire liturgical season of Epiphany, immediately following the twelve days of Christmas, is traditionally understood as a season about the revelation of Jesus Christ to the world.

A number of theologians have also written about the Out Christ in terms of speculating that Jesus Christ might have been an ancestor to LGBT people. In 1968, the Anglican priest Hugh W. Montefiore published an essay in the anthology *Christ for Us*

---

[3] Glaser, *Coming Out As Sacrament*, 82–84.

[4] Daniel Helminiak, *Sex and the Sacred: Gay Identity and Spiritual Growth* (Binghamton, NY: Harrington Park Press, 2006), 122.

[5] Matt. 16:15.

[6] Matt. 17:1–8.

Today suggesting that Jesus was gay.[7] In that essay—which created a "furore" and "spectacular publicity"[8]—Montefiore writes that the "homosexual explanation" of Jesus' celibacy is "one which we must not ignore." He notes that Jesus was friends with women in the gospels, but it was "men whom he is said to have loved." Furthermore, to the extent that Jesus was an "outsider" from birth (that is, conceived out of wedlock) to death (that is, executed as a criminal), it would make sense for God to disclose Godself in the person of a gay man. This, according to Montefiore, would be consistent with God's fundamental nature of "befriending the friendless, and identifying [God]self with the underprivileged."[9]

In 1973, the biblical scholar Morton Smith published a work, *Clement of Alexandria and a Secret Gospel of Mark*, that also created a huge controversy.[10] Smith discovered a manuscript of a lost letter from Clement of Alexandria that quotes from a passage from a secret Gospel of Mark. That passage, which is located in between the verses of canonical Mark 10:34 and Mark 10:35, refers to a secret all-night initiation rite in a tomb between Jesus Christ and a rich youth who "loved" Jesus and who had been resurrected by him. Interestingly, the youth is described as wearing only a "linen cloth over his naked body." Clement, however, denies in his letter that the words "naked man with naked man" is in the text of the secret gospel.[11] Although Smith's work has been accused of being an elaborate hoax, it does raise interesting issues about the Out Christ and helps to resolve the mystery of the naked youth who appears mysteriously in canonical Mark 14:51–52.

The late gay Episcopal priest Robert Williams also wrote about the Out Christ in his 1992 book, *Just as I Am*.[12] Williams, who was one of the first openly gay man ordained as a priest in the Episcopal Church, argued that Jesus was gay. He speculated that Jesus and the Beloved Disciple were lovers and that Lazarus was in fact the identity of the Beloved Disciple. Based upon the research of Morton Smith and the Secret Gospel of Mark, Williams also speculated that the rich young ruler mentioned in the gospels was

---

[7] H.W. Montefiore, "Jesus, The Revelation of God," in *Christ for Us Today*, ed. Norman Pittenger (London: SCM Press, 1968), 101–16.

[8] Montefiore, "Jesus, The Revelation of God," 109 n.2.

[9] Montefiore, "Jesus, The Revelation of God," 109–10.

[10] Morton Smith, *Clement of Alexandria and a Secret Gospel of Mark* (Cambridge, MA: Harvard University Press, 1973). Smith presented his findings to a non-academic audience in Morton Smith, *The Secret Gospel: The Discovery and Interpretation of the Secret Gospel According to Mark* (Middletown, CA: Dawn Horse Press, 1982).

[11] Smith, *Clement of Alexandria and a Secret Gospel of Mark*, 447.

[12] Williams, *Just as I Am*, 111–23.

the Beloved Disciple. Weaving the various stories together—of Jesus, the Beloved Disciple, Lazarus, and the rich young ruler—Williams paints a portrait of a gay Messiah who "makes it possible for you to be out and proud and still be a passionate follower of Jesus the Christ."[13]

Finally, Nancy Wilson has suggested in her 1995 book *Our Tribe* that Jesus Christ should be understood as an ancestor to LGBT people. Among other things, Wilson touches upon transgender and bisexual issues in her work. Citing Isaiah 53, Wilson argues that Jesus Christ should be understood as a "functional, if not physical, eunuch" to the extent that he was "cut off" from his people and died without heirs. Wilson then focuses on the rather queer Bethany household of Mary, Martha, and Lazarus, and how it was Jesus' family of choice. She speculates that Mary and Martha might have been secret lovers who were described as "sisters," and she also speculates, like Williams, that Jesus and Lazarus were lovers. Wilson concludes that, to the extent that Jesus was fully human and thus a sexual being, he should be seen as "bisexual in orientation, if not also in his actions."[14]

What do we make of these attempts of naming the Out Christ? Whether or not Jesus' sexuality or gender identity can be conclusively proved, these narratives of "outing" are helpful in terms of challenging our preconceptions and thinking about what it means to envision a God who "comes out" to us in the Christ event. These outing narratives are also helpful in terms of understanding the dynamics of revelation within the gospels.

2. Sin as the Closet

How should we think about sin in light of the Out Christ? If the Out Christ is understood as the One through whom God most fully reveals Godself to humanity, then sin—defined as what opposes the Out Christ—can be understood as the *closet*, or the refusal to reveal oneself fully to one's families, friends, co-workers, and other loved ones.[15] Not only does the closet prevent a person from truly connecting with others, but it has a corrosive effect on the self-esteem and well-being to the extent that she is constantly

[13] Williams, *Just as I Am*, 123.
[14] Wilson, *Our Tribe*, 132, 140, 147.
[15] For a key work in queer theory about the closet, see Eve Kosofsky Sedgwick, *Epistemology of the Closet*, updated ed. (Berkeley, CA: University of California Press, 2008).

forced to keep her life a secret to others.

As we have seen in recent years, the closet has a particularly toxic effect with respect to conservative Christian religious leaders who preach against same-sex or gender-variant acts and yet are secretly LGBT themselves. We have seen this in the case of Ted Haggard, the evangelical pastor who paid a male escort to give him sexual massages as well as crystal meth. I have written elsewhere about George Rekers, a prominent proponent of reparative therapy and board member of the anti-gay National Association for Research and Therapy of Homosexuality (NARTH), who was found returning from vacation with a male escort whom he had hired from Rentboy.com, allegedly for helping him to lift his luggage.[16] And there is the case of Eddie Long, the pastor of a black megachurch who had been accused by four young men of coercing them into sexual acts.[17]

The closet is also a serious and sinful issue for the Roman Catholic Church. In his book *The Silence of Sodom*, Mark Jordan has written about the deep closets within Roman Catholicism and the resulting tension between extreme homophobia and homoeroticism within the Roman Catholic priesthood.[18] The closet is not limited to homosexuality, however. Elsewhere, Jordan and others have written about the recent sexual abuse crisis in the Roman Catholic Church and the problems that have arisen out of the ecclesial closet and the extreme repression and inability to speak openly and honestly about issues of sexuality.[19] Mary Hunt has written about how the Roman Catholic Church is "suffused with secrecy and deception, and rewarding of duplicity." She writes that the system "works" because of the "collusion of those schooled in obedience to law and authority, who adhere to codes of behavior that preserve the priesthood and the institutional church at the expense of children."[20]

The sin of the closet also manifests itself in LGBT communities of color. For many LGBT people of color, coming out to

---

[16] Patrick S. Cheng, "'Ex-Gays' and the Ninth Circle of Hell," *Huffington Post* (May 20, 2010), available at http://www.huffingtonpost.com/rev-patrick-s-cheng-phd/ex-gays-and-the-ninth-cir_b_582825.html (accessed on December 11, 2011).

[17] For more homophobic individuals who were caught in gay sex scandals, see the Gay Homophobe website, available at http://gayhomophobe.com (accessed on December 11, 2011).

[18] Mark D. Jordan, *The Silence of Sodom: Homosexuality in Modern Catholicism* (Chicago: University of Chicago Press, 2000).

[19] See Mark D. Jordan, *Telling Truths in Church: Scandal, Flesh, and Christian Speech* (Boston: Beacon Press, 2003); Donald L. Boisvert and Robert E. Goss, eds., *Gay Catholic Priests and Clerical Sexual Misconduct* (Binghamton NY: Harrington Park Press, 2005).

[20] Hunt, "New Feminist Catholics," 270.

families and friends can be a particularly difficult process as a result of condemnation from theologically conservative churches, cultural expectations of traditional gender roles, and the anxieties of bringing shame to their families and ethnic communities.[21] For example, "Michael Kim," the pseudonym of a young Korean American gay Christian man, has written about the difficulties of coming out in the Korean American community.[22] According to Kim: "It is a single-elimination game—I could go to Harvard, Harvard Medical, do a surgical residency at Massachusetts General Hospital, and if in the end, I am still gay, I end up with a big fat zero." He writes about how others in the Korean community would say "Well, my son didn't go to Harvard, but at least he's not gay."[23]

It should be noted that the closet does not only relate to sexuality or gender identity. For example, it can take the form of downplaying other characteristics such as one's race or ethnicity. The gay Japanese American law professor Kenji Yoshino has written about this phenomenon of blending into the mainstream in his book *Covering: The Hidden Assault on Our Civil Rights*.[24] For example, LGBT people of color often experience an additional closet—the ethnic closet—in trying to hide or downplay their minority status within the predominantly white LGBT community. That is, they try to "blend in" as a result of the fetishization and marginalization described in the previous chapter.

3. Grace as Coming Out

By contrast, grace in the context of the Out Christ can be understood as the courage to come out of the closet, or sharing one's sexual orientation and/or gender identity with others. For LGBT people, the process of coming out can only be understood as grace, or an unmerited gift, on the part of God. There is no one correct pattern or single path to coming out. Some people come out very early in life; others wait until much later. For some people it is a slow and private process. For others, it is a fast

---

[21] Eunai Shrake, "Homosexuality and Korean Immigrant Protestant Churches," in *Embodying Asian/American Sexualities*, ed. Gina Masequesmay and Sean Metzger (Lanham, MD: Lexington Books, 2009), 145–56.

[22] Michael Kim, "Out and About: Coming of Age in a Straight White World," in *Asian American X: An Intersection of 21st Century Asian American Voices*, ed. Arar Han and John Hsu (Ann Arbor, MI: University of Michigan Press, 2004), 139–48.

[23] Kim, "Out and About," 146.

[24] Kenji Yoshino, *Covering: The Hidden Assault on Our Civil Rights* (New York: Random House, 2006).

and public announcement. Furthermore, coming out is not just a one-time process. Indeed, it is an ongoing process that unfolds in different situations and contexts throughout one's life.

Regardless of how one ultimately comes out, the act of coming out reflects the very nature of a God who is also constantly coming out and revealing Godself to us in the Out Christ. Coming out is a gift that is accompanied by other gifts such as self-love, the love for others, and the overcoming of shame and internalized homophobia. Coming out is not something that can be "willed" or "earned"; it can only happen as an act of grace from God.

A number of LGBT spiritual writers have noted the connection between coming out and the spiritual growth of LGBT people. That is, coming out is the first step to spiritual maturity. For example, the former Jesuit priest and current psychotherapist John McNeill has written in his book *Freedom, Glorious Freedom* about a three-step process for creating an authentic LGBT self: (1) a passage from the closet to self-acceptance; (2) a passage into intimacy with another; and (3) a public passage. For McNeill, these steps are necessary in order for LGBT "health and holiness." McNeill further recognizes that movement through these passages is not something that one can achieve through one's own resources; rather, it is a "gift of God's"—that is, a matter of grace.[25]

McNeill's model is echoed in the works of other writers who work on issues relating to LGBT spirituality. For example, Daniel Helminiak argues that sexual self-acceptance, including the coming-out process, is necessary for spiritual growth. That is, "sexual self-acceptance leads to self-esteem, which advances human development, which includes spiritual development."[26] James Empereur, a Jesuit professor of liturgy and theology, has noted that spiritual maturity begins with challenging a "conformist" model of spirituality (that is, basing one's values solely on external authorities), which often includes dealing with the coming-out process.[27] The connection between coming out and spiritual maturity is echoed in the autobiographies of closeted evangelical Christians such as Mel White—the former ghostwriter to Jerry Falwell—who have found their true vocational calling after coming out of the closet.[28]

---

[25] John J. McNeill, *Freedom, Glorious Freedom: The Spiritual Journey to the Fullness of Life for Gays, Lesbians, and Everybody Else* (Boston: Beacon Press, 1995), 61, 65.

[26] Helminiak, *Sex and the Sacred*, 55 ("Sexual Self-Acceptance and Spiritual Growth").

[27] James L. Empereur, *Spiritual Direction and the Gay Person* (New York: Continuum Publishing, 1998), 119–21.

[28] See generally White, *Stranger at the Gate*.

Justin Tanis, an ordained minister with the Metropolitan Community Churches, has written in his book *Trans-Gendered* about the ways in which congregations and other communities of faith can help transgender people come out about their gender identities. Tanis lists a number of characteristics of welcoming communities, including the "visible and audible presence of trans people and programs," which highlights the importance of creating spaces that allow trans people to come out.[29] Other resources for helping transgender people to come out within communities of faith include the "MCC TRANSFormative Church Ministry Program," which is a guide produced by the Metropolitan Community Churches Transgender Ministries.[30]

As noted above, there is not just one model for coming out with respect to the LGBT community. In fact, sometimes the "standard" model of coming out—that is, sitting down with family and friends and making the big announcement—does not work for immigrant communities or communities of color. In the Asian American community, for example, one rarely talks about sexuality, let alone LGBT issues. There are also complex social, cultural, and linguistic challenges with respect to coming out. I know of queer Asian American grassroots activists who are—and look—extremely out in their everyday lives, but they "tone down" their appearance whenever they go home and visit their families. It's not because they are closeted, but rather it is out of respect for their cultures.

When LGBT Asians come out, however, they also help their families, friends, and those around them to discover the gift of God's grace. Wei Ming Dariotis, a bisexual young woman of mixed Chinese and European heritage, wrote about how her coming out has allowed her mother to make the connections between homophobia and racism. When Dariotis came out, she told her Chinese mother—who had made a number of homophobic comments in the past—what it was like to be bisexual and Asian American. Some time later, her mother heard Dariotis' younger brother calling someone a "fag" and told him to stop. Her mother called Dariotis and said: "You would be very proud of me. I told Alex he can't talk like that. I told him he might be very popular

---

[29] Tanis, *Trans-Gendered*, 122.

[30] Metropolitan Community Church Transgender Ministries, *MCC TRANSFormative Church Ministry Program*, available through MCCTM@MCCChurch.net.

right now, but tomorrow it could turn around and then, because he is Chinese, they could call him a Chink, and it is just like calling the other kid a fag." Dariotis said that she was very proud of her mother for "making a connection between racism and homophobia—they are oppressions that support each other."[31] By coming out, Dariotis allowed her mother to discover God's grace by challenging and disrupting patterns of racist and homophobic behavior in herself and in those around her.

In the end, communities of color have their unique ways of dealing with the coming out issue, which can take the form of God's amazing grace. For example, I never had to "come out" to my Wai Puo (that is, my maternal grandmother). Early on in our relationship, I had simply invited Michael over to have lunch with Wai Puo. He loved her cooking, and she in turn loved cooking for him. Wai Puo always treated us like we were together and in the same way that she treated the other married members of my extended family. She just knew. Because she was so accepting of Michael, this set an example for the other members of our family. We have been blessed with the grace of coming out.

Study Questions

1. Who is the Out Christ? What does it mean to say that God comes out of the closet with respect to Jesus Christ?
2. Which depiction of the Out Christ in this chapter appeals to you the most? The least?
3. What is sin in light of the Out Christ? How does this sin affect closeted conservative Christian leaders? The Roman Catholic Church? Communities of color?
4. What is grace in light of the Out Christ? How does this grace help with respect to the spiritual growth of LGBT people?
5. Have you experienced the grace of coming out in your own life? If so, how? If not, how might you experience the grace of coming out in other contexts?

[31] Wei Ming Dariotis, "On Becoming a Bi Bi Grrl," in *Restoried Selves: Autobiographies of Queer Asian/Pacific American Activists*, ed. Kevin K. Kumashiro (Binghamton, NY: Harrington Park Press, 2004), 46.

For Further Study

The Out Christ

- Glaser, *Coming Out As Sacrament*
- Helminiak, *Sex and the Sacred*, 111–28
- Montefiore, "Jesus, The Revelation of God"
- Smith, *Clement of Alexandria and a Secret Gospel of Mark*
- Smith, *The Secret Gospel*
- Williams, *Just as I Am*, 111–23
- Wilson, *Our Tribe*, 132–48

Sin as the Closet

- Boisvert, *Gay Catholic Priests and Clerical Sexual Misconduct*
- Hunt, "New Feminist Catholics"
- Jordan, *Silence of Sodom*
- Jordan, *Telling Truths in Church*
- Kim, "Out and About"
- Shrake, "Homosexuality and Korean Immigrant Protestant Churches"
- Yoshino, *Covering*

Grace as Coming Out

- Dariotis, "On Becoming a Bi Bi Grrl"
- Empereur, *Spiritual Direction and the Gay Person*
- Helminiak, *Sex and the Sacred*, 53–64
- McNeill, *Freedom, Glorious, Freedom*, 51–89
- Metropolitan Community Church Transgender Ministries, "MCC TRANSFormative Church Ministry Program"
- Tanis, *Trans-Gendered*
- White, *Stranger at the Gate*

Chapter 7

Model Three: The Liberator Christ

1. The Liberator Christ

The third christological model of sin and grace for LGBT people is the Liberator Christ. In other words, Jesus Christ can be understood as the One who frees all who are enslaved to systematic oppressions, including heterosexism and homophobia. This model is rooted in liberation and contextual theologies, which started in the late 1960s with Latin American and black theologians such as Gustavo Gutiérrez and James Cone, and these theologies have since covered a wide number of identities and groups, including LGBT people.[1]

Jesus Christ announces at the beginning of his ministry that his mission is to set the oppressed free. By reading from the Book of Isaiah, Jesus proclaims that he has been anointed by God to "bring good news to the poor," to "proclaim release to the captives," and to "let the oppressed go free."[2] Indeed, a central theme of the gospel—if not Christian theology—is that of liberation, whether it relates to freedom from sin or from suffering. As such, the Liberator Christ is an important model of the Queer Christ.

[1] For an overview of liberation theologies in the United States, see Miguel A. De La Torre, ed., *Handbook of U.S. Theologies of Liberation* (St. Louis, MO: Chalice Press, 2004); Stacey M. Floyd-Thomas and Anthony B. Pinn, eds., *Liberation Theologies in the United States: An Introduction* (New York: New York University Press, 2010).

[2] Luke 4:18–19 (quoting Isa. 61:1–2).

The work of the Liberator Christ is reinforced by the parable of sheep and goats in Matthew 25, in which Jesus establishes an ethic of ministering to—and liberating—those who are hungry, thirsty, marginalized, naked, sick, and/or imprisoned.[3] Ironically, these are the criteria upon which Christians will be judged at the end of time, and not the issues of sexual morality that many churches and denominations have spent countless hours debating.

The Liberator Christ can also be seen in Jesus' challenge to the religious authorities of his day. Jesus is constantly liberating those from legalism, whether it is healing on the Sabbath or touching bleeding women, people possessed by demons, and others who are viewed as being unclean. Furthermore, Jesus challenges these authorities not only in word, but also in deed. For example, he cleanses the Temple by using physical force in overturning the tables of the money changers and driving out those who were selling animals for sacrifice.[4] Jesus' challenge to the religious authorities is what ultimately gets him convicted of blasphemy by the Sanhedrin, the assembly of religious leaders.[5]

Just as the ancient Israelites were freed from their slavery to the Egyptians, the Liberator Christ frees LGBT people from the enslavement of heterosexism and homophobia. In 1960, Robert Wood, the gay United Church of Christ minister, wrote a groundbreaking book, *Christ and the Homosexual*, that challenged the negative attitudes of the institutional church with respect to homosexuals. Wood dedicated this book to "the lonely and rejected homosexuals who feel damned" and hoped that they would find the "Light that is Jesus Christ." Wood wrote about the Liberator Christ when he argued that the church "has not always followed Christ in dealing with the homosexual."[6]

Three decades later, Robert E. Shore-Goss wrote about the Liberator Christ in *Jesus Acted Up: A Gay and Lesbian Manifesto*. In that book, which was written during the height of the HIV/AIDS pandemic, Shore-Goss defended the work of lesbian and gay, feminist, and HIV/AIDS activist groups from a Christian perspective. In particular, he argued that such activism is consistent with the Jesus Christ of the gospels, as opposed to the Jesus Christ of the institutional churches.

---

[3] Matt. 25.
[4] Mark 11:15–17; John 2:14–16.
[5] Mark 14:64.
[6] Wood, *Christ and the Homosexual*, 1, 97.

For Shore-Goss, it is critical that we deconstruct traditional christologies of institutional churches and, in particular, Roman Catholicism. For example, he cites how the celibacy of Jesus has been "used by Catholic doctrine and practice to buttress control of the church by celibate men."[7] Goss calls LGBT people to overthrow the erotophobic and sex-negative model of "Christ the Oppressor," and move to the LGBT-empowering model of "Jesus the Liberator."[8]

Other LGBT theologians have focused on different aspects of the Liberator Christ. For example, Gary Comstock, the gay theologian and retired university Protestant chaplain at Wesleyan University, writes about our need to be liberated from traditional notions of a hierarchical Jesus Christ that lords over us. In his book *Gay Theology Without Apology*, Comstock argues that Jesus liberates us from seeing him as a "master." Rather, Jesus invites us to be his "friend." Jesus gives us a "nudge to get on without him," and he urges us to take on the ethical responsibility of loving one another.[9] Thus, the Liberator Christ for Comstock is not so much an all-powerful sovereign, but rather a friend who empowers us to leave behind unhealthy behaviors with respect to abusive religions.

For me, the Liberator Christ is the One who liberates us from binary thinking about sexuality and gender identity. As I have written in *Radical Love*, queer theology is about a radical love that is so extreme that it dissolves existing binaries such as gay/straight, masculine/feminine, and male/female.[10] Thus, the Liberator Christ for me is found in the bisexual, transgender, and intersex christologies that free us from traditional sexual and gender binaries. These include the bisexual christologies of Nancy Wilson, Marcella Althaus-Reid, and Laurel Dykstra; the transgender christologies of Eleanor McLaughlin and Justin Tanis; and the intersex christology of Virginia Mollenkott.[11]

It should be noted that the Liberator Christ is *not* found in false notions of liberation, such as the "ex-gay" or reparative therapies advocated by organizations like Exodus International. These

---

[7] Robert E. Goss, *Jesus Acted Up: A Gay and Lesbian Manifesto* (San Francisco: HarperSanFrancisco, 1993), 69.

[8] Goss, *Jesus Acted Up*, 61–85.

[9] See Comstock, *Gay Theology Without Apology*, 91–103.

[10] See Cheng, *Radical Love*.

[11] For a detailed discussion of these christologies, see Cheng, *Radical Love*, 78–86. Ultimately, I believe that even LGBT categories themselves are dissolved by the Liberator Christ; neither sexuality nor gender identity has ultimate significance in the larger Christian narrative of creation, reconciliation, and redemption.

treatments, which are discredited by mainline psychological and psychiatric professional organizations, purport to free LGBT people from their sexualities and gender identities by "praying the gay away." As Wayne Besen has documented in his book *Anything But Straight*, these therapies simply do not work. For example, the two founders of Exodus International fell in love with each other and left the organization. Similarly, other poster-children for the "ex-gay" movement like John Paulk have been caught secretly cruising for men in gay bars.[12] This is not a question of being freed from one's sexual orientation or gender identity from the Liberator Christ; rather, it is an issue of being freed from self-loathing and self-hate.

In sum, the Liberator Christ is an important aspect of the Queer Christ, whether it frees LGBT people from the toxic heterosexism and homophobia that still pervades our institutional churches, from the hierarchical notion of a Jesus Christ that lords over us, or from false binaries with respect to sexuality, gender identity, and biological sex. We now turn to thinking about sin and grace in light of the Liberator Christ.

2. Sin as Apathy

What is sin in light of the Liberator Christ? If the Liberator Christ is understood as the One who frees all those who are enslaved to systemic oppressions, then sin—defined as that which opposes the Liberator Christ—can be understood as *apathy*. That is, sin with respect to the model of the Liberator Christ can be seen as the refusal to work towards the elimination of the systemic oppressions that affect *all* members of the LGBT community, including those LGBT people who are the "least among us," such as those who are marginalized on the basis of class, sex, race, gender identity, age, ability, and other factors.

One challenge that faces LGBT people is a lack of understanding about the interconnected nature of oppressions, even within our "community." As some of us obtain more legal rights and political representation, it is critical not to leave behind those who have not yet received those rights. For example, in 2006 transgender rights protections were dropped from the federal Employment Non-Discrimination Act (ENDA), the proposed federal civil rights

[12] See Besen, *Anything But Straight*.

legislation relating to sexual orientation. The rationale was that a bill that included gender identity protections would not have enough votes to pass Congress. This for me raises the question of apathy by some members of the LGBT community (here, lesbians and gay men) with respect to other more marginalized members of our community (transgender folk).

Indeed, some people have questioned the need for what they call the "alphabet soup" of letters in the LGBT acronym (which also can include additional letters such as IQQATS, which stand for intersex, queer, questioning, allies, and two-spirit people). The alphabet soup is actually very important to the extent that it reminds lesbians and gay men that sexual orientation is not the same thing as gender identity (as in the case of transgender people). Furthermore, the various letters also remind lesbians and gay men that sexuality is not a binary issue (as in the case of bisexuals), and neither is biological sex (as in the case of intersex people). The reluctance to be inclusive because of issues of expediency or convenience is for me an example of the sin of apathy. This is ironic because many LGBT people have suffered from the apathy of those who have failed to speak up or act on their behalf, such as bystanders who remain silent in the face of bullying.[13]

A similar issue of apathy relates to the same-sex marriage laws that have passed in a number of states, most recently New York State. Specifically, will LGBT people continue to fight for protections and rights with respect to *alternative* forms of relationships within the LGBT community, once they have obtained marriage rights themselves? Or will they no longer be concerned about broader issues of justice? For example, Mary Hunt has written a thought-provoking piece explaining why she is concerned that same-sex marriage legislation may fall short of true relational justice and leave behind those who cannot benefit from the marriage laws (as opposed to granting access to employer-provided health care benefits to individuals other than just spouses and dependents of the employee).[14]

The sin of apathy can take a number of other forms in the LGBT community. One such form is racism and the failure to

---

[13] See Barbara Coloroso, *The Bully, the Bullied, and the Bystander: From Preschool to High School—How Parents and Teachers Can Help Break the Cycle of Violence*, updated ed. (New York: Collins Living, 2008), 159–75 (discussing the role of bystanders in bullying situations). For a theological critique of the bullying of LGBT youth, see Cheng, "Faith, Hope, and Love."

[14] See Mary E. Hunt, "Same-Sex Marriage and Relational Justice," *Journal of Feminist Studies in Religion* 20, no. 2 (Fall, 2004): 83–92.

be inclusive with respect to LGBT communities of color. For example, in 1991, one of the major organizations in the LGBT community—Lambda Legal Defense and Education Fund—held its annual fundraiser at the Broadway musical *Miss Saigon*. That musical had been roundly condemned by the Asian American community for its stereotypical portrayal of Asians as "submissive 'Orientals,' self-erasing women, and asexual, contemptible men." The Asian American community was also angry that a major role that was written for an Asian person was played by a white actor in yellow face. Although Lambda refused to cancel the event for financial reasons, the incident did help to galvanize the LGBT Asian community in New York City in protesting the fundraiser.[15]

Twenty years later, things have not necessarily improved. In 2001, another major organization in the LGBT community—the Human Rights Campaign—was criticized by LGBT Asian American activists for failing to include any people of color in its testimony to Congress on the Defense of Marriage Act (DOMA). This was a particularly troubling oversight to the extent that DOMA significantly affects bi-national couples whose marriages were not recognized for purposes of immigration law. And one of the major LGBT publications—*Out Magazine*—profiled only two people of color (and no African Americans or Asian Americans) in its 2010 annual "Power 50" issue of the most influential people in the LGBT community.[16] We still have a long way to go with respect to the issue of race.

The sin of apathy can take a number of other forms in the LGBT community. For example, there is often a lack of concern about broader issues of economic justice by out lesbians and gays who live a comfortable middle- to upper-class existence in urban gay enclaves such as San Francisco and New York. Despite the fact that these individuals have benefitted greatly from the liberation work of past LGBT activists (for example, our courageous transgender ancestors at the Stonewall Riots), many of these "A-List Gays" do very little—if anything—towards the further liberation of *all* who suffer from systemic oppressions.

---

[15] See Yoko Yoshikawa, "The Heat Is on *Miss Saigon* Coalition: Organizing Across Race and Sexuality," in Eng and Hom, *Q&A*, 41–56.

[16] The two people of color were Anthony Romero and Perez Hilton. For the complete list of names, see "The Fifth Annual Power 50," available at http://www.out.com/out-exclusives/power-50/2011/04/11/fifth-annual-power-50#slide-1 (accessed on December 11, 2011).

3. Grace as Activism

If sin is apathy, then grace in the context of the Liberator Christ can be understood as *activism*, or the willingness to challenge the powers and principalities that result in systemic oppressions. That is, grace can be understood as a gift by God to challenge not only issues of traditional concern to LGBT people, but also many other issues that result in social and economic injustices.[17]

In many ways, the contemporary LGBT movement in the United States was born as a result of activism. The Stonewall Riots occurred during the evening of June 27–28, 1968, in the Stonewall Inn, a bar in Greenwich Village, New York City, and it is viewed as the founding event of the modern-day LGBT rights movement. On that night, patrons of the bar and other residents in Greenwich Village refused to accept a routine police raid of the Stonewall Inn and fought back. This event is commemorated each year with Pride marches around the world.[18]

Although the Stonewall Riots are seen as a pivotal moment in the modern LGBT rights movement, many events of activism led up to the Stonewall Riots, including the founding of the Mattachine Society and the Daughters of Bilitis—social and educational organizations for gay men and lesbians respectively—both in the 1950s. These were significant acts of courage, given that lesbians and gay men could be terminated from their jobs and were prohibited from dancing together in public places.

One early homophile activist was Kiyoshi Kuromiya, a gay Japanese American man who participated in one of the first gay rights demonstrations in 1965 at Independence Hall in Philadelphia to protest discrimination against homosexuals in the federal government and the military. Kuromiya was involved with LGBT activism for thirty-five years. Not only did he participate in the early homophile and gay liberation movements, but towards the end of his life he became involved with HIV/AIDS

---

[17] One such LGBT group is Queers for Economic Justice, which is a "progressive non-profit organization committed to promoting economic justice in a context of sexual and gender liberation." See http://q4ej.org/about (accessed on December 11, 2011). The grace of activism has taken on particular significance in light of the Occupy Wall Street movement that, as of December 2011, has held demonstrations for economic justice in hundreds of cities around the world.

[18] For histories of the Stonewall Riots and the founding of the LGBT rights movement in the United States, see Dudley Clendinen and Adam Nagourney, *Out for Good: The Struggle to Build a Gay Rights Movement in America* (New York: Touchstone, 1999); Eric Marcus, *Making Gay History: The Half-Century Fight for Lesbian and Gay Rights* (New York: Harper, 2002); Neil Miller, *Out of the Past: Gay and Lesbian History: From 1869 to the Present*, rev. ed. (New York: Alyson Books, 2006). For a general history of LGBT people and our queer ancestors, see Martin Duberman, Martha Vicinus, and George Chauncey, eds., *Hidden from History: Reclaiming the Gay and Lesbian Past* (New York: Meridian, 1989).

activism, including the AIDS Coalition to Unleash Power (ACT-UP), an LGBT activist organization that was founded in 1987 to protest the United States government's apathy with respect to the growing HIV/AIDS pandemic. Kuromiya died in 2000 from complications of HIV/AIDS and cancer, but his memory lives on as one of the first gay Asian American activists.[19]

Other LGBT activist organizations included Queer Nation, founded in 1990, which used confrontational tactics (for example, outing closeted individuals) to protest the continuing discrimination and violence against LGBT people. As noted above, there are a number of more "mainstream" LGBT political and legal activist organizations such as the Human Rights Campaign and the Lambda Legal Defense and Education Fund that have been working towards issues like marriage equality and the repeal of DOMA.

The grace of activism also can be seen in the grass roots work of many LGBT communities of color that acknowledge the interconnected nature of systemic oppressions. For example, the National Queer API Alliance (NQAPIA), the national coalition of queer Asian organizations, is committed not only to addressing traditional LGBT issues of sexual orientation and gender identity discrimination, but it also addresses issues of racism and classism within the LGBT community as well as immigration reform.[20]

Guy Nakatani is an example of the grace of activism within the queer Asian community. Nakatani, a young Japanese American gay man, was diagnosed with full-blown AIDS at the age of twenty. Although Nakatani's diagnosis in the late 1980s was initially a shock to him and his family, he decided to become an activist with respect to his HIV/AIDS status and become a peer AIDS educator. Over the course of the next six years, Nakatani gave numerous live presentations to local high school students in the San Francisco Bay Area about HIV prevention. When he died at the age of twenty-six, Nakatani had made presentations to approximately 40,000 people, which likely saved numerous lives. Nakatani's story is a powerful example of how the grace of activism manifested itself in a young, HIV+ gay Asian man.[21]

Finally, the grace of activism can be seen in the founding of

---

[19] Liz Highleyman, "Kiyoshi Kuromiya: Integrating the Issues," in *Smash the Church, Smash the State!: The Early Years of Gay Liberation*, ed. Tommi Avicolli Mecca (San Francisco: City Lights Books, 2009).

[20] For the NQAPIA website, see http://www.nqapia.org (accessed on December 11, 2011).

[21] See Molly Fumia, *Honor Thy Children: One Family's Journey to Wholeness* (Berkeley, CA: Conari Press, 1997).

LGBT religious organizations such as the Metropolitan Community Churches (MCC). MCC was founded in 1968 in the living room of Troy Perry, a gay Pentecostal minister who had been expelled from his ministry because of his sexuality. Perry wrote about his religious activism in his autobiography, *The Lord Is My Shepherd and He Knows I'm Gay*. In that book, Perry traced his journey from his "personal wilderness" to the "oasis in God's garden."[22] In the last four decades, MCC has since grown to become an international organization of churches that is open to all.[23]

The grace of activism can also be seen in the founding of LGBT affinity groups in mainline denominations. One of the most prominent of such groups is Integrity, the national LGBT organization of the Episcopal Church, which was founded by Dr. Louie Crew in rural Georgia in 1974.[24] Integrity was founded at a time when even Grace Cathedral in San Francisco did not know where lesbian and gay Episcopalians could gather together. A few decades later, Integrity witnessed the consecration of the Rt. Rev. Gene Robinson in 2003 and the Rt. Rev. Mary Glasspool in 2010, the first openly gay and openly lesbian persons, respectively, to be elected and consecrated bishops in the Anglican Communion.

Indeed, the grace of LGBT activism—from the Stonewall Riots to the founding of ACT-UP and Queer Nation to the founding of MCC and Integrity—is a gift from God that recognizes that we are all interconnected within the Body of Christ and that we cannot say to another that "I have no need of you."[25]

---

[22] Troy Perry, *The Lord Is My Shepherd and He Knows I'm Gay* (Los Angeles: Nash Publishing, 1972), 6.

[23] For an online archive of LGBT religious history, including key figures in MCC, see the LGBT Religious Archive Network at http://www.lgbtran.org (accessed on December 11, 2011).

[24] For the story of the founding of Integrity, see Louie Crew, "The Founding of Integrity," available at http://www.rci.rutgers.edu/~lcrew/pubd/founding.html (accessed on December 11, 2011).

[25] 1 Cor. 12:21.

Study Questions

1. Who is the Liberator Christ? What are some examples of the Liberator Christ in the gospels?
2. Which depiction of the Liberator Christ in this chapter appeals to you the most? The least?
3. What are some false notions of liberation with respect to LGBT people?
4. What is sin in light of the Liberator Christ? How might this sin be manifested in the LGBT community today?
5. What is grace in light of the Liberator Christ? What are some examples of this grace in the LGBT community, both historically and today?

For Further Study

U.S. Liberation Theologies

- De La Torre, *Handbook of U.S. Theologies of Liberation*
- Floyd-Thomas and Pinn, *Liberation Theologies in the United States*

Liberator Christ

- Cheng, *Radical Love*, 78–86
- Comstock, *Gay Theology Without Apology*, 91–103
- Goss, *Jesus Acted Up*
- Wood, *Christ and the Homosexual*

Ex-Gays and False Liberation

- Besen, *Anything But Straight*

Sin as Apathy

- Coloroso, *The Bully, the Bullied, and the Bystander*
- Hunt, "Same-Sex Marriage and Relational Justice"
- Yoshikawa, "The Heat Is on *Miss Saigon* Coalition"

Grace as Activism

- Clendinen and Nagourney, *Out for Good*
- Crew, "The Founding of Integrity"
- Duberman, Vicinus, and Chauncey, *Hidden from History*
- Fumia, *Honor Thy Children*
- Highleyman, "Kiyoshi Kuromiya"
- Marcus, *Making Gay History*
- Miller, *Out of the Past*
- Perry, *The Lord Is My Shepherd and He Knows I'm Gay*

Chapter 8

Model Four: The Transgressive Christ

1. The Transgressive Christ

The fourth christological model of sin and grace for LGBT people is the Transgressive Christ. The Transgressive Christ arises out of the understanding that Jesus Christ was crucified by the religious and political authorities of his day for refusing to conform to—and in some cases actively subverting—their standards of behavior. Jesus Christ is described as a "pervert" in the Gospel of Luke; he is brought before Pontius Pilate and accused by the people of "perverting" (in the Greek, *diastrephonta*, meaning to "twist," "turn away," or "mislead") their nation.[1]

From the beginning of the gospels, Jesus Christ is portrayed as an outsider. For example, the genealogy in the Gospel of Matthew names or alludes to several unconventional or sexually "transgressive" woman ancestors, including Tamar (who disguised herself as a prostitute and tricked her father-in-law into having sex with her), Rahab (who was a prostitute and a Canaanite), Bathsheba (who committed adultery with King David while she was married to Uriah the Hittite), and Ruth (who pledged her devotion to another woman and was a Moabite). And Jesus is born, of course, to Mary, who was unmarried when she became pregnant with him.[2]

---

[1] Luke 23:2, 14.

[2] Matt. 1:1–16.

In his ministries, Jesus is constantly seen as transgressing the commonly accepted religious and legal boundaries of his day. In a world obsessed by purity codes, he touches and heals those who are considered to be unclean, including lepers,[3] bleeding women,[4] those possessed by demons, and the disabled.[5] He challenges the teachings of the religious authorities, such as the prohibition against healing on the Sabbath[6] and the grounds for divorce.[7] He is criticized for eating and drinking with outcasts such as tax collectors and sinners.[8]

Jesus pushes the boundaries of conventional behavior. He was an unmarried rabbi in his early thirties, he rejected his biological family,[9] and he is rejected by his own hometown.[10] He tells parables about many people who are on the margins of Israelite society, such as the Samaritans.[11] In sum, the Transgressive Christ can be understood as God's solidarity with the suffering of LGBT people and others who refuse to conform to the rules of the principalities and powers of this world.

Robert Shore-Goss has written extensively about the Transgressive Christ in his groundbreaking books on LGBT christology, *Jesus Acted Up* and *Queering Christ*.[12] In *Jesus Acted Up*, which was an angry manifesto written in response to the silence and inaction of the church with respect to the HIV/AIDS pandemic, Shore-Goss argued that Jesus Christ should be seen as a model of "transgressive practice" with respect to those who advocate for sexual justice today.

Specifically, Shore-Goss compared Jesus' actions in driving out the animal merchants and overturning the tables of the money changers in the Temple to the ACT UP/New York protest in St. Patrick's Cathedral. That protest, which occurred during the height of the HIV/AIDS crisis, created an uproar when a protester crumbled up a consecrated host instead of eating it. For Shore-Goss, both actions "violated sacred space, transgressed sacred ritual, and offended sensibilities." Yet, according to Shore-Goss,

---

3 Matt. 8:1–4; Luke 17:11–19.
4 Matt. 9:18–26; Mark 5:21–43.
5 Mark 7:31–37.
6 Mark 3:1–6.
7 Mark 10:2–12.
8 Matt. 9:9–13. See generally Carey, *Sinners*; see also Edward P. Wimberly, *Moving from Shame to Self-Worth: Preaching and Pastoral Care* (Nashville, TN: Abingdon Press, 1999), 76–78.
9 Mark 3:31–35.
10 Matt. 13:53–58.
11 Luke 10:29–37.
12 See Goss, *Jesus Acted Up*; Robert E. Goss, *Queering Christ: Beyond Jesus Acted Up* (Cleveland, OH: Pilgrim Press, 2002).

both acts exhibited a "profound reverence for the sacred based on God's justice-doing."[13]

In *Queering Christ*, Shore-Goss argued that the idea of transgression can be seen as a metaphor—if not *the* metaphor—for queer theologies today.[14] In a provocative chapter, "Expanding Christ's Wardrobe of Dresses," Shore-Goss describes a number of queer christologies in popular culture, including what he calls "obscene" representations of Jesus Christ that deconstruct the "heterosexual and patriarchal constructions of Christ."[15]

One of these popular representations is Terrence McNally's controversial off-Broadway play, *Corpus Christi*, which depicts a gay young man, Joshua, as a queer Christ figure.[16] Another such depiction is Swedish photographer Elisabeth Ohlson Wallin's exhibit, Ecce Homo, which depicts images such as Jesus being baptized in a bathhouse and appearing at a drag Last Supper.[17] (The trangressive representations of Jesus have continued to this day, with Lady Gaga's recent video of *Judas* in which Jesus is portrayed as a svelte, well-coiffed, and somewhat-feminized leather biker who wears a lot of gold jewelry.[18])

Finally, the Transgressive Christ can be seen in bisexual, transgender, and intersex christologies that respectively challenge binary thinking with respect to sexuality, gender identity, and biological sex. For example, Marcella Althaus-Reid, the late bisexual Argentinean theologian and professor at the University of Edinburgh, wrote about the Bi/Christ in her groundbreaking book, *Indecent Theology*. For Althaus-Reid, the Bi/Christ is not so much about the "sexual performances of Jesus." Rather, it is about challenging the Mono/Christ, or the "patterns of hierarchical, binary constructive organised thought" that treat heterosexuality and homosexuality (or straight and gay) as polar opposites.[19]

Similarly, transgender theologians such as Justin Tanis have written about a transgender Christ who challenges the gender

---

[13] Goss, *Jesus Acted Up*, 149–50.
[14] See Goss, *Queering Christ*, 223–38.
[15] Goss, *Queering Christ*, 179.
[16] See Terrence McNally, *Corpus Christi: A Play* (New York: Grove Press, 1998).
[17] Goss, *Queering Christ*, 171–72.
[18] For a theological discussion of the Judas video, see Patrick S. Cheng, "Lady Gaga and the Gospel of Judas," *Huffington Post* (May 16, 2011), at http://www.huffingtonpost.com/rev-patrick-s-cheng-phd/lady-gaga-and-the-gospel-_b_862104.html (accessed on December 11, 2011).
[19] Marcella Althaus-Reid, *Indecent Theology: Theological Perversions in Sex, Gender, and Politics* (London: Routledge, 2000), 114. For another bisexual christology, see Laurel Dysktra, "Jesus, Bread, Wine and Roses: A Bisexual Feminist at the Catholic Worker," in *Blessed Bi Spirit: Bisexual People of Faith*, ed. Debra R. Kolodny (New York: Continuum, 2000), 78–88.

binaries of masculine and feminine. Tanis develops a trans-christology that focuses on Jesus Christ's breaking through "barriers of gender" during his ministry, including speaking with women, performing traditionally female acts such as washing feet, and having women as followers. Furthermore, Jesus experienced harassment and a sense of homelessness, in much the same way that trans folk do today. Tanis also draws connections between the resurrected body of Christ and the process of transition that trans people go through.[20]

Finally, Virginia Mollenkott has articulated an intersex christology in her book *Omnigender* that challenges the binaries of male and female with respect to biological sex. Mollenkott notes that if Jesus Christ was truly the product of a virgin, or parthenogenetic, birth, then there would be no biological male to contribute any Y chromosomes to the XX chromosomes of his mother Mary. Accordingly, Jesus Christ would be a male-bodied person with XX chromosomes, which would make him an intersex person.[21] Susannah Cornwall, a queer theologian and postdoctoral research associate at the University of Manchester in the United Kingdom, has proposed another intersex christology; she has written on the relationship between intersex people and the Body of Christ in her book *Sex and Uncertainty in the Body of Christ*.[22]

In sum, the Transgressive Christ is manifested in many contemporary LGBT christologies. These christologies share a common goal of challenging conventional boundaries, whether they relate to sexuality, gender identity, or biological sex. We now turn to what sin and grace mean in the context of the Transgressive Christ.

2. Sin as Conformity

What is sin in light of the Transgressive Christ? If the Transgressive Christ is the One who is tortured and executed for daring to break society's rules, then sin—as that which opposes the Transgressive Christ—can be understood as mindless *conformity*

---

[20] See Tanis, *Trans-Gendered*, 138–43. Other articulations of trans christologies include Eleanor McLaughlin, "Feminist Christologies: Re-Dressing the Tradition," in *Reconstructing the Christ Symbol: Essays in Feminist Christology*, ed. Maryanne Stevens (New York: Paulist Press, 1993), 118–49; and Sheridan, *Crossing Over*, 93–97. See also Virginia Ramey Mollenkott and Vanessa Sheridan, *Transgender Journeys* (Cleveland, OH: Pilgrim Press, 2003).

[21] Mollenkott, *Omnigender*, 105–07.

[22] Susannah Cornwall, *Sex and Uncertainty in the Body of Christ: Intersex Conditions and Christian Theology* (London: Equinox, 2010). For other works on intersex theology, see Susannah Cornwall, "Apophasis and Ambiguity: The 'Unknowingness' of Transgender," in *Trans/Formations*, ed. Marcella Althaus-Reid and Lisa Isherwood (London: SCM Press, 2009), 13–40.

with the dominant culture. The sin of conformity is something that occurs within all groups, including the LGBT community. It may be the case, however, that certain individuals who have been rejected and shamed in the past for being different—such as LGBT people—are particularly susceptible to the sin of conformity.

For example, it is easy for gay men to get caught up in the white, middle-class gay male "scene" in gay meccas like San Francisco, West Hollywood, Manhattan, Fire Island, or Provincetown, where certain standards of beauty, body types, and material possessions are the primary measure of a person's worth. The pressure to conform to a certain look or lifestyle can be very difficult for gay men of color. For example, many gay Asian American men try to "downplay" their racial identities, sometimes to the point of disowning their own ethnic backgrounds and avoiding contact with other Asian Americans. However, no matter how hard a person of color tries to do this, he still will never become "just like" a member of the dominant culture.

There is another way, however, in which the sin of conformity manifests itself in the LGBT and other communities. This is the scapegoating mechanism, based upon the writings of the literary theorist René Girard,[23] through which the dominant society bands together through conformity and sacrifices an innocent victim who is usually seen as different or an outsider.[24] The scapegoat, of course, is the goat in the Hebrew Bible that bears the sins of the community and is expelled from it on the Day of Atonement.[25]

According to Girard, competing factions within a given society develop hostilities that would normally erupt into violence. However, instead of directing the violence at each other, these factions unconsciously select an innocent scapegoat—usually someone who is different or an outsider—upon whom violence and blame is directed. As a result of this channeling, the scapegoat is expelled, the competing factions make peace, and order is restored to society.[26] This scapegoating mechanism can occur on a wide scale (for example, the Holocaust or widespread ethnic cleansing) or on a narrow basis (for example, a hate crime or bullying incident involving just a few people).

---

[23] See René Girard, *The Scapegoat*, trans. Yvonne Freccero (Baltimore, MD: Johns Hopkins University Press, 1986).

[24] See Tom Douglas, *Scapegoats: Transferring Blame* (London: Routledge, 1995); Gordon W. Allport, *ABC's of Scapegoating*, rev. ed. (Chicago: Anti-Defamation League of B'Nai B'rith, 1948).

[25] Lev. 16.

[26] See Girard, *The Scapegoat*; Raymund Schwager, *Must There Be Scapegoats?: Violence and Redemption in the Bible*, trans. Maria L. Assad (San Francisco: Harper and Row, 1987).

For Girard, the ultimate example of this scapegoating mechanism was the crucifixion of Jesus Christ. That is, Jesus Christ was sacrificed as an innocent victim by the religious and political elements of his society. The significance of the Christ event, however, is that it announced God's rejection of the scapegoating mechanism. Instead of perpetuating this mechanism, God said "No!" to scapegoating by means of the resurrection. As I have written elsewhere, the doctrine of atonement can be understood as the ending of scapegoating through radical love.[27] The gay Roman Catholic theologian James Alison also has written about Girard and scapegoating from a gay perspective in his book *Faith Beyond Resentment*.[28]

The sin of conformity often occurs when LGBT people are scapegoated by religious fundamentalists who are unable to accept their own sexual sins. That is, LGBT people are sacrificed on the altar of Christianity so that such fundamentalists can blame someone else and be purged of their guilt. However, the sin of conformity also occurs *within* the LGBT community. For example, even though there are many gay men in the Roman Catholic priesthood,[29] the Roman Catholic Church has chosen to scapegoat LGBT people in order to deflect attention from their own closets and sexual crimes.[30] Sadly, just because a group has suffered from discrimination in the past does not mean that it is immune from the sin of conformity, particularly when it tries to distance itself from those who are deemed to be too different, either out of fear or simply to "fit in."

3. Grace as Deviance

If sin is conformity, then grace in the context of the Transgressive Christ can be understood as *deviance*, or the transgression of social, legal, and religious boundaries and norms. Like the act of coming out, one's ability to challenge such boundaries and norms is not something that can be "willed" or "earned," but is rather a gift of grace from God. Although there is always the very real

---

[27] Cheng, *Radical Love*, 94–98.

[28] James Alison, *Faith Beyond Resentment: Fragments Catholic and Gay* (New York: Crossroad Publishing, 2001), 147–69 ("On Learning to Say that 'Jesus is Lord': A 'Girardian' Confession").

[29] See Jordan, *Silence of Sodom*, 103 (citing interviews with gay priests, religious, and seminarians who estimate that 40 to 60 percent of the Roman Catholic clergy "as a whole" are gay).

[30] For a discussion of the sin of heterosexism in the Roman Catholic Church, see Mary E. Hunt, "Eradicating the Sin of Heterosexism," in *Heterosexism in Contemporary World Religion: Problem and Prospect*, ed. Marvin M. Ellison and Judith Plaskow (Cleveland, OH: Pilgrim Press, 2007), 155–76.

risk of crucifixion for challenging societal norms, there is also the promise of resurrection on the other side in terms of being true to one's own God-given sexuality and gender identity.[31]

Deviance is not a matter of essentialism or identifying certain "inherent" or "biological" deviant qualities in a person. Rather, deviance is understood by sociologists to be a "culturally relative phenomenon" that depends upon the larger society as well as "political, economic, and cultural factors."[32] Furthermore, although there are many factors that might lead to labeling someone as deviant, ultimately deviance is a relational concept. That is, deviance is defined in opposition to what is dominant or normal.

The gay writer and psychotherapist John Fortunato has written about the gift of grace that is found within the social location of deviance. In his book *Embracing the Exile*, Fortunato describes his experience of confronting God about the hatred that people on the margins—including LGBT people—often experience. Fortunato asks God why anyone should be subjected to such vitriol. Could those who hate us actually be right? In speaking with God, however, Fortunato realizes that our deviance or marginality is actually a gift. Specifically, our deviance is a gift that gives us the opportunity to "love them anyway."[33] God is in solidarity with us because God has experienced precisely the same sense of rejection in the person of Jesus Christ on the cross.

I have often thought that my own queerness has been an incredible gift of grace from God. Although I experienced much suffering and loneliness when I was struggling with my sexuality as a teenager—and wondered why God would ever make me gay—ultimately my social location as a gay man has helped me to hear the gospel and recognize the solidarity of the Transgressive Christ with all those who are seen as outsiders by the world. Indeed, I suspect that my own marginality was what allowed me to follow my passion for theology, notwithstanding my trajectory towards success and wealth as defined by the powers and principalities of this world. In that sense, being a theologian is very much a transgressive thing.

---

[31] The queer theorist Michael Warner has critiqued attempts by the LGBT community to seek "normalcy," which he argues ultimately reproduces—rather than eliminates—a hierarchy of stigma and shame. See Michael Warner, *The Trouble with Normal: Sex, Politics, and the Ethics of Queer Life* (Cambridge, MA: Harvard University Press, 1999).

[32] Jack P. Gibbs, "Conceptions of Deviant Behavior: The Old and the New," in *Deviance Across Cultures*, ed. Robert Heiner (New York: Oxford University Press, 2008), 41–45.

[33] John E. Fortunato, *Embracing the Exile: Healing Journeys of Gay Christians* (San Francisco: Harper and Row, 1982), 126–27.

Furthermore, the fact that I am twice marginalized—that is, not just as a gay person in a predominantly straight world, but also as an Asian American person in a predominantly white LGBT world—has allowed me to critique *both* communities in a unique way. That is, as a gay Asian American man, I am able to challenge *both* the homophobia in the Asian American community *as well as* the racism in the gay community. Although this perspective often arises out of a painful place of exclusion, my experience as a dual outsider has been a unique gift from God.

The grace of deviance can be seen in various sub-communities within the LGBT community that normally are marginalized, such as the transgender community. Although these communities are often seen as deviant, they are in fact gifts to the wider LGBT community and the world. For example, many transgender people are deeply committed to social justice and "ministering" to marginalized communities that are otherwise ignored by the larger society.

For example, Pauline Park, a transgender Korean American woman, has talked about her work with marginalized communities in the *Embodying Asian/American Sexualities* anthology. Park notes that to be transgender is to "transgress" gender boundaries; she has been an outspoken advocate for transgender folk as well as transgender Asian Americans who face multiple challenges relating to ethnicity, language, citizenship status, and religious prejudice.[34]

Other transgender Asian Americans have talked about the graces of deviance in their particular contexts. For example, Rhode, a Filipino American trans man, believes that understanding what life is like from the perspective of both genders is a gift; that is, "people who are more androgynous are more capable of overcoming a lot of the obstacles in life."[35] Being transgender can still be a challenge, however; Bryan, a Vietnamese American trans man, still struggles with his Catholic beliefs: "I keep thinking, 'It's a sin! It's a sin!'"[36]

Kaui, a transgender woman of Hawaiian, Chinese, Filipino, and Samoan descent, has described the grace of deviance in a powerful way. According to her, the *Mahu* (that is, the trans people

[34] See Pauline Park, "An Interview with Pauline Park," in Masequesmay and Metzger, *Embodying Asian/American Sexualities*, 105–13.

[35] Diep Khac Tran, Bryan, and Rhode, eds., "Transgender/Transsexual Roundtable," in Eng and Hom, *Q&A*, 229.

[36] Tran, Bryan, and Rhode, "Transgender/Transsexual Roundtable," 231.

in Hawai'i) are God's gift to the world: "We're actually angels. We were sent down to earth to soak up all of man's sins. I was sent up to earth to make people laugh and happy, to give them counseling that they need."[37] Kaui, along with the other transgender Asian Americans in this chapter, speaks powerfully about the grace of deviance in the context of the Transgressive Christ.

Study Questions

1. Who is the Transgressive Christ? What are some examples of the Transgressive Christ in the gospels?
2. Which depiction of the Transgressive Christ in this chapter speaks to you the most? The least?
3. What is sin in light of the Transgressive Christ? How does this sin manifest itself in the LGBT community?
4. What is the scapegoating mechanism? Describe a situation in which you may have observed the scapegoating mechanism in action.
5. What is grace in light of the Transgressive Christ? How does this grace manifest itself in the LGBT community?
6. How do Asian American transgender voices shed light on the grace of deviance? What encounters or experiences have you had with the transgender community?

---

[37] Kaui, "Kaui," in Andrew Matzner, *'O Au No Keia: Voices From Hawai'i's Mahu and Transgender Communities* (Bloomington, IN: Xlibris Corporation, 2001), 112–13.

For Further Study

Transgressive Christ

- Althaus-Reid, *Indecent Theology*
- Carey, *Sinners*
- Cornwall, *Sex and Uncertainty in the Body of Christ*
- Goss, *Jesus Acted Up*
- Goss, *Queering Christ*
- Mollenkott, *Omnigender*
- Tanis, *Trans-Gendered*

Sin as Conformity

- Alison, *Faith Beyond Resentment*, 147–69
- Allport, *ABC's of Scapegoating*
- Cheng, *Radical Love*, 94–98
- Douglas, *Scapegoats*
- Girard, *The Scapegoat*
- Hunt, "Eradicating the Sin of Heterosexism"
- Schwager, *Must There Be Scapegoats?*

Grace as Deviance

- Eng and Hom, *Q&A*, 227–43
- Fortunato, *Embracing the Exile*
- Gibbs, "Conceptions of Deviant Behavior"
- "Kaui" in Matzner, *'O Au No Keia*
- Park, "An Interview with Pauline Park"
- Tran, Bryan, and Rhode, "Transgender/Transsexual Roundtable," in Eng and Hom, *Q&A*, 227–43

Chapter 9

Model Five: The Self-Loving Christ

1. The Self-Loving Christ

The fifth Christ-based model of sin and grace for LGBT people is the Self-Loving Christ. The Self-Loving Christ is the One who, even in the face of intense adversity and hatred, has sufficient self-love to persist in his ministry and vocational calling. This focus on self-love may be surprising for some people who have thought about Jesus Christ only in terms of self-sacrifice and ministering to others. As anyone who has been in a long-term relationship or friendship knows, however, it's not possible to love another person authentically without also having a healthy amount of love for oneself. True love for the other—whether it is God or neighbor—requires a positive sense of the self as a starting point.[1]

As the pastoral theologian Edward Wimberly has noted, Jesus Christ's life experiences were filled with potential instances of shame that could have paralyzed him. This was particularly significant because he lived in a society in which honor and shame were central motivating factors for behavior. For example, Jesus was born to a young mother who became pregnant before she was married, a stigmatizing situation. He worked as a carpenter, which was considered a lower-class occupation. Jesus was rejected

[1] As the gay theologian and psychotherapist John McNeill has noted: "Without self-love we cannot fulfill the most important commandment: to love God, and one's neighbor as oneself. If you hate yourself, you will hate your neighbor." McNeill, *Freedom, Glorious Freedom*, 68–69.

by the people of his own town, and his boundary-transgressing interactions with women and others subjected him to ridicule.[2] As Wimberly put it, Jesus "constantly faced rejection, ridicule, and hostility in his interpersonal and group encounters."[3]

Nevertheless, Jesus had enough self-love to get through these moments of potential shame and move ahead with his ministries and vocational calling. Ironically, having sufficient self-love is actually what allows a person to transcend moments of suffering and shame and to pray for the well-being of his persecutors. Even while he is dying a horrific death on the cross, Jesus Christ is able to transcend his own situation and pray for the forgiveness of his enemies: "Father, forgive them; for they do not know what they are doing."[4] It is Jesus' self-love that allows him to "love them anyway," in the words of the gay psychotherapist John Fortunato.[5]

The Self-Loving Christ is present in a number of other aspects of Jesus' ministry. For example, Jesus Christ is able to resist the temptations of Satan in the wilderness at the beginning of his ministry because of self-love. That is, instead of needing or relying on external rewards such as food, wealth, and power, Jesus has a sufficiently positive sense of himself internally to resist Satan and to carry himself forward in his ministry. He does not think of himself as being defective; in fact, he has everything that he needs because he knows that he is the beloved child of God. Also, Jesus exercises self-love when he withdraws from the crowds from time to time; he takes the time to recharge and take care of himself.

Wimberly also has written about how Jesus taught those around him to love themselves, despite their own shame and marginality. For example, Jesus constantly broke through religious and societal boundaries of purity and impurity in order to heal others. This included his healing of those who were considered to be unclean, outcasts, and sinners.[6] For me, the Self-Loving Christ is able to model self-love for others by breaking through taboos and social boundaries, notwithstanding the negative societal messages of unworthiness and defectiveness.

A number of LGBT theologians have written about different aspects of the Self-Loving Christ. For example, Gary Comstock

---

[2] See Wimberly, *Moving from Shame to Self-Worth*, 37–39, 76–78.
[3] Wimberly, *Moving from Shame to Self-Worth*, 40.
[4] Luke 23:34.
[5] Fortunato, *Embracing the Exile*, 126–27.
[6] Wimberly, *Moving from Shame to Self-Worth*, 61–95.

has written in *Gay Theology Without Apology* about the Jesus who wants us to see him as a "friend, not master." Citing John 15:15, in which Jesus calls his disciples "friends" and not "servants," Comstock argues that Jesus was not interested in establishing an organization that "would be preoccupied with fawning over him and perfecting his image."[7] For me, this implies a Jesus Christ who has a sufficiently positive sense of self so as to treat those around him as colleagues and not inferiors. That is, Jesus' self love is what frees him of controlling, abusive behaviors. My only wish is that more church institutions and religious leaders would behave in the same way.

Mark Jordan has written about how a fully embodied corpus of Jesus Christ, complete with realistic genitals, might be one way in which LGBT people can encounter the Self-Loving Christ. In *Telling Truths in Church*, Jordan writes about the extreme realism of many Roman Catholic crucifixes; each bodily wound from the passion and crucifixion of Christ is depicted in gory detail. However, this realism stops at the loincloth of Jesus Christ. Inevitably there is nothing underneath but a smooth groin area. For Jordan, this refusal to depict the entire body of Jesus Christ—who was, after all, fully human as well as fully divine—perpetuates the shame that many Roman Catholic LGBT people (and others) continue to harbor about their bodies.[8]

For me, Jordan's discussion about an anatomically correct corpus implies a Self-Loving Christ who has sufficient self-love for his own body and is not ashamed of his full humanity, including his sexuality. As such, an anatomically correct corpus would heal our "original shame" about nudity that followed the opening of Adam and Eve's eyes in the Book of Genesis. (On a side note, Leo Steinberg has written about how the artistic depiction of Jesus' genitals was an important motif in Renaissance art because it affirmed the full humanity of Jesus.[9])

Finally, Robert Shore-Goss has written about the Self-Loving Christ in the context of masturbation and fantasizing about Jesus Christ. For Goss, masturbation is a spiritual exercise in which one can join mystically with Christ through self-love.[10] A number of

---

[7] Comstock, *Gay Theology Without Apology*, 99.
[8] See Jordan, *Telling Truths in Church*, 84–87.
[9] See Leo Steinberg, *The Sexuality of Christ in Renaissance Art and in Modern Oblivion*, 2nd ed. (Chicago: University of Chicago Press, 1996).
[10] See Goss, *Queering Christ*, 17 n.9, 56–71.

other gay spiritual practitioners have done work in the area of erotic Christianity, including Joseph Kramer, a former Jesuit and the founder of the Body Electric School, as well as Michael Kelly, a gay bishop in the Old Catholic Church from Australia who has produced a popular series of tapes about erotic spirituality called the *Erotic Contemplative*.[11]

Having explored the Self-Loving Christ from a number of different perspectives, we now move to thinking about sin and grace in the context of the Self-Loving Christ.

2. Sin as Shame

What is sin in the context of the Self-Loving Christ? If the Self-Loving Christ is the One who teaches us to love ourselves, then sin is that which opposes this teaching, or *shame*. Shame is a particularly pernicious form of self-hatred. It is the feeling that somehow one is intrinsically defective or that somehow one's existence is fundamentally a mistake. Shame is different from guilt. Guilt is the feeling that one has *done* something wrong (for example, violating a law). Shame, on the other hand, is the feeling that one *is* something wrong. Although guilt can be eradicated through punishment or absolution, shame is much harder to "cure."

The sin of shame is closely connected with feminist theologies about sin. As mentioned above, Valerie Saiving wrote a groundbreaking article in 1960 on sin from the perspective of women. That article, "The Human Situation: A Feminine View," argued that although pride might be the quintessential sin for men, sin for women can be thought of as "underdevelopment or negation of the self."[12] That is, instead of sinning by reaching too high, women sin by not reaching high enough.[13]

Indeed, Elizabeth Stuart has suggested that the "sin" of LGBT people is not so much "individual disobedience rooted in pride," but rather "not loving ourselves enough, of not having enough

---

[11] For more about Kelly's work, see Michael Bernard Kelly, *Seduced By Grace: Contemporary Spirituality, Gay Experience and Christian Faith* (Melbourne, Australia: Clouds of Magellan Publishing, 2007).

[12] Saiving Goldstein, "The Human Situation," 109.

[13] For feminist and womanist theologies of sin, see Kathryn Green-McCreight, "Gender, Sin and Grace: Feminist Theologies Meet Karl Barth's Hamartiology," *Scottish Journal of Theology* 50, no. 4 (1997): 415–32; Daphne Hampson, "Reinhold Niebuhr on Sin: A Critique," in *Reinhold Niebuhr and the Issues of Our Time*, ed. Richard Harries (Grand Rapids, MI: William B. Eerdmans Publishing, 1986), 46–60; Serene Jones, *Trauma and Grace: Theology in a Ruptured World* (Louisville, KY: Westminster John Knox Press, 2009); Margaret D. Kamitsuka, "Toward a Feminist Postmodern and Postcolonial Interpretation of Sin," *Journal of Religion* 84, no. 2 (April 2004): 179–211; Christine M. Smith, "Sin and Evil in Feminist Thought," *Theology Today* 50, no. 2 (July 1993): 208–19; Emilie M. Townes, ed., *A Troubling in My Soul: Womanist Perspectives on Evil and Suffering* (Maryknoll, NY: Orbis Books, 1993).

pride in ourselves." Many LGBT people have not been allowed to be "proud or self-loving." According to Stuart, many of us have "failed to have a sense of self," in part due to the "association of the body and sexuality with sin."[14]

Perhaps this notion of shame as original sin can be traced back to the Book of Genesis, when Adam and Eve are ashamed of their nakedness after their eyes are opened as a result of eating the forbidden fruit. They sewed fig leaves together to make loincloths, and they attempted to hide themselves from God, in part due to their nakedness.[15] Instead of original sin being defined solely as pride and disobedience, original sin in this context can be understood as Adam and Eve's fall into shame and wanting to hide from God. Jesus Christ, by contrast, can be understood as taking on and overcoming this shame in the crucifixion. That is, he "endured the cross, disregarding its shame."[16] Thus, the crucifixion is not so much a question of atonement or payment exacted for a crime, but it is rather a recapitulation in which our "original shame" is reversed through the Christ event.

As someone who has served as a pastor to the LGBT community for over a decade—and as someone who teaches LGBT pastoral care to seminarians—I strongly believe that the sin of shame is at the root of most LGBT suffering. That is, the trauma of growing up LGBT in a straight world contributes to a sense of shame about oneself that is deeply rooted and not easily eradicated. This sense of shame is reinforced by religious teachings against same-sex and gender-variant acts as "intrinsically disordered." Because these teachings actually touch upon fundamental aspects of personhood such as sexual orientation and gender identity—as opposed to just acts—this becomes a matter of shame and not guilt. This shame can lead to depression, anxiety, addictive behaviors, and even suicide.[17]

A number of LGBT psychologists and social workers have written about the toxic effects of this shame on the LGBT community in general, and with respect to gay men in particular. For example, the gay psychologist Alan Downs has written in *The Velvet Rage* that unresolved shame is often at the core of the gay

---

[14] Stuart, "Salvation," 89.
[15] Gen. 3:7–10.
[16] Heb. 12:2.
[17] For a helpful book on shame and the LGBT community, see Gershen Kaufman and Lev Raphael, *Coming Out of Shame: Transforming Gay and Lesbian Lives* (New York: Doubleday, 1996).

male experience. Although we may attempt to avoid this shame by ignoring it or becoming the "best" at what we do, this shame will still rear its ugly head in the form of rage or other emotions.[18] Similarly, the gay social worker Robert Weiss has written in *Cruise Control* that shame, or a lack of self-esteem, often lies at the heart of sex addiction.[19]

Furthermore, the sin of shame may be particularly strong for LGBT people of color. As we have seen, LGBT people often experience a strong sense of shame from their upbringing. However, this is magnified by the shame felt by many people of color who live in a predominantly white world. Thus, there is a sense of double shaming in the lives of LGBT people of color.

Finally, it is my experience that the LGBT community is often shamed into a heteronormative view of sex. The cultural anthropologist Gayle Rubin has described a "charmed circle" of socially accepted sexual practices: heterosexual, married, monogamous, procreative, non-commercial, in pairs, in a relationship, same generation, in private, no pornography, bodies only, and vanilla. Anything falling outside of this charmed circle—that is, LGBT or queer, unmarried, promiscuous, non-procreative, commercial, alone or in groups, casual, older/younger adult relationships, in public, pornography, with manufactured objects, sadomasochistic—is viewed as shameful, sometimes even by the LGBT community.[20] A recent volume called *Gay Shame* examines the ways in which the LGBT community might reclaim the ways in which certain sexual practices have been shamed by the larger society.[21]

It is important to note that by calling shame a sin, I am not intending to further shame or judge people who already feel shamed. Rather, by labeling shame as sin, I hope that LGBT Christians might reexamine how we have often distanced or separated ourselves from the queer Christ by shame and, in particular, from the Self-Loving Christ.

---

[18] See Alan Downs, *The Velvet Rage, Overcoming the Pain of Growing Up Gay in a Straight Man's World*, (Cambridge, MA: Da Capo Press, 2005).

[19] See Weiss, *Cruise Control*, 60–62.

[20] For a diagram of Rubin's "charmed circle," see Deborah T. Meem, Michelle A. Gibson, and Jonathan F. Alexander, eds., *Finding Out: An Introduction to LGBT Studies* (Los Angeles: SAGE Publications, 2010), 210–12.

[21] See David M. Halperin and Valerie Traub, eds., *Gay Shame* (Chicago: University of Chicago Press, 2009).

3. Grace as Pride

If sin is shame, then grace in the context of the Self-Loving Christ is *pride*. Pride is a central theme for the LGBT community. Every June, numerous pride marches are held all around the world to commemorate the Stonewall Riots of 1969 and to celebrate LGBT pride. The pride flag, which is a rainbow-striped flag, is a universally acknowledged symbol for the LGBT community. Indeed, pride is at the heart of the collective LGBT consciousness.

Ironically, pride has been traditionally understood in Christian theology as the root of all sin. That is, according to the theological tradition, Adam and Eve's pride resulted in their disobedience of God's command not to eat of the forbidden fruit. As such, this pride unleashed original sin, which became the cause of all subsequent sin. Some anti-LGBT people have criticized LGBT pride events precisely because of this association between pride and original sin.

However, as noted above, feminist and womanist theologians have noted that, for many marginalized communities, sin can take the form of self-negation or shame. In those cases, what is needed is not to condemn, but instead to affirm feelings of self-love or pride. JoAnne Marie Terrell, a womanist theologian and professor at Chicago Theological Seminary, has noted that "self-love is the critical principle of effecting liberation" and that "black women need to love themselves so they can genuinely love others."[22] Thus, pride is not a sin, but rather a manifestation of God's grace that heals and lifts up those who are in need of self-love. In other words, Jesus did not teach us to love our neighbors *more than* ourselves. Rather, we are taught to love our neighbors *as* ourselves.[23]

In their book *Coming Out of Shame*, Gershen Kaufman and Lev Raphael have a chapter called "From Gay Shame to Gay Pride."[24] In that chapter, they discuss a number of ways in which gay shame can be transformed into gay pride. One of these ways is developing an "*inner* source of self-esteem" so that we can be proud of ourselves regardless of what others say or do. Pride,

---

[22] JoAnne Marie Terrell, *Power in the Blood?: The Cross in the African American Experience* (Maryknoll, NY: Orbis Books, 1998), 139.

[23] For more about healthy pride for LGBT people, see Patrick S. Cheng, "The Grace of Pride" (June 26, 2011), available at http://www.patrickcheng.net/uploads/7/0/3/7/7037096/the_grace_of_pride.pdf (accessed on December 11, 2011).

[24] Kaufman and Raphael, *Coming Out of Shame*, 122–86.

according to Kaufman and Raphael, is "feeling joy" about oneself and one's accomplishments. It is also about "turning the very thing that society condemns" into a source of self-esteem. This kind of pride is not contempt, or the diminishment of others, but rather a means of nurturing self-love.[25]

Healthy pride is the affirmation of one's intrinsic value and self-worth. Pride is a matter of grace—that is, a gift of God—because it is not possible for shamed people (or anyone, for that matter) simply to will it into existence. As Lewis Smedes writes in *Shame and Grace*, the healing of shame must begin with a "spiritual experience of grace."[26] Specifically, one must have an experience of being accepted "without regard to whether we are acceptable."[27] The grace of pride—that is, knowing that we are accepted "at the ultimate depth of our being"—is something that breaks into our lives in unexpected ways.[28] We must experience pride in our bodies before we can root out the negative messages of shame that we have carried with us since our childhood.

The grace of pride can be especially important with LGBT people of color, many of whom experience a great deal of shame because of their ethnicities. For example, David Lee, a young Chinese American gay man, wrote about how he dyed and curled his hair in high school so that he would seem more "American."[29] William Tran, also a young Chinese American gay man, wrote about how he would avoid chatting with other Asian Americans online because he thought they were unattractive.[30] However, both Lee and Tran have since come to realize the beauty of other LGBT Asians through the grace of pride. Lee writes: "The truth is, Asians are HOT! Asian men *are* sexy, dateable, and very delectable."[31] Tran writes: "I'm beginning to get rid of this stigma that I've attached to Asian Americans . . . . Why on earth should I hate my own kind?"[32]

Recently a white gay party promoter in New York City advertised an orientalist-themed party called "Mr. Wong's Dong Emporium"—complete with a "Sum Hung Boys erotic dance

---

[25] Kaufman and Raphael, *Coming Out of Shame*, 173–75.
[26] Lewis B. Smedes, *Shame and Grace: Healing the Shame We Don't Deserve* (New York: HarperSanFrancisco, 1993), 105.
[27] Smedes, *Shame and Grace*, 107–08.
[28] Smedes, *Shame and Grace*, 109.
[29] David C. Lee, "All-American Asian," in Kumashiro, *Restoried Selves*, 73–80.
[30] William Tran, "GAM4GWM," in *Troubling Intersections of Race and Sexuality: Queer Students of Color and Anti-Oppressive Education*, ed. Kevin K. Kumashiro (Lanham, MD: Rowman and Littlefield Publishers, 2001), 81–82.
[31] Lee, "All-American Asian," 76.
[32] Tran, "GAM4GWM," 82.

troupe" and a "Happy Ending massage den"—that invoked all kinds of highly offensive Asian stereotypes. This caused an uproar in the LGBT Asian American community, and numerous people demanded that the name of the party be changed. Instead of feeling ashamed, LGBT Asian Americans showed pride and self-love by refusing to be silent about the racism in the white gay male community. The Gay Asian Pacific Islander Men of New York wrote an open letter to the promoter and offered suggestions on how to host a party that truly celebrated Asian American heritages instead of exploiting them.[33]

Even though I have been "out" for nearly a quarter century and I have been involved with grassroots advocacy and ministry to the LGBT community for over a decade, I still experience the toxic feelings of shame from time to time. For example, despite the fact that my husband Michael and I have been together for two decades and we are legally married, sometimes I feel ashamed when we walk hand-in-hand in predominantly straight neighborhoods. Sometimes I feel ashamed when I am one of the few people of color in a large gathering of LGBT people—or one of the few LGBT people in a large gathering of people of color—and I wonder whether my feelings of exclusion or rejection are real or imagined.

I experience the grace of the Self-Loving Christ in these situations when I am able to acknowledge my feelings of shame and not run away from or bury them. I experience grace when I can experience pride with respect to my relationship or my identity as an LGBT person of color. But, most importantly, I experience grace when I experience that God loves and accepts me just the way that I am, no more and no less.

---

[33] Gay Asian Pacific Islander Men of New York, "An Open Letter to Cazwell and Joey Izrael" (September 21, 2011), available at http://www.gapimny.org/2011/09/21/an-open-letter-to-cazwell-and-joey-izrael/ (accessed on December 11, 2011).

Study Questions

1. Who is the Self-Loving Christ? Where does the Self-Loving Christ appear in the gospels?
2. Which depiction of the Self-Loving Christ in this chapter appeals to you the most? The least?
3. What is sin in light of the Self-Loving Christ? How does this sin manifest itself in the LGBT community?
4. What are some ways in which you have experienced shame in your own life? How is this similar or different than the shame often experienced by LGBT people of color?
5. What is grace in light of the Self-Loving Christ? How does this grace manifest itself in the LGBT community?
6. What are some ways in which you have experienced healthy pride in your own life?

For Further Study

Self-Loving Christ

- Comstock, *Gay Theology Without Apology*, 91–103
- Fortunato, *Embracing the Exile*, 126–27
- Goss, *Queering Christ*, 56–71
- Jordan, *Telling Truths in Church*, 84–87
- Steinberg, *The Sexuality of Christ in Renaissance Art and Modern Oblivion*
- Wimberly, *Moving from Shame to Self-Worth*

Sin as Shame

- Downs, *The Velvet Rage*
- Halpern and Traub, *Gay Shame*
- Kaufman and Raphael, *Coming Out of Shame*
- Stuart, "Salvation"
- Weiss, *Cruise Control*

Feminist and Womanist Theologies of Sin

- Green-McCreight, "Gender, Sin and Grace"
- Hampson, "Reinhold Neibuhr on Sin"
- Jones, *Trauma and Grace*
- Kamitsuka, "Toward a Feminist Postmodern and Postcolonial Interpretation of Sin"
- Smith, "Sin and Evil in Feminist Thought"
- Townes, *A Troubling in My Soul*

Grace as Pride

- Kaufman and Raphael, *Coming Out of Shame*, 122–86
- Smedes, *Shame and Grace*
- Terrell, *Power in the Blood?*

LGBT Asian American Pride

- Lee, "All-American Asian"
- Tran, "GAM4GWM"

Chapter 10

Model Six: The Interconnected Christ

1. The Interconnected Christ

The sixth christological model for LGBT people is the Interconnected Christ. The Interconnected Christ is the One in whom all things cohere, or "hold together" (that is, *synestēken* in the Greek),[1] whether it be the cosmos, the ecosystem, or the world's religions and spiritual traditions. The Interconnected Christ is the antithesis of a globalized, imperial, or colonialist Christ in which one part of the whole triumphs over the others. Rather, the Interconnected Christ recognizes that all of us on this earth are dependent on each other, not just for survival but also for flourishing.

The Interconnected Christ is grounded in the notion of the cosmic Christ, or the pre-existent Christ who is divine Wisdom, the creator and reconciler of the universe.[2] This can be seen in the Letter to the Colossians in which Jesus Christ is described as the "firstborn of all creation" in whom "all things on heaven and earth were created," and in whom the "fullness of God was pleased to dwell."[3] Similarly, the Interconnected Christ can be seen in the Gospel of John as the divine Word or *logos* who was with God "in

---

[1] Col. 1:17.

[2] For an overview of the cosmic Christ in Christian theology, see George A. Maloney, *The Cosmic Christ: From Paul to Teilhard* (New York: Sheed and Ward, 1968).

[3] Col. 1:15–20.

the beginning,"[4] as well as in the Letter to the Hebrews in which Jesus Christ is described as the One who "sustains all things by his powerful word."[5]

Indeed, the entire cosmos can be thought of as the "Body of Christ" that is mentioned in the First Letter to the Corinthians. In other words, all parts of the cosmos make up "one body," and one part cannot say to the other that "I have no need of you."[6] In fact, instead of limiting the Body of Christ to the Christian church, what if we conceived of the Body of Christ as the sum of the created order and *all* world religions and spiritual traditions? That is, rather than thinking about the Christian church as the sole end of all faith traditions, what if we thought about it as simply one tradition among many in the multi-membered body of the Interconnected Christ?[7]

Lisa Isherwood, an openly lesbian theologian at the University of Winchester, has written about the Interconnected Christ in a chapter entitled "Ecological Christ" in her book *Introducing Feminist Christologies*. For Isherwood, an incarnational religion such as Christianity must "pay attention to the whole of the created order and the very fibres of the universe itself." She criticizes the dominant Christian tradition for "preferring to prioritize the experience of men," and lifts up the christological work of ecofeminist theologians such as Rosemary Ruether, Kwok Pui-lan, Anne Primavesi, Sallie McFague, and Ivone Gebara.[8]

Denis Edwards, an Australian theologian, also has written about the Interconnected Christ in his book *Jesus the Wisdom of God*. For Edwards, Jesus Christ is the personification of divine Wisdom and can "undergird a Christian approach to ecology and form the basis of a cosmic Christology." This view of Jesus Christ requires us to ponder a "new bodily relationship with the Earth and all its living creatures and with the whole material universe."[9] It requires us to shift from an androcentric, or human-centered, view of the universe, to a creation-centered view. Indeed, LGBT

---

[4] John 1:1.

[5] Heb. 1:3.

[6] 1 Cor. 12:20–21.

[7] This is not to erase or absorb other faith traditions into the Body of Christ. Rather, it is to acknowledge that the Body of Christ may transcend the institutional church and even Christianity itself.

[8] For a discussion of these ecofeminist christologies, see Lisa Isherwood, *Introducing Feminist Christologies* (Cleveland, OH: Pilgrim Press, 2002), 71–86. For an introduction to ecofeminist theology, see Rosemary Radford Ruether, *Gaia and God: An Ecofeminist Theology of Earth Healing* (New York: HarperOne, 1992); and Sallie McFague, *The Body of God: An Ecological Theology* (Minneapolis, MN: Fortress Press, 1993).

[9] Denis Edwards, *Jesus the Wisdom of God: An Ecological Theology* (Maryknoll, NY: Orbis, 1995), 86.

people often have a special relationship with our pets as four-legged members of our families, and the Interconnected Christ reminds us that they are part of the Body of Christ as well.

The Interconnected Christ is also present in the context of people with disabilities. Nancy Eiesland, who was a professor of theology at Emory University, argued in *The Disabled God* for the importance of "holding our bodies together" (that is, "face-to-face interaction between people with disabilities and the able-bodied").[10] Eiesland described the "disabled God" in terms of a resurrected Jesus Christ who had impaired hands, feet, and side.[11] Interdependence for this disabled God—as well as people with disabilities—is "a necessary condition of life." Interdependence is required for both "justice and survival."[12]

A number of LGBT theologians and ethicists have written about ecological theology, and their work is also highly relevant to the Interconnected Christ. Dan Spencer, a gay environmental ethicist who teaches at the University of Montana, proposes an erotic ethic of ecojustice in his book *Gay and Gaia*. Instead of seeing the world as divided into human and non-human elements, Spencer argues for an ethic of right relation "at all levels of human and nonhuman nature."[13] This has many ethical implications for LGBT people, including rethinking our patterns of consumption, our views of sexual practices as being disconnected from others and nature, our practices of eating animals, and perhaps even the use of leather in gay eroticism.[14]

Echoes of the Interconnected Christ also can be seen in the work of the gay theologian J. Michael Clark. In his book *Beyond Our Ghettos*, Clark writes about the importance for LGBT people to be aware of the "fundamental interconnectedness, relationality, and interdependence of all things within the web of being." Clark draws upon the Jewish notion of *tikkun olam*—that is, "repairing the world"—as a challenge to LGBT people to repair the world in its "human and nonhuman, its biospheric and geospheric aspects."[15]

In addition to issues of ecology and environmentalism, the

---

[10] Nancy L. Eiesland, *The Disabled God: Toward a Liberatory Theology of Disability* (Nashville, TN: Abingdon Press, 1994), 94.

[11] Eiesland, *The Disabled God*, 101.

[12] Eiesland, *The Disabled God*, 103. For another theology of disability, see Thomas E. Reynolds, *Vulnerable Communion: A Theology of Disability and Hospitality* (Grand Rapids, MI: Brazos Press, 2008).

[13] Daniel T. Spencer, *Gay and Gaia: Ethics, Ecology, and the Erotic* (Cleveland, OH: Pilgrim Press, 1996), 324.

[14] See Spencer, *Gay and Gaia*, 348–61.

[15] J. Michael Clark, *Beyond Our Ghettos: Gay Theology in Ecological Perspective* (Cleveland, OH: Pilgrim Press, 1993), 89.

Interconnected Christ also speaks to the issues of religious plurality.[16] In recent decades, many Asian, African, and other two-thirds world and indigenous theologians have written about christology in the context of other world religions and spiritual traditions. For example, the anthology *Asian Faces of Jesus* contains a number of essays ranging from "Jesus and Krishna" to "Christ and Buddha" to "Confessing Christ in the Islamic Context."[17] Other anthologies that address similar questions of christology and religious pluralism include *Faces of Jesus in Africa*; *Jesus of Africa*; and *Hope Abundant*.[18]

Stanley Samartha in his essay "The Cross and the Rainbow" notes that "to claim that the Judeo-Christian-Western tradition has the only answer to all problems in all places and for all persons in the world is presumptuous, if not incredible."[19] As such, he proposes a "Mystery-centered" christology that provides "more theological space for Christians to live together with neighbors of other faiths."[20]

In the LGBT context, a number of works have focused on queer spirituality in the context of a variety of faith traditions.[21] For example, one helpful resource in the area of queer world spiritualities is *Cassell's Encyclopedia of Queer Myth, Symbol and Spirit*, which provides nearly four hundred pages of resources on LGBT themes in world religions.[22] Another resource is *Homosexuality and World Religions*, a survey of LGBT issues in world faith traditions.[23] However, most of such works do not expressly address the question of religious pluralism as raised by the model of the Interconnected Christ. One exception is the recent book *Jewish/Christian/Queer: Crossroads and Identities*, which addresses the

---

[16] For an introduction to the theology of religious pluralism, see Paul F. Knitter, *Introducing Theologies of Religions* (Maryknoll, NY: Orbis Books, 2002).

[17] R.S. Sugirtharajah, ed., *Asian Faces of Jesus* (Maryknoll, NY: Orbis Books, 1993); Ovey N. Mohammed, "Jesus and Krishna," in Sugirtharajah, *Asian Faces of Jesus*, 9–24; Seiichi Yagi, "Christ and Buddha," in Sugirtharajah, *Asian Faces of Jesus*, 25–45; Alexander J. Malik, "Confessing Christ in the Islamic Context," in Sugirtharajah, *Asian Faces of Jesus*, 75–84.

[18] Robert J. Schreiter, ed., *Faces of Jesus in Africa* (Maryknoll, NY: Orbis Books, 1991); Diane B. Stinton, *Jesus of Africa: Voices of Contemporary African Christology* (Maryknoll, NY: Orbis Books, 2004); Kwok Pui-lan, *Hope Abundant: Third World and Indigenous Women's Theology* (Maryknoll, NY: Orbis Books, 2010), 165–215.

[19] Stanley J. Samartha, "The Cross and the Rainbow: Christ in a Multireligious Culture," in Sugirtharajah, *Asian Faces of Jesus*, 104–23, at 113.

[20] Samartha, "The Cross and the Rainbow," 115, 116.

[21] See, e.g., Robert Barzan, ed., *Sex and Spirit: Exploring Gay Men's Spirituality* (San Francisco: White Crane Newsletter, 1995); Christian de la Huerta, *Coming Out Spiritually: The Next Step* (New York: Jeremy P. Tarcher/Putnam, 1999); Kolodny, *Blessed Bi Spirit*; Catherine Lake, ed., *Recreations: Religion and Spirituality in the Lives of Queer People* (Toronto, Canada: Queer Press, 1999); Ronald E. Long, *Men, Homosexuality, and the Gods: An Exploration into the Religious Significance of Male Homosexuality in World Perspective* (Binghamton, NY: Harrington Park Press, 2004).

[22] Randy P. Conner, David Hatfield Sparks, and Mariya Sparks, eds., *Cassell's Encyclopedia of Queer Myth, Symbol and Spirit: Gay, Lesbian, Bisexual and Transgender Lore* (London: Cassell, 1997).

[23] Arlene Swidler, ed., *Homosexuality and World Religions* (Valley Forge, PA: Trinity Press International, 1993).

"queerness of where the Jewish and Christian intersect."[24] But there is still much work to be done in this area.

Having explored the significance of the Interconnected Christ to issues like ecological theology as well as religious pluralism, we now turn to what sin and grace might look like in light of the Interconnected Christ.

2. Sin as Isolation

What is sin for LGBT people in the context of the Interconnected Christ? If the Interconnected Christ is a symbol of the fundamental interrelatedness of all creation, then sin can be understood as *isolation*, or the illusion of one's own self-sufficiency. Isolation in this context differs from the isolation of the closet. Here, isolation is not just a feeling of loneliness, but it is the refusal—or inability—to see the ways in which all of creation is connected with each other. It may seem like we have little, if nothing, to do with people halfway around the world, but in fact we all breathe the same air and consume resources from the same planet, which ultimately will have an impact on our respective well-being.

One way in which the sin of isolation manifests itself in the LGBT community is through a mentality of overconsumption.[25] We often focus primarily on ourselves and not on how our consumption is affecting the larger world, including the environment and the situation of global warming. Flip through any glossy national LGBT magazine such as *Out Magazine* or *The Advocate*, and you will see numerous ads for international travel, boat cruises, designer-brand clothing, gambling, and alcohol. Although this advertising may be a reflection of our larger national culture, I do think it is fair to say that many middle- and upper-class LGBT people live a lifestyle of overspending and overconsumption. This overconsumption results in a devastating impact on both humans and nonhuman species.[26]

In addition to living in a culture of overconsumption, there is also competition in the LGBT community with respect to material wealth. It is often a race to see who has the biggest house, newest

[24] Frederick Roden, ed., *Jewish/Christian/Queer: Crossroads and Identities* (Farnham, UK: Ashgate, 2009), 1.

[25] Ironically, according to the Book of Ezekiel, the true sin of Sodom was "excess of food," "prosperous ease," and the failure to "aid the poor and needy." Ezek. 16:49.

[26] For an anthology on feminist ethics and animal rights, see Lisa Kemmerer, ed., *Sister Species: Women, Animals, and Social Justice* (Urbana, IL: University of Illinois Press, 2011).

cars, best jobs, and most fabulous lifestyles. This is reinforced by media images that portray LGBT people as having lots of disposable income. One such example is the Logo channel's reality show *A-List: New York*, which follows the lives of six bisexual and gay men in New York City, all of whom are fairly well-to-do and are focused on advancing their careers in fields like modeling and the arts.[27] One of the problems with this kind of media portrayal, however, is that it often erases the experience of lower-class LGBT people as well as the complexity and economic diversity of the LGBT community. Nevertheless, there is some truth to the existence of a culture of overconsumption, especially with respect to the middle-class gay male community.

As we have seen earlier, there is also often a sense of isolation in the LGBT community with respect to activism and seeing the interconnectedness of oppressions. That is, LGBT people are often very active in terms of fighting for our own rights such as same-sex marriage or the repeal of "Don't Ask, Don't Tell." However, once these victories have been achieved, we are often no longer interested in building political coalitions with other marginalized groups, including some groups (for example, transgender people, undocumented immigrants, people of color) who are within our own community.

I experienced the sin of isolation first-hand when I worked as a tax and employee benefits lawyer for two New York City firms. The work hours were long, and I represented many multinational corporations and private equity firms in their mergers and acquisitions work. My work quickly became my life. Without realizing it, I had become isolated and cut off from the rest of the world—not only with respect to the social justice issues that I cared about in college and law school, but also with respect to my friends and families, as well as the neighborhoods in which I lived and worked. It was only when I started transitioning out of law firm life that I became more involved with the LGBT Asian community as well as the larger LGBT community. In light of my background, I have observed with great interest the Occupy Wall Street movement and the ways in which that movement challenges the economic isolationism of the top 1% of earners in the United States and around the world.

The sin of isolation also can occur in the religious sphere. In

27 In October 2011, Logo expanded its reality television franchise with a new show, *A-List: Dallas*.

particular, many LGBT Christian religious leaders are all but oblivious to the spiritual lives of non-Christian LGBT people. Often, the word "faith" or "religion" really means just "Christian." The fact is that there are many LGBT people from different faith traditions, as indicated by such diverse resources as *Torah Queeries: Weekly Commentaries on the Hebrew Bible* (Judaism);[28] *Homosexuality in Islam: Critical Reflection on Gay, Lesbian, and Transgender Muslims* (Islam);[29] *Queer Dharma: Voices of Gay Buddhists* (Buddhism);[30] and *A Lotus of Another Color: An Unfolding of the South Asian Gay and Lesbian Experience* (Hinduism).[31] Nevertheless, LGBT Christian religious leaders—including theologians—rarely draw upon or enter into dialogue with these communities within the LGBT community. It is time for us Christian LGBT theologians to change this state of affairs.

This sin of isolation is reminiscent of the theological isolation of the Vatican and the Roman Catholic curia—and their secular spokespersons, such as the Catholic League for Religious and Civil Rights—with respect to issues relating to homosexuality. The Roman Curia refuses to engage in any theological, moral, or scientific dialogue on LGBT issues; it simply repeats the same circular arguments over and over again, without any regard to whether in fact its assertions are true.[32] This isolation is particularly ironic given the widespread existence of homosexuality within the Roman Catholic Church's own priestly and episcopal ranks.[33] To me, this idolatry of the self from a theological perspective is a repudiation of the Interconnected Christ. In the fall of 2011, four educational institutions—Fairfield University, Fordham University, Union Theological Seminary in New York, and Yale Divinity School—challenged the Roman Catholic Church's sin of isolation by sponsoring a series of conferences called "More than a Monologue: Sexual Diversity and the Catholic Church." It remains to be seen whether such conferences will have any effect on moving the conversation forward.

---

[28] Gregg Drinkwater, Joshua Lesser, and David Shneer, *Torah Queeries: Weekly Commentaries on the Hebrew Bible* (New York: New York University Press, 2009).

[29] Scott Siraj al-Haqq Kugle, *Homosexuality in Islam: Critical Reflection on Gay, Lesbian, and Transgender Muslims* (Oxford, UK: Oneworld Publications, 2010).

[30] Winston Leyland, ed., *Queer Dharma: Voices of Gay Buddhists* (San Francisco: Gay Sunshine Press, 1998).

[31] Rakesh Ratti, ed., *A Lotus of Another Color: An Unfolding of the South Asian Gay and Lesbian Experience* (Boston: Alyson Publications, 1993).

[32] See Gareth Moore, *A Question of Truth: Christianity and Homosexuality* (London, UK: Continuum, 2003), 243 (asking whether the teaching of the Roman Catholic Church on homosexuality is "actually true").

[33] See generally Jordan, *Silence of Sodom*.

3. Grace as Interdependence

If sin is isolation, then grace in the context of the Interconnected Christ is *interdependence*. Interdependence is a recognition that we are all different, yet we are all part of one cosmic body, and thus we cannot afford to say to any other part of that body that "I have no need of you."[34] Interdependence can take a number of forms. For example, interdependence can manifest itself in the context of ecological issues, and it can also manifest itself in the context of interfaith issues. A deep understanding of interdependence is a gift; it is not something that can be willed or earned, but only experienced through the amazing grace of God.[35]

I personally have experienced the grace of interdependence in the great outdoors. Since I was a young boy, I have always loved nature. One of my favorite places growing up was Cutter Scout Reservation, the local Boy Scout camp for our scouting council. I have fond memories of attending Camp Cutter both as a scout as well as a camp counselor. By the end of my tenure there, I knew the trails well enough that I could find my way around at night without a flashlight. Although we had Sunday religious services at Cutter in an A-frame chapel, I often experienced God's presence more intensely in the trails and mountains. For me, there was something mysterious and holy about the way in which the plants, animals, birds, insects, terrain, water, and air all worked together as one interdependent ecosystem.[36]

Even today, some of my most powerful experiences of the divine have occurred in the great outdoors. One of my favorite places in the world is Acadia National Park in Maine. Michael and I have visited there often, and we have walked—and climbed—many of the trails. For me, one of the most powerful "proofs" of the existence of God—akin to the divine watchmaker argument[37]—is climbing to the top of a mountain and looking out as far as the eye can see at the amazing beauty and grace of creation.

---

[34] 1 Cor. 12:21.

[35] A number of theological and ethical works about the grace of interdependence have been published in recent years. These include Joseph Sittler, *Evocations of Grace: Writings on Ecology, Theology, and Ethics* (Grand Rapids, MI: William B. Eerdmans Publishing, 2000); and Willis Jenkins, *Ecologies of Grace: Environmental Ethics and Christian Theology* (Oxford, UK: Oxford University Press, 2008). See also Steven Bouma-Prediger, *For the Beauty of the Earth: A Christian Vision for Creation Care*, 2nd ed. (Grand Rapids, MI: Baker Academic, 2010).

[36] For a collection of feminist interfaith essays on ecological issues, see Carol J. Adams, ed., *Ecofeminism and the Sacred* (New York: Continuum, 1993). For a collection of essays by two-thirds world women on ecofeminist theologies, see Rosemary Radford Ruether, *Women Healing Earth: Third World Women on Ecology, Feminism, and Religion* (Maryknoll, NY: Orbis Books, 1996).

[37] See Laura L. Garcia, "Teleological and Design Arguments," in *A Companion to Philosophy of Religion*, ed. Philip L. Quinn and Charles Taliaferro (Malden, MA: Blackwell Publishing, 1997), 338–44.

The interdependence of the ecosystem is both an unfathomable mystery and also something that is tangible and close at hand.

Finally, I have experienced the grace of interdependence through our puppy, Chartres. As I mentioned earlier, animals are an important part of many LGBT families. Since Chartres came into our lives two and a half years ago, Michael and I have become much more aware of the non-human aspects of creation and our relationship to animals, especially while walking Chartres each day.[38] One of great blessings and joys of teaching at my seminary has been designing and leading the annual blessing of the animals on St. Francis's Day. This past year, we opened up the chapel to all kinds of animals—from dogs to cats to goldfish to stuffed toys—and celebrated the grace of interdependence through liturgy. For me, the challenge of the grace of interdependence is how to translate the above anecdotes about my encounters with God's creation into better creation care of our planet in my day-to-day life, from what I eat and wear to what I buy and recycle.

A second context in which I've experienced the grace of interdependence has been in the interfaith realm. Indeed, the very idea of interdependence is a central theme in many East Asian religions and philosophies, from the ultimate oneness of Hinduism to the interdependence of all things in Buddhism. A few years ago, I attended the conference of the National Queer Asian Pacific Islander Association (NQAPIA) in Seattle, Washington. The organizers asked me to put together an interfaith meditation service that would honor a variety of religious and spiritual traditions. With the help of some of my friends, I prepared a service that involved Asian drumming, silent meditation, and readings from holy texts of various religious and spiritual traditions. It was a simple yet powerful service, and it allowed me to experience the Interconnected Christ, despite the fact that it was not exclusively a "Christian" service.

Another interfaith context in which I've experienced the grace of interdependence was a seminary course that I took on Jewish-Christian dialogue. A number of us students from Union Theological Seminary in New York met each week with our counterparts at the Jewish Theological Seminary, which was located right across the street. It was through this course that I met my good friend Faith, now an ordained rabbi in the Conservative

[38] For a powerful theological reflection on dog walking, see Carter Heyward, *Touching Our Strength: The Erotic as Power and Love of God* (New York: HarperSanFrancisco, 1989), 93.

Jewish movement. I attended Shabbat services and dinners with Faith and her friends; she visited local church services with me and heard me preach. We talked about queer theology and feminist readings of the Talmud, and we remain friends to this day. I was forever transformed by this interfaith encounter. I am grateful for the grace of interdependence that occurred between a gay Asian American male doctoral student of Christian theology on the one hand, and a straight Conservative Jewish woman rabbinical student on the other.

Finally, it is important to note that interdependence in the interfaith context is not strictly limited to religious issues. As Rosemary Radford Ruether has shown in her book *Integrating Ecofeminism, Globalization, and World Religions*, interfaith issues also touch upon issues of ecology, feminism, and corporate globalization. Ruether notes that the intersections of these issues can lead to imagining a "different way of interrelating human and nature as an interdependent matrix of life."[39]

In sum, the Interconnected Christ can be experienced through the grace of interdependence, which is the notion that we are all dependent on each other for our survival and flourishing. This grace can take many forms, including ecological and interfaith awareness.

Study Questions

1. Who is the Interconnected Christ? What are some examples of the Interconnected Christ in the New Testament?
2. How might the Interconnected Christ be manifested in ecological, disability, and interreligious theologies?
3. What is sin in light of the Interconnected Christ? How is this sin manifested in the LGBT community?
4. What are some examples of overconsumption that you have experienced or observed within the LGBT community?

[39] Rosemary Radford Ruether, *Integrating Ecofeminism, Globalization, and World Religions* (Lanham, MD: Rowman and Littlefield Publishers, 2005), x.

5. What is grace in light of the Interconnected Christ? How is this sin manifested in the LGBT community?
6. Have you experienced faith traditions other than your own? In what forms have these encounters taken place? Worship services? Interfaith discussions?

For Further Study

Interconnected Christ

- Clark, *Beyond Our Ghettos*
- Edwards, *Jesus the Wisdom of God*
- Eiesland, *The Disabled God*
- Isherwood, *Introducing Feminist Christologies*, 71–86
- Kwok, *Hope Abundant*, 165–216
- Maloney, *The Cosmic Christ*
- Schreiter, *Faces of Jesus in Africa*
- Spencer, *Gay and Gaia*
- Stinton, *Jesus of Africa*
- Sugirtharajah, *Asian Faces of Jesus*

LGBT Interfaith Resources

- Barzan, *Sex and Spirit*
- Connor, Sparks, and Sparks, *Cassell's Encyclopedia of Queer Myth, Symbol and Spirit*
- de la Huerta, *Coming Out Spiritually*
- Drinkwater, Lesser, and Shneer, *Torah Queeries*
- Kolodny, *Blessed Bi Spirit*
- Kugle, *Homosexuality in Islam*
- Lake, *Recreations*
- Leyland, *Queer Dharma*
- Long, *Men, Homosexuality, and the Gods*
- Ratti, *A Lotus of a Different Color*
- Roden, *Jewish/Christian/Queer*
- Swidler, *Homosexuality and World Religions*

Sin as Isolation

- Jordan, *The Silence of Sodom*
- Kemmerer, *Sister Species*
- Moore, *A Question of Truth*

Grace as Interdependence

- Adams, *Ecofeminism and the Sacred*
- Bouma-Prediger, *For the Beauty of the Earth*
- Garcia, "Teleological and Design Arguments"
- Heyward, *Touching Our Strength*
- Jenkins, *Ecologies of Grace*
- Ruether, *Integrating Ecofeminism, Globalization, and World Religions*
- Ruether, *Women Healing Earth*
- Sittler, *Evocations of Grace*

Chapter 11

Model Seven: The Hybrid Christ

1. The Hybrid Christ

The seventh and final Christ-based model of sin and grace is the Hybrid Christ. The Hybrid Christ is the One who occupies a space that is "in-between" binary categories and can be understood as a "third thing." Take, for example, the binary categories of divine and human. Normally we think of these categories as being mutually exclusive—one is either divine or human. The Hybrid Christ challenges these categories, however, because he is neither purely divine, nor is he purely human. Rather, as a result of the incarnation and the Word made flesh, the Hybrid Christ is *both* divine *and* human. As such, the Hybrid Christ occupies the interstitial space between these categories; he is a hybrid being.

Hybridity is a concept from postcolonial theory that describes the simultaneous coexistence of two things that leads to the creation of a third "hybrid" thing.[1] For example, Homi Bhabha, in his book *The Location of Culture*, has described hybridity in terms of the "liminal space" of the stairwell that lies between two floors. This space challenges the normal binary divisions of upper/

[1] See, for example, "Hybridity," in Bill Ashcroft, Gareth Griffiths, and Helen Tiffin, *Post-Colonial Studies: The Key Concepts* (London: Routledge, 2000), 118–21.

lower, superior/inferior, and colonizer/colonized; in this space, these binary categories are deconstructed and transformed.[2]

For me, the Hybrid Christ arises out of the theological understanding that Jesus Christ is simultaneously divine *and* human in nature. He is neither purely one nor the other. In the words of the Athanasian Creed, Jesus Christ is simultaneously both "God and human," and yet he is "not two, but one Christ."[3] As such, he is the ultimate hybrid being. In other words, the Hybrid Christ challenges binary and either/or ways of seeing the world.

This hybrid nature is reflected in the double consciousness—that is, living simultaneously in a white world and a non-white world—that is experienced by many racial minorities and immigrants in the United States such as African Americans, Latino/as, Asian Americans, Native Americans, and others. In the case of Asian Americans, we are neither purely "Asian" (because we no longer live in Asia, but rather in the United States), nor are we purely "American" (because we do not have European American bodies, but rather we are signified as "foreigners" by our Asian bodies). Rather, we are a third "hybrid" or "in-between" thing, which ultimately challenges the binary and hierarchical nature of the original two categories of "Asian" (normally seen as the outsider) and "American" (normally seen as the insider).[4]

Marcella Althaus-Reid has written about the Hybrid Christ in her book *Indecent Theology*. Specifically, Althaus-Reid writes about the Bi/Christ, in which a bisexual Jesus challenges the "heterosexual patterns of thought" of hierarchical and binary categories. Just as the bisexual person challenges the heterosexual binaries of "male/female" and "straight/gay," the Bi/Christ challenges the either/or way of thinking with respect to theology (for example, by deconstructing "poor" and "rich" as mutually exclusive categories

---

[2] Homi Bhabha, *The Location of Culture* (London: Routledge, 1994), 5. Emilie Townes has warned against a false kind of postmodern hybridity in which a culture—such as Black culture—is appropriated solely for "marketing and the acquisition of wealth and privilege." There is no reciprocity in this kind of appropriation. Townes cites a number of examples of this false hybridity, including the white rappers Eminem and Vanilla Ice. Emilie M. Townes, *Womanist Ethics and the Cultural Production of Evil* (New York: Palgrave Macmillan, 2006), 42.

[3] "*Symbolum Quicunque*: The Athanasian Creed," in Philip Schaff, *The Greek and Latin Creeds*, vol. 2 of *The Creeds of Christendom: With a History and Critical Notes*, 6th ed. (Grand Rapids, MI: Baker Books, 2007), 66–71.

[4] For a theological reflection on race and hybridity, see Brian Bantum, *Redeeming Mulatto: A Theology of Race and Christian Hybridity* (Waco, TX: Baylor University Press, 2010). For other works on hybridity, see Avtar Brah and Annie E. Coombes, *Hybridity and Its Discontents: Politics, Science, Culture* (London: Routledge, 2000); Peter Burke, *Cultural Hybridity* (Cambridge, UK: Polity Press, 2009); Virinder S. Karla, Raminder Kaur, and John Hutnyk, *Diaspora and Hybridity* (London: SAGE Publications, 2005); Marwan M. Kraidy, *Hybridity, or the Cultural Logic of Globalization* (Philadelphia, PA: Temple University Press, 2005); Anjali Prabhu, *Hybridity: Limits, Transformations, Prospects* (Albany, NY: State University of New York Press, 2007).

in liberation theology). As such, the Bi/Christ can be understood as an example of the Hybrid Christ.[5]

Indeed, the queer identities of "bisexual," "transgender," and "intersex" are all hybrid concepts because they respectively deconstruct the binaries of heterosexuality/homosexuality, masculine/feminine, and male/female. Each of these three identities occupies an interstitial space with respect to sexuality, gender identity, and biological sex, respectively. For example, "bisexual" challenges the conventional notion that sexuality exists only in terms the heterosexuality/homosexuality binary. Similarly, transgender challenges the notion that gender identity exists only in terms of the masculine/feminine binary. Finally, intersex challenges the notion that biological sex exists only in terms of the male/female binary. As such, whenever LGBT theologians write about the Bisexual Christ, the Transgender Christ, or the Intersex Christ, they are also writing about the Hybrid Christ.

Another manifestation of the Hybrid Christ is the Queer Asian Christ. Although many queer theologians have written about the Queer Christ, and many Asian and Asian American theologians have written about the Asian Christ, there has been virtually no reflection on the Queer Asian Christ, which is a *blending* of these two christologies. I believe that the passion narrative in the Gospel according to John can be a source for constructing a queer Asian christology. Both the Beloved Disciple and Jesus' mother, Mary, are present at the foot of the cross.[6] For me, the Beloved Disciple—who laid his head on Jesus' breast at the Last Supper—represents the Queer Christ. Mary, on the other hand, represents Jesus' biological family and ethnic heritage, which for me is the Asian Christ. Before Jesus dies, he says to Mary: "Woman, here is your son."[7] He then says to the Beloved Disciple: "Here is your mother."[8] For me, this chiastic exchange at the foot of the cross is at the heart of a Queer Asian christology because it represents the coming together—that is, a hybrid blending—of both the Queer Christ and the Asian Christ.[9]

[5] Althaus-Reid, *Indecent Theology*, 114–16. Similarly, Halvor Moxnes has argued that Jesus' kingdom sayings establish a "queer space" that challenge binaries of male/female, we/them, inside/outside, and central/marginal. See Halvor Moxnes, *Putting Jesus in His Place: A Radical Vision of Household and Kingdom* (Louisville, KY: Westminster John Knox Press, 2003), 104–07.

[6] John 19:25–27.

[7] John 19:26.

[8] John 19:27.

[9] See Patrick S. Cheng, "Jesus, Mary, and the Beloved Disciple: Towards a Queer Asian Pacific American Christology" (2001), at http://www.patrickcheng.net/uploads/7/0/3/7/7037096/jesus_mary_and_the_beloved_disciple.pdf (accessed on December 11, 2011).

The Queer Asian Christ also can be understood in the context of Kuan Yin, the Asian bodhisattva (that is, an enlightened being in Buddhism who defers entering into Nirvana in order to help others get there). Historically speaking, Kuan Yin is a transgender being; she first appears in India as the *male* bodhisattva Avalokiteshvara, but when her story eventually reaches China, she becomes a *female* bodhisattva and takes on the name Kuan Yin. Because of this gender fluidity, Kuan Yin is *queer*. Because of her connections to South Asia and East Asia, Kuan Yin is *Asian*. Finally, because the bodhisattva in Buddhism has a sacrificial role (that is, she or he defers enlightenment in order to help others), Kuan Yin can be understood as a *Christ* figure. Thus, Kuan Yin can be understood as a manifestation of the Queer Asian Christ, both in terms of her multiple identities, but also from a Buddhist and Christian interfaith perspective.[10]

In sum, a theology of the Hybrid Christ recognizes that Jesus Christ exists simultaneously in both the human and the divine worlds. This can be seen most clearly in the post-resurrection narratives. As a resurrected person with a human body, Jesus Christ is "in-both" worlds (that is, his resurrected body is both human and divine), and yet he is also "in-between" worlds (that is, he is neither purely human nor purely divine).[11] Although this can be a painful experience—metaphorically speaking, Jesus Christ has no place to lay down his head[12]—his hybridity is what ultimately allows him to build a bridge between the human and divine.

2. Sin as Singularity

If the Hybrid Christ is the One who exists simultaneously within multiple categories (such as humanity *and* divinity), then sin—defined as what opposes the Hybrid Christ—can be understood as *singularity*. The sin of singularity is a refusal to acknowledge the complex interplay of identity categories. Singularity is our desire to simplify multiple overlapping and intersecting categories—say, race, gender, and sexuality—into separate and distinct

---

[10] Patrick S. Cheng, "Kuan Yin: Mirror of the Queer Asian Christ" (2003), at http://www.patrickcheng.net/uploads/7/0/3/7/7037096/kuan_yin_mirror_of_the_queer_asian_christ.pdf (accessed on December 11, 2011).

[11] The late Asian American theologian Jung Young Lee coined the term "in-beyond" to describe the simultaneous state of being "in-both" and "in-between." See Jung Young Lee, *Marginality: The Key to Multicultural Theology* (Minneapolis, MN: Fortress Press, 1995), 55–99.

[12] Matt. 8:20.

categories. For example, Laurel Schneider, a lesbian professor of theology at the Chicago Theological Seminary, has challenged singularity in theological discourse by asking the question "What race is your sex?"[13] By posing this question, Schneider challenges the conventional wisdom that race and sex are two separate and distinct categories as opposed to being inextricably intertwined.

The sin of singularity is manifested in either/or thinking. According to this way of thinking, there is only a *single* choice possible between two binaries; for example, one can choose *either* humanity *or* divinity to describe Jesus Christ, but not both. In christological terms, the sin of singularity is the heresy of Arianism on the one hand (that is, understanding Jesus Christ *only* in human terms), as well as the heresy of Docetism on the other (that is, understanding Jesus Christ *only* in divine terms). I have written elsewhere about sin as reinforcing the false choice of binaries instead of challenging or deconstructing them.[14]

The sin of singularity also extends to the realm of Christian theology. A number of contemporary theologians have critiqued the traditional doctrine of sin as being too singular or one-dimensional. For example, the Asian American theologian Andrew Park has criticized traditional ways of thinking about sin because they focus exclusively on the guilt of the sinner and not on the suffering, or *han*, of the "sinned-against" or victims.[15] Similarly, the feminist theologian Margaret Kamitsuka has challenged the traditional division of sin into "male" and "female" forms of sin (for example, Valerie Saiving's feminist critique of Reinhold Niebuhr's anthropology) by using a Butlerian and Foucauldian analysis.[16] Both Park and Kamitsuka advocate for a more multidimensional way of thinking about sin.

The sin of singularity also can be manifested in the failure to recognize the complex reality of multiple intersecting and shifting identities within a single person. For example, postcolonial scholars Clayton Crockett and Jay McDaniel have characterized sin as "making idols of identities"; that is, defining personhood through only fixed or singular identities and "clinging to identities

[13] See Laurel C. Schneider, "What Race Is Your Sex?," in *Disrupting White Supremacy from Within: White People on What We Need to Do*, ed. Jennifer Harvey, Karin A. Case, and Robin Hawley Gorsline (Cleveland, OH: Pilgrim Press, 2004), 142–62.

[14] See Cheng, *Radical Love*, 70–78.

[15] See Andrew Sung Park, *The Wounded Heart of God: The Asian Concept of Han and the Christian Doctrine of Sin* (Nashville, TN: Abingdon Press, 1993).

[16] See Kamitsuka, "Toward a Feminist Postmodern and Postcolonial Interpretation of Sin."

as if they defined a person."[17] As a result, those of us who exist at the intersections of marginalized racial, gender, sexual orientation, age, religious, and other categories often find that our experiences are rendered invisible or erased. The sin of singularity does violence to our lives; we experience fragmentation as a result of this erasure, much like the unnamed concubine in the Book of Judges who is gang-raped and dismembered.[18]

For example, the LGBT rights debate is often reduced to a false binary between sexual minorities (that is, white queer people who support such rights) vs. ethnic minorities (that is, straight people of color who are opposed to such rights). Unfortunately, there is no room for LGBT people of color in this binary way of thinking. Kelly Brown Douglas, a womanist theologian and professor at Gaucher College, has argued in *Sexuality and the Black Church: A Womanist Perspective* that homophobia—and not homosexuality—is the real "sin and betrayal of Black faith," particularly since its "venomous rhetoric" alienates black LGBT people from God.[19] Traci West, a black feminist ethicist and professor at the Drew University Theological School, has also noted the "condemnations from the pulpit about certain expressions of sexuality and sexual identity" within many black churches.[20]

In recent years, a number of LGBT black theologians and religious scholars have started to challenge the virulent homophobia in the black church that often forces its LGBT members to choose between their ethnicities and their sexualities. For example, Horace Griffin, a gay Episcopal priest and professor at the Pacific School of Religion in Berkeley, California, has written in his book *Their Own Receive Them Not* about the ways in which the black church often forces its LGBT members to "live as heterosexual" or risk "ridicule or punishment."[21] Similarly, Roger Sneed, a gay professor of religion at Furman University in Greenville, South

---

[17] Clayton Crockett and Jay McDaniel, "From an Idolatry of Identity to a Planetization of Alterity: A Relational-Theological Approach to Hybridity, Sin, and Love," *Journal of Postcolonial Theory and Theology* 1, no. 3 (November 2010), 11.

[18] See Patrick S. Cheng, "Multiplicity and Judges 19: Constructing a Queer Asian Pacific American Biblical Hermeneutic," *Semeia* 90/91 (2002), 119–33.

[19] Kelly Brown Douglas, *Sexuality and the Black Church: A Womanist Perspective* (Maryknoll, NY: Orbis Books, 1999), 126–27. See also Kelly Brown Douglas, "Heterosexism and the Black American Church Community: A Complicated Reality," in Ellison and Plaskow, *Heterosexism in Contemporary World Religion*, 177–200.

[20] Traci C. West, "A Space for Faith, Sexual Desire, and Ethical Black Ministerial Practices," in *Loving the Body: Black Religious Studies and the Erotic*, ed. Anthony B. Pinn and Dwight N. Hopkins (New York: Palgrave Macmillan, 2004), 33.

[21] Horace L. Griffin, *Their Own Receive Them Not: African American Lesbians and Gays in Black Churches* (Cleveland, OH: Pilgrim Press, 2006), 145. For an anthology of LGBT-positive African American voices, see Gary David Comstock, *A Whosoever Church: Welcoming Lesbians and Gay Men into African American Congregations* (Louisville, KY: Westminster John Knox Press, 2001).

Carolina, has criticized the ways in which conservative African American Christians continue to believe in a "God who created a heteronormative social order."[22] Traci West has highlighted the work of eleven black women leaders, including several lesbian pastors, who are committed to challenging heterosexism and refuse to "reinforce a hierarchy of moral worth based upon sexuality, race, gender, or any other category of social identity."[23]

The gay Latino Roman Catholic theologian Orlando Espín has similarly written about the destructive consequences of homophobia in the Latino/a community. In his book *Grace and Humanness*, Espín calls for a new theological anthropology that would recognize the *humanitas*, or humanity, of *all* members of the Latino/a community, including LGBT Latinos/as. He calls upon Latino/a theologians to recognize the complex intersections of gender, social class, history, and sexual orientation in all bodies and to break the sinful silences that arise out of a singular focus on racism.[24] Espín has written more broadly elsewhere about grace and sin from a Latino/a perspective, and he challenges singularity in that theological context as well. He writes that "*there cannot be one single way of being Catholic or of experiencing grace and sin.*"[25] These experiences, according to Espín, are shaped by a multiplicity of different "conflicts, social places, classes, cultures, genders" and other factors.[26]

I have personally experienced the sin of singularity when I have tried to downplay one aspect of myself to appear more acceptable to a particular community. For example, I have downplayed my Asian American identity in predominantly white LGBT settings, and I have similarly downplayed my gay identity in predominantly straight Asian American settings. As noted earlier, this phenomenon of "covering" can have negative effects on the well-being of those who are affected.[27]

Eric Wat, a Chinese American gay man, has written about

---

[22] Roger A. Sneed, *Representations of Homosexuality: Black Liberation Theology and Cultural Criticism* (New York: Palgrave Macmillan, 2010), 179.

[23] See Traci C. West, *Disruptive Christian Ethics: When Racism and Women's Lives Matter* (Louisville, KY: Westminster John Knox Press, 2006), 141–79. A number of allies, including James Cone, have acknowledged the struggles that are faced by LGBT African Americans in the black community. See Comstock, *A Whosoever Church*, 205–17 (interview with Rev. Dr. James H. Cone).

[24] Orlando O. Espín, *Grace and Humanness: Theological Reflections Because of Culture* (Maryknoll, NY: Orbis Books, 2007), 51–79.

[25] Orlando O. Espín, "An Exploration into the Theology of Grace and Sin," in *From the Heart of Our People: Latino/a Explorations in Catholic Systematic Theology*, ed. Orlando O. Espín and Miguel H. Díaz (Maryknoll, NY: Orbis Books, 1999), 135 (emphasis in original).

[26] Espín, "An Exploration into the Theology of Grace and Sin," 135.

[27] See Yoshino, *Covering*.

experiencing the sin of singularity in the form of being rejected by both the white LGBT community and the straight Asian American community. Because of the one-dimensional nature of singularity, Wat's racial identity as an Asian American is erased within the predominantly white LGBT world, whereas his sexual identity as a gay man is erased within the predominantly straight Asian American world. For Wat, LGBT Asian Americans are "nobody's children," and we are "forever left in the middle of the road, unacceptable to those at either side of the street."[28]

3. Grace as Hybridity

If sin is singularity in the context of the Hybrid Christ, then grace can be understood as *hybridity*. That is, grace is found in the simultaneous holding together of two or more intersecting worlds. Instead of an either/or approach (for example, forcing a choice between *either* race *or* sexuality), the grace of hybridity allows for a both/and approach (for example, identifying with *both* race *and* sexuality). Indeed, hybridity can be a wonderfully unexpected gift for those of us who constantly exist at the intersections of multiple marginalities.[29]

In an essay entitled "Disrupted/Disruptive Moments: Black Theology and Black Power 1969/1999," the lesbian and womanist theologian Renée Hill has written about how her theological reflection has been shaped by her existence at the "intersections, in-between places, and borderlands" of her identities of race, gender, and sexual orientation. Hill's own experience of this hybridity as an "African American lesbian, Christian, theologian, and worker for justice" has convinced her of the need to create new "multireligious and multidialogical" processes for doing theologies and to embrace "questions, disruptions, and moments of ambiguity and uncertainty."[30]

Similarly, the bisexual and biracial theologian elias farajajé-jones has written about the grace of hybridity in his life and in the life of LGBT people. farajajé-jones argues that our minds must be

---

[28] See Eric Wat, "Preserving the Paradox: Stories From a *Gay-Loh*," in *Asian American Sexualities: Dimensions of the Gay and Lesbian Experience*, ed. Russell Leong (New York: Routledge, 1996), 78.

[29] For a theology of multiplicity, see Catherine Keller and Laurel C. Schneider, eds., *Polydoxy: Theology of Multiplicity and Relation* (London: Routledge, 2011).

[30] See Renée Leslie Hill, "Disrupted/Disruptive Movements: Black Theology and Black Power 1969/1999," in *Black Faith and Public Talk: Critical Essays on James H. Cone's* Black Theology and Black Power, ed. Dwight N. Hopkins (Maryknoll, NY: Orbis Books, 1999), 138, 147–48.

decolonized from the "violence" that separates the sacred from the erotic. The two in fact cannot be separated; farajajé-jones refers to the intermingling of the two as "sexspiritualities, or spiritsexualities." He describes how holding together the sacred and the erotic is ultimately about wholeness and "transcending apparent opposites." farajajé-jones describes himself as a someone "dancing on the edge, ruining your categories, your boxes, your party, because they don't even really exist."[31]

Indeed, as the womanist Roman Catholic theologian Shawn Copeland reminds us in her book *Enfleshing Freedom*, the Body of Christ can in fact be understood as the ultimate hybrid body. Because we are all incorporated into it,[32] the Body of Christ is the only body that is "capable of taking us all in as we are with *all* our different body marks," including those of LGBT people.[33] Although it is one body, the Body of Christ does not require erasure or uniformity. It preserves the integrity of the bodies of "black, brown, red, yellow, poorwhite, and queer folk,"[34] while at the same time all of these marks are "relativized, reoriented, and reappropriated" under the sign of the cross. The Body of Christ is a hybrid of not only racial and sexual identities, but a hybrid of all of our collective "body marks."[35]

Like Hill and farajajé-jones, LGBT Asian Americans have written about the grace of hybridity in our lives. For example, Eric Wat writes that, instead of being caught in the middle of the race/sexuality divide, "gay Asian men must find that *third side of the street* where we can grow, find our voices, learn about ourselves, and educate others about who we are, so that eventually we can join them at both sides of the street."[36] Ann Yuri Uyeda, a queer Asian American activist, wrote about the grace of hybridity in her "overwhelming" experiences in being in a room of nearly two hundred queer Asian American women for the first time: "[We were] Asian and Pacific Islander. And queer. All at once. And all together."[37]

My own vocational and theological journey has reflected an

---

[31] elias farajajé-jones, "Holy Fuck," in *Male Lust: Pleasure, Power, and Transformation*, ed. Kerwin Kay, Jill Nagle, and Baruch Gould (Binghamton, NY: Harrington Park Press, 2000), 330–32, 334.
[32] 1 Cor. 12:27.
[33] M. Shawn Copeland, *Enfleshing Freedom: Body, Race, and Being* (Minneapolis, MN: Fortress Press, 2010), 83.
[34] Copeland, *Enfleshing Freedom*, 81.
[35] Copeland, *Enfleshing Freedom*, 83.
[36] Wat, "Preserving the Paradox," 80 (emphasis added).
[37] Ann Yuri Uyeda, "All at Once, All Together: One Asian American Lesbian's Account of the 1989 Asian Pacific Lesbian Network Retreat," in Lim-Hing, *The Very Inside*, 121.

increasing awareness of the grace of hybridity. My first class in systematic theology at Union Theological Seminary—taught by Professor James Cone—opened my eyes to the wonders of contextual theologies. Although I had spent many years in higher education prior to arriving at Union, I realized that I rarely had an opportunity to reflect on the hybrid nature of my own racial and sexual identities. It was also in that systematic theology class that I realized that neither white queer theologies nor straight Asian American theologies spoke fully to me as a gay Asian man. I discovered my theological voice by reflecting upon the hybrid nature of my existence.[38]

As a result of my theological reflections, I became involved with the queer Asian activist community in New York City. My experience with groups like Gay Asian Pacific Islander Men of New York (GAPIMNY), Q-Wave, and NQAPIA allowed me to hold my sexual and racial identities together, and I did not have to choose one identity over the other.[39] Something was still missing, however, in terms of the religious and spiritual dimensions of my experience. That changed when I walked into an amazing eucharistic celebration at MCC New York for the Chinese Lunar New Year. That was the first time in which my various fragmented identities—queer, Asian, and Christian—came together in one place. Shortly thereafter, I founded an e-mail list and website—Queer Asian Spirit—that still exists today as a pastoral and information resource for LGBT Asians of faith around the world.[40]

It has taken a decade, but the voices of queer Asian theologians are finally emerging as a result of the grace of hybridity. In 2010, a number of queer Asian theologians and religion scholars from around the world formed the Emerging Queer Asian Religion Scholars (EQARS) group. We meet monthly via Skype and, for all intents and purposes, EQARS has been my theological "home."[41] Several of our members—such as Mike Campos and Lai Shan

[38] See, e.g., Patrick S. Cheng, "Gay Asian Masculinities and Christian Theologies," *CrossCurrents* 61, no. 4 (December 2011): 540–48. See also Patrick S. Cheng, "Hybridity and the Decolonization of Asian Ameican and Queer Theologies," Postcolonial Theology Network (October 17, 2009), available at https://www.facebook.com/topic.php?uid=23694574926&topic=11026 (accessed on December 11, 2011).

[39] For a history of the founding of LGBT Asian American groups in Southern California, see Eric C. Wat, *The Making of a Gay Asian Community: An Oral History of Pre-AIDS Los Angeles* (Lanham, MD: Rowman and Littlefield Publishers, 2002).

[40] See http://www.queerasianspirit.org (accessed on December 11, 2011).

[41] These scholars include Michael Sepidoza Campos, Joseph Goh, Elizabeth Leung, Hugo Córdova Quero, Miak Siew, Lai Shan Yip, and myself. For more information about EQARS, see http://www.eqars.org (accessed on December 11, 2011).

Yip—are making significant contributions to LGBT theological anthologies.[42] Our hybrid voices are increasingly being heard,[43] and the 2011 annual meeting of the American Academy of Religion in San Francisco will have a groundbreaking panel session, "Coming Home," which is dedicated to theological reflections on the LGBT Asian experience. Finally, the grace of hybridity also includes groundbreaking work on LGBT Asian theological issues by our straight allies such as Professor Kwok Pui-lan of the Episcopal Divinity School[44] and Dean Tat-siong Benny Liew of the Pacific School of Religion.[45]

In sum, the Hybrid Christ can be found in the grace of hybridity. Instead of reducing complex identities to a single factor or characteristic, hybrid thinking delights in multiplicities, intersections, and interstitial spaces. The grace of hybridity can be especially important for LGBT people of color, who occupy those spaces every day. I close with a poem, "The Burning Bush," that I wrote about the deep connections between hybridity, Christian theology, and the LGBT Asian experience in my own life:

I AM
an inner dance
of interwoven identities
perichoretic
cappadocian
chalcedonian:
Asian, ever ancient
ancestral ethnic cultural
Queer, ever new

[42] See Michael Sepidoza Campos, "The *Baklâ*: Gendered Religious Performance in Filipino Cultural Spaces," in *Queer Religion*, ed. Donald L. Boisvert and Jay Emerson Johnson (Santa Barbara, CA: Praeger, 2012), 2:167-91; Lai Shan Yip, "Listening to the Passion of Catholic *nu-tongzhi*: Developing a Catholic Lesbian Feminist Theology in Hong Kong," in Boisvert and Johnson, *Queer Religion*, 2:63-80.

[43] On April 28, 2011, I delivered the Fourth Annual John E. Boswell Lecture at the Center for Lesbian and Gay Studies in Religion and Ministry at the Pacific School of Religion in Berkeley, California. The lecture was entitled "The Rainbow Connection: Bridging Asian American and Queer Theologies." For more information about the lecture, see http://www.clgs.org/events/fourth-annual-boswell-lecture-rainbow-connection (accessed on December 11, 2011).

[44] See Kwok Pui-lan, "Asian and Asian American Churches," in *Homosexuality and Religion: An Encyclopedia*, ed. Jeffrey S. Siker (Westport, CT: Greenwood Press, 2007); Kwok Pui-lan, "Body and Pleasure in Postcoloniality," in *Dancing Theology in Fetish Boots: Essays in Honour of Marcella Althaus-Reid*, ed. Lisa Isherwood and Mark D. Jordan (London: SCM Press, 2010); Kwok Pui-lan, *Postcolonial Imagination and Feminist Theology* (Louisville, KY: Westminster John Knox Press, 2005), 100–21.

[45] See Tat-siong Benny Liew, "(Cor)Responding: A Letter to the Editor," in Stone, *Queer Commentary and the Hebrew Bible*, 182–92; Tat-siong Benny Liew, "Queering Closets and Perverting Desires: Cross-Examining John's Engendering and Transgendering Word Across Different Worlds," in *They Were All Together in One Place?: Toward Minority Biblical Criticism*, ed. Randall C. Bailey, Tat-siong Benny Liew, and Fernando F. Segovia (Atlanta, GA: Society of Biblical Literature, 2009), 251–88.

youthful incarnational erotic sexual I AM
Spirit, ever timeless
community church ecclesial
unmixed unchanged
indivisible
inseparable
image and likeness of the
trinitarian
Godhead
I AM[46]

Study Questions

1. Who is the Hybrid Christ? Where does the Hybrid Christ appear in the gospels and Christian theological reflection?
2. What is hybridity? How is hybridity manifested in your life and/or in the lives of those around you?
3. How can the Bi/Christ and the Queer Asian Christ be understood as manifestations of the Hybrid Christ?
4. What is sin in light of the Hybrid Christ? How is this sin manifested within the LGBT community?
5. What are some examples of false binaries involving LGBT people and communities of color? How does this impact LGBT people of color?
6. What is grace in light of the Hybrid Christ? How is this grace manifested within the LGBT community? How might the work of Renée Hill and elias farajajé-jones shed light on this grace?

[46] Patrick S. Cheng, "The Burning Bush" (2009).

For Further Study

Hybrid Christ

- Althaus-Reid, *Indecent Theology*, 114–16
- Bantum, *Redeeming Mulatto*
- Cheng, "Jesus, Mary, and the Beloved Disciple"
- Cheng "Kuan Yin"
- Copeland, *Enfleshing Freedom*, 55–84

Hybridity

- Ashcroft, Griffiths, and Tiffin, *Post-Colonial Studies*, 118–21
- Bhabha, *The Location of Culture*
- Brah and Coombes, *Hybridity and Its Discontents*
- Burke, *Cultural Hybridity*
- Karla, Kaur, and Hutnyk, *Diaspora and Hybridity*
- Kraidy, *Hybridity, or the Cultural Logic of Globalization*
- Prabhu, *Hybridity*

Sin as Singularity

- Cheng, "Multiplicity and Judges"
- Cheng, *Radical Love*, 70–78
- Comstock, *A Whosoever Church*
- Crockett and McDaniel, "From an Idolatry of Identity to a Planetization of Alterity"
- Douglas "Heterosexism and the Black American Church Community"
- Douglas, *Sexuality and the Black Church*
- Espin, "An Exploration into the Theology of Grace and Sin"
- Espin, *Grace and Humanness*, 51–79
- Griffin, *Their Own Receive Them Not*
- Kamitsuka, "Toward a Feminist Postmodern and Postcolonial Interpretation of Sin"
- Park, *The Wounded Heart of God*
- Schneider, "What Race Is Your Sex?"
- Sneed, *Representations of Homosexuality*
- Wat, "Preserving the Paradox"
- Yoshino, *Covering*

Grace as Hybridity

- Campos, "The *Baklâ*"
- Cheng, "Gay Asian Masculinities and Christian Theologies"
- Cheng, "Hybridity and the Decolonization of Asian American and Queer Theologies"
- Cheng, "The Burning Bush"
- farajajé-jones, "Holy Fuck"
- Hill, "Disrupted/Disruptive Movements"
- Keller and Schneider, *Polydoxy*
- Kwok, "Asian and Asian American Churches"
- Kwok, "Body and Pleasure in Postcoloniality"
- Kwok, *Postcolonial Imagination and Feminist Theology*, 100–21
- Liew, "(Cor)Responding"
- Liew, "Queering Closets and Perverting Desires"
- Uyeda, "All at Once, All Together"
- Wat, *The Making of a Gay Asian Community*
- Yip, "Listening to the Passion of Catholic *nu-tongzhi*"

Conclusion

As an openly gay Christian theologian, I have wrestled with the doctrines of sin and grace for much of my adult life. At one point in my life, I was so repulsed by the language of sin as used by the church that I could no longer see the good news of God's grace in my life. And, as an ordained minister who has pastored to the LGBT community for over a decade, I have seen firsthand the emotional and psychological damage inflicted by the constant use of sin-talk by the Christian right.

However, in this book I have argued for a new way of thinking about sin and grace for LGBT people—as well as for anyone who has struggled with these doctrines, including our allies. Rather than throw out these doctrines completely, I have proposed that we must move from a *crime-based* view to a *Christ-based* view of sin and grace. That is, instead of understanding sin as crime, and grace as acquittal and rehabilitation, we should understand sin as immaturity, and grace as deification (that is, becoming divine) or being conformed to the image of Christ. In traditional theological terms, I have argued for a shift from an Augustinian model (that is, Western and crime-based) to a Irenaean model (that is Eastern and Christ-centered) of sin and grace.

The traditional crime-based model of sin and grace has developed into a sadistic paradigm in which our first parents fell from a state of perfection into eternal damnation, and all subsequent human beings have suffered the consequences of their crime. By contrast, the Christ-based model of sin and grace is a much more compassionate paradigm in which the human race is understood to be in a process of constant growth. Adam and Eve's disobedience was caused by their spiritual immaturity, just as children and adolescents are in a constant process of growth towards adulthood. We are still in the process of becoming divine; we may lose our way from time to time, but with God's help we will find our way back home.

What are the implications of this fundamental shift in thinking about sin and grace? Instead of understanding sin as a laundry list of prohibited crimes, we can understand sin as opposing what God has revealed to us in the incarnation of Christ Jesus. Instead of relying on vice lists, we are challenged to interpret the gospel in our own particular contexts. Thus, we can define sin and grace in relationship to our experiences of the Queer Christ.

In light of this Christ-centered approach, I have proposed seven different models of the Queer Christ based upon the writings of LGBT theologians over the last few decades. These seven models are: (1) the Erotic Christ; (2) the Out Christ; (3) the Liberator Christ; (4) the Transgressive Christ; (5) the Self-Loving Christ; (6) the Interconnected Christ; and (7) the Hybrid Christ. It is my hope that these models of the Queer Christ can result in further conversation within the LGBT community—as well as other communities—about Jesus' question of "But who do you say that I am?"[1]

From these seven models of the Queer Christ, I have proposed seven new deadly sins and seven new amazing graces for LGBT people. The following chart summarizes these sins and graces:

Model of the Queer Christ	Sin	Grace
1. Erotic Christ	Exploitation	Mutuality
2. Out Christ	The Closet	Coming Out
3. Liberator Christ	Apathy	Activism
4. Transgressive Christ	Conformity	Deviance
5. Self-Loving Christ	Shame	Pride
6. Interconnected Christ	Isolation	Interdependence
7. Hybrid Christ	Singularity	Hybridity

A Christ-centered model of sin and grace can help LGBT Christians—and, in fact, all Christians—to once again hear the Good News. Such a model also allows us to reclaim the language of sin and grace, which to date has been monopolized by the Christian right. Furthermore, this model challenges us to think theologically about what it means to be separated from—and reunited with—God.

As I was completing this book manuscript, I attended a memorial service in Cambridge, Massachusetts, that commemorated the tenth anniversary of the 9-11 attacks on the World Trade Center

[1] Mark 8:29.

in New York City. It was a joint service planned by the Episcopal communities in Harvard Square—the Episcopal Divinity School, Christ Church Cambridge, the Society of Saint John the Evangelist, and the Episcopal Chaplaincy at Harvard. The service brought back vivid memories of my being in Manhattan on September 11, 2001, and the utter horror and fear that Michael and I—and many of our friends—experienced in the days, weeks, months, and even years following the attacks.

The 9-11 attacks shook me to the core—as well my relationship with God. A part of me died that day. How could God have allowed this to happen to the nearly three thousand people who died as an immediate result of those attacks, as well as the countless number of people who died in the subsequent wars in Afghanistan and Iraq? What did it mean for our country to be so hated by so many people around the world—and for so many of us to be utterly ignorant of the depth of this hatred? Many of my feelings of being separated from God resurfaced as I sat through the service and relived the events from a decade ago.

To my surprise, the memorial service ended with the hymn "Amazing Grace."[2] I was incredibly moved to hear a church full of people sing the hymn at full voice along with the pipe organ and choir. (And, no, the word "wretch" was not changed or deleted from the first verse.) The hymn was a remarkably appropriate ending for a service that was called "From Horror to Hope." In fact, I thought the service could have just as easily been called "From Sin to Amazing Grace." I had never heard the hymn in quite the same way before, and it helped to move me from a place of being separated from God to being reunited with God through God's amazing grace.

I am convinced that, more than ever, it is important for LGBT people—and many others—to wrestle deeply with the doctrines of sin and grace, as opposed to throwing them out. It is my hope that a Christ-centered model of sin and grace will allow LGBT people of faith, as well as our allies, to enter into a more meaningful theological dialogue among ourselves as well as with the broader theological community about the amazing grace of our lives and loves.

---

[2] Newton, "Amazing Grace."

Bibliography

Adams, Carol J., ed. *Ecofeminism and the Sacred.* New York: Continuum, 1993.

Alison, James. *Faith Beyond Resentment: Fragments Catholic and Gay*. New York: Crossroad Publishing, 2001.

Allport, Gordon W. *ABC's of Scapegoating*. Revised ed. Chicago: Anti-Defamation League of B'Nai B'rith, 1948.

Althaus-Reid, Marcella. *Indecent Theology: Theological Perversions in Sex, Gender, and Politics*. London: Routledge, 2000.

Althaus-Reid, Marcella, and Lisa Isherwood, eds. *Trans/Formations*. London: SCM Press, 2009.

Anderson, Gary A. *Sin: A History*. New Haven, CT: Yale University Press, 2009.

Anselm of Canterbury. "Why God Became Man." In Fairweather, *A Scholastic Miscellany*, 100–183.

Apostolic Constitutions. In Roberts and Donaldson, *Ante-Nicene Fathers*, 7:385–508.

Aquinas, Thomas. *Summa Theologiae*. 61 vols. Cambridge, UK: Cambridge University Press, 2006.

Ashcroft, Bill, Gareth Griffiths, and Helen Tiffin. *Post-Colonial Studies: The Key Concepts*. London: Routledge, 2000.

Athanasius. *On the Incarnation.* In Schaff and Wace, *Nicene and Post-Nicene Fathers 2nd*, 4:31–67.

Augustine of Hippo. *Against Julian* 4.4.34. In Clark, *St. Augustine on Marriage and Sexuality*, 91.

__________. *Confessions*. In Schaff, *Nicene and Post-Nicene Fathers 1st*, 1:27–207.

__________. *On Nature and Grace* 3.3. In Harmless, *Augustine in His Own Words*, 403.

__________. *The City of God.* In Schaff, *Nicene and Post-Nicene Fathers 1st*, 2:ix-511.

__________. *To Simplicianus* 1.2. In Harmless, *Augustine in His Own Words*, 386–87.

Ayres, Tony. "China Doll—The Experience of Being a Gay Chinese Australian." In Jackson and Sullivan, *Multicultural Queer*, 87–97.

Bailey, Derrick Sherwin. *Homosexuality and the Western Christian Tradition*. London: Longmans, Green, and Company, 1955.

Bailey, Randall C., Tat-siong Benny Liew, and Fernando F. Segovia, eds. *They Were All Together in One Place?: Toward Minority Biblical Criticism*. Atlanta, GA: Society of Biblical Literature, 2009.

Bantum, Brian. *Redeeming Mulatto: A Theology of Race and Christian Hybridity.* Waco, TX: Baylor University Press, 2010.

Barth, Karl. "A Theological Dialogue." *Theology Today* 19, no. 2 (July 1962): 171–77.

__________. *Church Dogmatics*. Volume III/4. Edinburgh: T&T Clark, 1961.

__________. *Church Dogmatics*. Volume IV/1. Edinburgh: T&T Clark, 1956.

__________. "Freedom for Community." In Rogers, *Theology and Sexuality*, 115.

Barzan, Robert, ed. *Sex and Spirit: Exploring Gay Men's Spirituality*. San Francisco: White Crane Newsletter, 1995.

Beinert, Wolfgang, and Francis Schüssler Fiorenza. *Handbook of Catholic Theology*. New York: Herder and Herder, 1995.

Berkhof, Louis. *The History of Christian Doctrines*. Carlisle, PA: Banner of Truth Trust, 1937.

Berkouwer, G.C. *The Triumph of Grace in the Theology of Karl Barth: An Introduction and Critical Appraisal.* Grand Rapids, MI: Wm. B. Eerdmans Publishing, 1956.

Besen, Wayne R. *Anything But Straight: Unmasking the Scandals and Lies Behind the Ex-Gay Myth*. Binghamton, NY: Harrington Park Press, 2003.

Bhabha, Homi. *The Location of Culture*. London: Routledge, 1994.

Biddle, Mark E. *Missing the Mark: Sin and Its Consequences in Biblical Theology*. Nashville, TN: Abingdon Press, 2005.

Bieler, Andrea, and Hans-Martin Gutmann. *Embodying Grace: Proclaiming Justification in the Real World*. Minneapolis, MN: Fortress Press, 2010.

Blocher, Henri. *Original Sin: Illuminating the Riddle*. Downer's Grove, IL: InterVarsity Press, 1997.

Bohache, Thomas. *Christology from the Margins*. London: SCM Press, 2008.

Boisvert, Donald L. *Sanctity and Male Desire: A Gay Reading of Saints*. Cleveland, OH: Pilgrim Press, 2004.

Boisvert, Donald L., and Robert E. Goss, eds. *Gay Catholic Priests and Clerical Sexual Misconduct*. Binghamton NY: Harrington Park Press, 2005.

Boisvert, Donald L., and Jay Emerson Johnson, eds. *Queer Religion*. 2 vols. Santa Barbara, CA: Praeger Publishers, forthcoming 2011.

Bonaventure. "Christ, The One Teacher of All." In Johnson, *Bonaventure*, 152–66.

Bonhoeffer, Dietrich. *The Cost of Discipleship*. New York: Touchstone, 1995.

Boswell, John. *Christianity, Social Tolerance, and Homosexuality: Gay People in Western Europe from the Beginning of the Christian Era to the Fourteenth Century*. Chicago: University of Chicago Press, 1980.

Bouma-Prediger, Steven. *For the Beauty of the Earth: A Christian Vision for Creation Care*. 2nd edition. Grand Rapids, MI: Baker Academic, 2010.

Brah, Atar, and Annie E. Coombes. *Hybridity and Its Discontents: Politics, Science, Culture*. London: Routledge, 2000.

Brooten, Bernadette, J. *Love Between Women: Early Christian Responses to Female Homoeroticism*. Chicago: University of Chicago Press, 1996.

Brown, Joanne Carlson, and Carole R. Bohn, eds. *Christianity, Patriarchy, and Abuse: A Feminist Critique*. Cleveland, OH: Pilgrim Press, 1989.

Brown, Judith C. *Immodest Acts: The Life of a Lesbian Nun in Renaissance Italy*. New York: Oxford University Press, 1986.

Brown, Peter. *The Body and Society: Men, Women, and Sexual Renunciation in Early Christianity*. 20th anniversary edition. New York: Columbia University Press, 2008.

Buber, Martin. *I and Thou*. Edinburgh: T&T Clark, 1937.

Burke, Peter. *Cultural Hybridity*. Cambridge, UK: Polity Press, 2009.

Calvin, John. *Genesis*. Edited by Alister McGrath and J.I. Packer. Wheaton, IL: Crossway Books, 2001.

__________. *The Epistles of Paul the Apostle to the Romans and to the Thessalonians*. Edited by David W. Torrance and Thomas F. Torrance. Translated by Ross Mackenzie. Grand Rapids, MI: William B. Eerdmans Publishing, 1995.

__________. *Institutes of the Christian Religion*. Edited by John T. McNeill. Louisville, KY: Westminster John Knox Press, 1960.

Campos, Michael Sepidoza. "The *Baklâ*: Gendered Religious Performance in Filipino Cultural Spaces." In Boisvert and Johnson, *Queer Religion*, 2:167–91.

Carey, George. *Sinners: Jesus and His Earliest Followers*. Waco, TX: Baylor University Press, 2009.

Carpenter, James A. *Nature and Grace: Toward an Integral Perspective*. New York: Crossroad, 1988.

Catechism of the Catholic Church. 2nd edition. Washington, DC: United States Catholic Conference, 1997.

Cheng, Patrick S. "'Ex-Gays' and the Ninth Circle of Hell." *Huffington Post* (May 20, 2010). Available at http://www.huffingtonpost.com/rev-patrick-s-cheng-phd/ex-gays-and-the-ninth-cir_b_582825.html. Accessed on December 11, 2011.

__________. "Faith, Hope, and Love: Ending LGBT Teen Suicide." *Huffington Post* (October 6, 2010). Available at http://www.huffingtonpost.com/rev-patrick-s-cheng-phd/faith-hope-and-love-endin_b_749160.html. Accessed on December 11, 2011.

_________. "Gay Asian Masculinities and Christian Theologies." *CrossCurrents* 61, no. 4 (December 2011): 540–48.

_________. "Hybridity and the Decolonization of Asian Ameican and Queer Theologies." *Postcolonial Theology Network* (October 17, 2009). Available at https://www.facebook.com/topic.php?uid=23694574926&topic=11026. Accessed on December 11, 2011.

_________. "'I Am Yellow and Beautiful': Reflections on Queer Asian Spirituality and Gay Male Cyberculture." *Journal of Technology, Theology, and Religion* 2, no. 3 (June 2011): 1–21.

_________. "Jesus, Mary, and the Beloved Disciple: Towards a Queer Asian Pacific American Christology" (2001). Available at http://www.patrickcheng.net/uploads/7/0/3/7/7037096/jesus_mary_and_the_beloved_disciple.pdf. Accessed on December 11, 2011.

_________. "Kuan Yin: Mirror of the Queer Asian Christ" (2003). Available at http://www.patrickcheng.net/uploads/7/0/3/7/7037096/kuan_yin_mirror_of_the_queer_asian_christ.pdf. Accessed on December 11, 2011.

_________. "Lady Gaga and the Gospel of Judas." *Huffington Post* (May 16, 2011). Available at http://www.huffingtonpost.com/rev-patrick-s-cheng-phd/lady-gaga-and-the-gospel-_b_862104.html. Accessed on December 11, 2011.

_________. "Multiplicity and Judges 19: Constructing a Queer Asian Pacific American Biblical Hermeneutic." *Semeia* 90/91 (2002), 119–33.

_________. *Radical Love: An Introduction to Queer Theology*. New York: Seabury Books, 2011.

_________. "Reclaiming Our Traditions, Rituals, and Spaces: Spirituality and the Queer Asian Pacific American Experience." *Spiritus* 6, no. 2 (Fall 2006): 234–40.

_________. "Rethinking Sin and Grace for LGBT People Today." In Ellison and Douglas, *Sexuality and the Sacred: Sources for Theological Reflection*, 105–18.

_________. "The Burning Bush" (2009).

_________. "The Grace of Pride" (June 26, 2011). Available at http://www.patrickcheng.net/uploads/7/0/3/7/7037096/the_grace_of_pride.pdf. Accessed on December 11, 2011.

_________. "The Values Voter Summit and the Idolatry of 'Family Values.'" *Huffington Post* (October 13, 2011). Available at http://www.huffingtonpost.com/rev-patrick-s-cheng-phd/values-voter-summit_b_1003623.html. Accessed on December 11, 2011.

Cherry, Kittredge. *Art That Dares: Gay Jesus, Woman Christ, and More*. Berkeley, CA: Androgyne Press, 2007.

Cho, Song, ed. *Rice: Explorations Into Gay Asian Culture and Politics*. Toronto, Canada: Queer Press, 1998.

Christensen, Michael J., and Jeffrey A. Wittung, eds. *Partakers of the Divine Nature: The History and Development of Deification in the Christian Traditions*. Grand Rapids, MI: Baker Academic, 2007.

Chrysostom, John. *Homilies on the Statues to the People of Antioch*. In Schaff, *Nicene and Post-Nicene Fathers 1st*, 9:315–489.

Clark, Elizabeth, ed. *St. Augustine on Marriage and Sexuality*. Washington, DC: Catholic University Press of America, 1996.

Clark, J. Michael. *Beyond Our Ghettos: Gay Theology in Ecological Perspective*. Cleveland, OH: Pilgrim Press, 1993.

Clement of Alexandria. *The Instructor*. In Roberts and Donaldson, *Ante-Nicene Fathers*, 2:207–98.

Clendinen, Dudley, and Adam Nagourney. *Out for Good: The Struggle to Build a Gay Rights Movement in America*. New York: Touchstone, 1999.

Coleman, Peter. *Gay Christians: A Moral Dilemma*. London: SCM Press, 1989.

Coloroso, Barbara. *The Bully, the Bullied, and the Bystander: From Preschool to High School—How Parents and Teachers Can Help Break the Cycle of Violence*. Updated edition. New York: Collins Living, 2008.

Comstock, Gary David. *A Whosoever Church: Welcoming Lesbians and Gay Men into African American Congregations*. Louisville, KY: Westminster John Knox Press, 2001.

_________. *Gay Theology Without Apology*. Cleveland, OH: Pilgrim Press, 1993.

Cone, James H. *A Black Theology of Liberation*. 20th anniversary edition. Maryknoll, NY: Orbis Books, 1990.

Conner, Randy P., David Hatfield Sparks, and Mariya Sparks, eds. *Cassell's Encyclopedia of Queer Myth, Symbol and Spirit: Gay, Lesbian, Bisexual and Transgender Lore*. London: Cassell, 1997.

Copeland, M. Shawn. *Enfleshing Freedom: Body, Race, and Being*. Minneapolis, MN: Fortress Press, 2010.

Cornwall, Susannah. "Apophasis and Ambiguity: The 'Unknowingness' of Transgender." In Althaus-Reid and Isherwood, *Trans/Formations*, 13–40.

_________. *Controversies in Queer Theology*. London: SCM Press, 2011.

_________. "*Ratum et Consummatum*: Refiguring Non-Penetrative Sexual Activity Theologically, in Light of Intersex Conditions." *Theology and Sexuality* 16.1 (2010): 77–93.

_________. *Sex and Uncertainty in the Body of Christ: Intersex Conditions and Christian Theology*. London: Equinox, 2010.

Countryman, L. William. *Dirt, Greed, and Sex: Sexual Ethics in the New Testament and Their Implications for Today*. Revised edition. Minneapolis, MN: Fortress Press, 2007.

Countryman, L. William, and M.R. Ritley. *Gifted By Otherness: Gay and Lesbian Christians in the Church*. Harrisburg, PA: Morehouse Publishing, 2001.

Cover, Robin C. "Sin, Sinners (OT)." In Freedman, *Anchor Yale Bible Dictionary*, 6:31–40.

Crew, Louie. "The Founding of Integrity." *Voice of Integrity* 3.4 (Fall 1993), 23. Available at http://www.rci.rutgers.edu/~lcrew/pubd/founding.html. Accessed on December 11, 2011.

Crockett, Clayton, and Jay McDaniel. "From an Idolatry of Identity to a Planetization of Alterity: A Relational-Theological Approach to Hybridity, Sin, and Love." *Journal of Postcolonial Theory and Theology* 1, no. 3 (November 2010): 1–26.

Cullen, Christopher M. *Bonaventure*. Oxford: Oxford University Press, 2006.

Daly, Mary. *Beyond God the Father: Toward a Philosophy of Women's Liberation*. Boston: Beacon Press, 1973.

Damian, Peter. *Book of Gomorrah: An Eleventh-Century Treatise Against Clerical Homosexual Practices*. Translated by Pierre J. Payer. Waterloo, Ontario: Wilfrid Laurier University Press, 1982.

Dariotis, Wei Ming, "On Becoming a Bi Bi Grrl." In Kumashiro, *Restoried Selves*, 37–46.

de la Huerta, Christian. *Coming Out Spiritually: The Next Step*. New York: Jeremy P. Tarcher/Putnam, 1999.

De La Torre, Miguel A., ed. *Handbook of U.S. Theologies of Liberation*. St. Louis, MO: Chalice Press, 2004.

Defranza, Megan. "Intersex and Imago: Sex, Gender, and Sexuality in Postmodern Theological Anthropology." Ph.D. diss., Marquette University, 2011.

Delio, Ilia. *Simply Bonaventure: An Introduction to His Life, Thought, and Writings*. Hyde Park, NY: New City Press, 2001.

_________. *The Humility of God: A Franciscan Perspective*. Cincinnati, OH: St. Anthony Messenger Press, 2005.

DeYoung, Rebecca Konydyk. *Glittering Vices: A New Look at the Seven Deadly Sins and Their Remedies*. Grand Rapids, MI: Brazos Press, 2009.

Douglas, Kelly Brown. "Heterosexism and the Black American Church Community: A Complicated Reality." In Ellison and Plaskow, *Heterosexism in Contemporary World Religion*, 177–200.

_________. *Sexuality and the Black Church: A Womanist Perspective*. Maryknoll, NY: Orbis Books, 1999.

Douglas, Tom. *Scapegoats: Transferring Blame*. London: Routledge, 1995.

Downs, Alan. *The Velvet Rage: Overcoming the Pain of Growing Up Gay in a Straight Man's World*. Cambridge, MA: Da Capo Press, 2005.

Drinkwater, Gregg, Joshua Lesser, and David Shneer. *Torah Queeries: Weekly Commentaries on the Hebrew Bible*. New York: New York University Press, 2009.

Duberman, Martin, Martha Vicinus, and George Chauncey, eds. *Hidden from History: Reclaiming the Gay and Lesbian Past*. New York: Meridian, 1989.

Duffy, Stephen J. *The Dynamics of Grace*. Collegeville, MN: Liturgical Press, 1993.

Dykstra, Laurel. "Jesus, Bread, Wine and Roses: A Bisexual Feminist at the Catholic Worker." In Kolodny, *Blessed Bi Spirit*, 78–88.

Easton, Dossie, and Janet W. Hardy. *The Ethical Slut: A Practical Guide to Polyamory, Open Relationships and Other Adventures*. 2nd edition. Berkeley, CA: Celestial Arts, 2009.

_________. *The New Bottoming Book*. Emeryville, CA: Greenery Press, 2001.

_________. *Radical Ecstasy: SM Journeys to Transcendence*. Oakland, CA: Greenery Press, 2004.

Edwards, Denis. *Jesus the Wisdom of God: An Ecological Theology*. Maryknoll, NY: Orbis, 1995.

Eiesland, Nancy L. *The Disabled God: Toward a Liberatory Theology of Disability*. Nashville, TN: Abingdon Press, 1994.

Ellingsen, Mark. *Sin Bravely: A Joyful Alternative to a Purpose-Driven Life*. New York: Continuum, 2009.

Ellison, Marvin M. *Erotic Justice: A Liberating Ethic of Sexuality*. Louisville, KY: Westminster John Knox Press, 1996.

_________. *Making Love Just: An Ethical Guide for the Sexually Perplexed*. Minneapolis, MN: Fortress Press, forthcoming 2012.

Ellison, Marvin M., and Kelly Brown Douglas, eds. *Sexuality and the Sacred: Sources for Theological Reflection*. 2nd edition. Louisville, KY: Westminster/John Knox Press, 2010.

Ellison, Marvin M., and Judith Plaskow, eds. *Heterosexism in Contemporary World Religion: Problem and Prospect*. Cleveland, OH: Pilgrim Press, 2007.

Ellison, Marvin M., and Sylvia Thorson-Smith, eds. *Body and Soul: Rethinking Sexuality as Justice-Love*. Cleveland, OH: Pilgrim Press, 2003.

Empereur, James L. *Spiritual Direction and the Gay Person*. New York: Continuum Publishing, 1998.

Eng, David L., and Alice Y. Hom. *Q&A: Queer in Asian America*. Philadelphia, PA: Temple University Press, 1998.

Erickson, Millard J. *Christian Theology*. 2nd edition. Grand Rapids, MI: Baker Books, 1983.

Espín, Orlando O. "An Exploration into the Theology of Grace and Sin." In Espín and Díaz, *From the Heart of Our People*, 121–52.

_________. *Grace and Humanness: Theological Reflections Because of Culture*. Maryknoll, NY: Orbis Books, 2007.

Espín, Orlando O., and Miguel H. Díaz, eds. *From the Heart of Our People: Latino/a Explorations in Catholic Systematic Theology*. Maryknoll, NY: Orbis Books, 1999.

Evans, Amie M., and Trebor Healey, eds. *Queer and Catholic*. New York: Routledge, 2008.

Fairweather, Eugene R., ed. *A Scholastic Miscellany: Anselm to Ockham*. Louisville, KY: Westminster John Knox Press, 1956.

farajajé-jones, elias. "Holy Fuck." In Kay, Nagle, and Gould, *Male Lust*, 327–35.

Farley, Wendy. *Gathering Those Driven Away: A Theology of Incarnation*. Louisville, KY: Westminster John Knox, 2011.

Fenway Health. "Glossary of Gender and Transgender Terms" (January 2010). Available at http://www.fenwayhealth.org/site/DocServer/Handout_7-C_Glossary_of_Gender_and_Transgender_Terms__fi.pdf?docID=7081. Accessed on December 11, 2011.

Finlan, Stephen, and Vladimir Kharlamov, eds. *Theōsis: Deification in Christian Theology*. Volume 1. Eugene, OR: Pickwick Publications, 2006.

Finstuen, Andrew S. *Original Sin and Everyday Protestants: The Theology of Reinhold Niebuhr, Billy Graham, and Paul Tillich in an Age of Anxiety*. Chapel Hill, NC: The University of North Carolina Press, 2009.

Floyd-Thomas, Stacey M., and Anthony B. Pinn. *Liberation Theologies in the United States: An Introduction*. New York: New York University Press, 2010.

Fone, Byrne. *Homophobia: A History*. New York: Picador USA, 2000.

Fortunato, John E. *Embracing the Exile: Healing Journeys of Gay Christians*. San Francisco: Harper and Row, 1982.

Freedman, David Noel, ed. *Anchor Yale Bible Dictionary*. New Haven, CT: Yale University Press, 2008.

Fumia, Molly. *Honor Thy Children: One Family's Journey to Wholeness*. Berkeley, CA: Conari Press, 1997.

Garcia, Laura L. "Teleological and Design Arguments." In Quinn and Taliaferro, *A Companion to Philosophy of Religion*, 338–44.

Gibbs, Jack P. "Conceptions of Deviant Behavior: The Old and the New." In Heiner, *Deviance Across Cultures*, 41–45.

Gilkey, Langdon. *On Niebuhr: A Theological Study*. Chicago: University of Chicago Press, 2001.

Girard, René. *The Scapegoat*. Translated by Yvonne Freccero. Baltimore, MD: Johns Hopkins University Press, 1986.

Glaser, Chris. *Coming Out As Sacrament*. Louisville, KY: Westminster John Knox Press, 1998.

Gomes, Peter J. *The Good Book: Reading the Bible with Mind and Heart*. New York: HarperSanFrancisco, 1996.

Gorell, Paul J. "Rite to Party: Circuit Parties and Religious Experience." In Thumma and Gray, *Gay Religion*, 313–26.

Goss, Robert E. *Jesus Acted Up: A Gay and Lesbian Manifesto*. San Francisco: HarperSanFrancisco, 1993.

_________. *Queering Christ: Beyond Jesus Acted Up*. Cleveland, OH: Pilgrim Press, 2002.

Goss, Robert E., and Mona West, eds. *Take Back the Word: A Queer Reading of the Bible*. Cleveland, OH: Pilgrim Press, 2000.

Green-McCreight, Kathryn. "Gender, Sin and Grace: Feminist Theologies Meet Karl Barth's Hamartiology." *Scottish Journal of Theology*, 50, no. 4 (1997): 415–32.

Griffin, Horace L. *Their Own Receive Them Not: African American Lesbians and Gays in Black Churches.* Cleveland, OH: Pilgrim Press, 2006.

Guest, Deryn, Robert E. Goss, Mona West, and Thomas Bohache, eds. *The Queer Bible Commentary*. London: SCM Press, 2006.

Gunton, Colin E. *The Barth Lectures*. London: T&T Clark, 2007.

Gutiérrez, Gustavo. *A Theology of Liberation: History, Politics, and Salvation*. Translated and edited by Caridad Inda and John Eagleson. 15th anniversary edition. Maryknoll, NY: Orbis Books, 1988.

Haight, Roger. *The Experience and Language of Grace*. New York: Paulist Press, 1979.

Haldeman, W. Scott. "A Queer Fidelity: Reinventing Christian Marriage." In Ellison and Douglas, *Sexuality and the Sacred*, 304–16.

Haller, Tobias Stanislas. *Reasonable and Holy: Engaging Same-Sexuality*. New York: Seabury Books, 2009.

Halperin, David M., and Valerie Traub, eds. *Gay Shame*. Chicago: University of Chicago Press, 2009.

Hampson, Daphne. "Reinhold Niebuhr on Sin: A Critique." In Harries, *Reinhold Niebuhr and the Issues of Our Time*, 46–60.

Han, Arar, and John Hsu, eds. *Asian American X: An Intersection of 21st Century Asian American Voices*. Ann Arbor, MI: University of Michigan Press, 2004.

Hardon, John. *History and Theology of Grace: The Catholic Teaching on Divine Grace*. Ave Maria, FL: Sapientia Press, 2002.

Harmless, William, ed. *Augustine in His Own Words* (Washington, DC: Catholic University of America Press, 2010).

Harries, Richard, ed. *Reinhold Niebuhr and the Issues of Our Time*. Grand Rapids, MI: William B. Eerdmans Publishing, 1986.

Harvey, Jennifer, Karin A. Case, and Robin Hawley Gorsline, eds. *Disrupting White Supremacy from Within: White People on What* We *Need to Do*. Cleveland, OH: Pilgrim Press, 2004.

Hayes, Zachary. *The Gift of Being: A Theology of Creation*. Collegeville, MN: Liturgical Press, 2001.

Heiner, Robert, ed. *Deviance Across Cultures*. New York: Oxford University Press, 2008.

Helminiak, Daniel A. *Sex and the Sacred: Gay Identity and Spiritual Growth*. Binghamton, NY: Harrington Park Press, 2006.

_________. *What the Bible* Really *Says About Homosexuality*. Millennium edition. Tajique, NM: Alamo Square Press, 2000.

Heyward, Carter. *Saving Jesus from Those Who Are Right: Rethinking What It Means to Be Christian*. Minneapolis, MN: Fortress Press, 1999.

_________. *Touching Our Strength: The Erotic As Power and the Love of God*. New York: HarperSanFrancisco, 1989.

Highleyman, Liz. "Kiyoshi Kuromiya: Integrating the Issues." In Mecca, *Smash the Church, Smash the State!*, 17–21.

Higton, Mike. *Christian Doctrine*. London: SCM Press, 2008.

Hill, Renée Leslie. "Disrupted/Disruptive Movements: Black Theology and Black Power 1969/1999," in Hopkins, *Black Faith and Public Talk*, 138–49.

Hopkins, Dwight N., ed. *Black Faith and Public Talk: Critical Essays on James H. Cone's* Black Theology and Black Power. Maryknoll, NY: Orbis Books, 1999.

Hornsby, Teresa J., and Ken Stone, eds. *Bible Trouble: Queer Reading at the Boundaries of Biblical Scholarship*. Atlanta: Society of Biblical Literature, 2011.

Horton, Michael. *Putting Amazing Back into Grace: Embracing the Heart of the Gospel*. 2nd edition. Grand Rapids, MI: Baker Books, 2002.

Hunt, Mary E. "Eradicating the Sin of Heterosexism." In Ellison and Plaskow, *Heterosexism in Contemporary World Religion: Problem and Prospect*, 155–76.

_________. *Fierce Tenderness: A Feminist Theology of Friendship*. New York: Crossroad, 1991.

_________. "New Feminist Catholics: Community and Ministry." In Hunt and Neu, *New Feminist Christianity*, 269–84.

_________. "Same-Sex Marriage and Relational Justice." *Journal of Feminist Studies in Religion* 20, no. 2 (Fall, 2004): 83–92.

Hunt, Mary E., and Diann L. Neu, eds. *New Feminist Christianity: Many Voices, Many Views*. Woodstock, VT: Skylight Paths, 2010.

Isherwood, Lisa. *Introducing Feminist Christologies*. Cleveland, OH: Pilgrim Press, 2002.

Isherwood, Lisa, and Mark D. Jordan. *Dancing Theology in Fetish Boots: Essays in Honour of Marcella Althaus-Reid*. London: SCM Press, 2010.

Jackson, Peter A., and Gerard Sullivan. *Multicultural Queer: Australian Narratives*. Binghamton, NY: Harrington Park Press, 1999.

Jacobs, Alan. *Original Sin: A Cultural History*. New York: HarperOne, 2008.

Jakobsen, Janet R., and Ann Pellegrini. *Love the Sin: Sexual Regulation and the Limits of Religious Tolerance*. New York: New York University Press, 2003.

Jeffery, Steve, Michael Ovey, and Andrew Sach. *Pierced for Our Transgressions: Rediscovering the Glory of Penal Substitution*. Wheaton, IL: Crossway Books, 2007.

Jenkins, Willis. *Ecologies of Grace: Environmental Ethics and Christian Theology*. Oxford, UK: Oxford University Press, 2008.

Jensen, David H., ed. *The Lord and Giver of Life: Perspectives on Constructive Pneumatology*. Louisville, KY: Westminster John Knox Press, 2008.

Jenson, Matt. *The Gravity of Sin: Augustine, Luther, and Barth on* Homo Incurvatus in Se. London: T&T Clark, 2006.

Johnson, Elizabeth A. *She Who Is: The Mystery of God in Feminist Theological Discourse*. New York: Crossroad, 1992.

Johnson, Timothy J., ed. *Bonaventure: Mystic of God's Word*. Hyde Park, NY: New City Press, 1999.

Jones, Serene. *Feminist Theory and Christian Theology: Cartographies of Grace*. Minneapolis, MN: Fortress Press, 2000.

_________. *Trauma and Grace: Theology in a Ruptured World*. Louisville, KY: Westminster John Knox Press, 2009.

Jordan, Mark D. *Telling Truths in Church: Scandal, Flesh, and Christian Speech*. Boston: Beacon Press, 2003.

_________. *The Invention of Sodomy in Christian Theology*. Chicago: University of Chicago Press, 1997.

_________. *The Silence of Sodom: Homosexuality in Modern Catholicism*. Chicago: University of Chicago Press, 2000.

Jorgenson, Allen. "Karl Barth's Christological Treatment of Sin." *Scottish Journal of Theology* 54, no. 4 (2001): 439–62.

Kaminsky, Joel S. *Corporate Responsibility in the Hebrew Bible*. Sheffield, UK: Sheffield Academic Press, 1995.

Kamitsuka, Margaret D. *Feminist Theology and the Challenge of Difference*. New York: Oxford University Press, 2007.

_________, ed. *The Embrace of Eros: Bodies, Desires, and Sexuality in Christianity*. Minneapolis, MN: Fortress Press, 2010.

_________. "Toward a Feminist Postmodern and Postcolonial Interpretation of Sin." *Journal of Religion* 84, no. 2 (April 2004): 179–211.

Kärkkäinen, Veli-Matti. *Christology: A Global Introduction*. Grand Rapids, MI: Baker Academic, 2003.

_________. *One with God: Salvation as Deification and Justification*. Collegeville, MI: Liturgical Press, 2004.

Karla, Virinder S., Raminder Kaur, and John Hutnyk. *Diaspora and Hybridity*. London: SAGE Publications, 2005.

Kaufman, Gershen, and Lev Raphael. *Coming Out of Shame: Transforming Gay and Lesbian Lives*. New York: Doubleday, 1996.

Kaui. "Kaui." In Matzner, *'O Au No Keia*, 90–113.

Kay, Kerwin, Jill Nagle, and Baruch Gould, eds. *Male Lust: Pleasure, Power, and Transformation*. Binghamton, NY: Harrington Park Press, 2000.

Keating, Daniel A. *Deification and Grace*. Ave Maria, FL: Sapientia Press, 2007.

Keller, Catherine, and Laurel C. Schneider, eds. *Polydoxy: Theology of Multiplicity and Relation*. London: Routledge, 2011.

Kelly, Michael Bernard. *Seduced By Grace: Contemporary Spirituality, Gay Experience and Christian Faith*. Melbourne, Australia: Clouds of Magellan Publishing, 2007.

Kelsey, David H. "Whatever Happened to the Doctrine of Sin?" *Theology Today* 50, no. 2 (July 1993): 169–78.

Kemmerer, Lisa, ed. *Sister Species: Women, Animals, and Social Justice*. Urbana, IL: University of Illinois Press, 2011.

Kharlamov, Vladimir, ed. *Theōsis: Deification in Christian Theology*. Volume 2. Eugene, OR: Pickwick Publications, 2011.

Kim, Michael. "Out and About: Coming of Age in a Straight White World." In Han and Hsu, *Asian American X*, 139–48.

Kleinberg, Aviad. *Seven Deadly Sins: A Very Partial List*. Cambridge, MA: Belknap Press, 2008.

Knitter, Paul F. *Introducing Theologies of Religions*. Maryknoll, NY: Orbis Books, 2002.

Kraidy, Marwan M. *Hybridity, or the Cultural Logic of Globalization*. Philadelphia: Temple University Press, 2005.

Kraus, Georg. "Grace." In Beinert and Fiorenza, *Handbook of Catholic Theology*, 302–10.

Kugle, Scott Siraj al-Haqq. *Homosexuality in Islam: Critical Reflection on Gay, Lesbian, and Transgender Muslims*. Oxford, UK: Oneworld Publications, 2010.

Kumashiro, Kevin K., ed. *Restoried Selves: Autobiographies of Queer Asian/Pacific American Activists*. Binghamton, NY: Harrington Park Press, 2004.

_________, ed. *Troubling Intersections of Race and Sexuality: Queer Students of Color and Anti-Oppressive Education*. Lanham, MD: Rowman and Littlefield Publishers, 2001.

Kwok Pui-lan. "Asian and Asian American Churches." In Siker, *Homosexuality and Religion*, 59–62.

_________. "Body and Pleasure in Postcoloniality." In Isherwood and Jordan, *Dancing Theology in Fetish Boots*, 31–43.

_________. *Hope Abundant: Third World and Indigenous Women's Theology*. Maryknoll, NY: Orbis Books, 2010.

_________. *Postcolonial Imagination and Feminist Theology*. Louisville, KY: Westminster John Knox Press, 2005.

Lake, Catherine, ed. *Recreations: Religion and Spirituality in the Lives of Queer People*. Toronto, Canada: Queer Press, 1999.

Lee, David C. "All-American Asian." In Kumashiro, *Restoried Selves*, 73–80.

Lee, Jung Young. *Marginality: The Key to Multicultural Theology*. Minneapolis, MN: Fortress Press, 1995.

Leong, Russell, ed. *Asian American Sexualities: Dimensions of the Gay and Lesbian Experience*. New York: Routledge, 1996.

Leyland, Winston, ed. *Queer Dharma: Voices of Gay Buddhists*. San Francisco: Gay Sunshine Press, 1998.

Liew, Tat-siong Benny. "(Cor)Responding: A Letter to the Editor." In Stone, *Queer Commentary and the Hebrew Bible*, 182–92.

_________. "Queering Closets and Perverting Desires: Cross-Examining John's Engendering and Transgendering Word Across Different Worlds." In Bailey, Liew, and Segovia, *They Were All Together in One Place?*, 251–88.

Lim-Hing, Sharon, ed. *The Very Inside: An Anthology of Writing by Asian and Pacific Islander Lesbian and Bisexual Women*. Toronto, Canada: Sister Vision Press, 1994.

Lohse, Bernhard. *A Short History of Christian Doctrine: From the First Century to the Present*. Revised American edition. Philadelphia, PA: Fortress Press, 1985.

Long, Ronald E. *Men, Homosexuality, and the Gods: An Exploration into the Religious Significance of Male Homosexuality in World Perspective*. Binghamton, NY: Harrington Park Press, 2004.

Lorde, Audre. "Uses of the Erotic: The Erotic as Power." In Ellison and Douglas, *Sexuality and the Sacred*, 73–77.

Lowe, Mary E. "Sin from a Queer, Lutheran Perspective." In Streufert, *Transformative Lutheran Theologies*, 71–86.

Luther, Martin. *Lectures on Genesis*. Vol. 3 of *Luther's Works*. Edited by Jaroslav Pelikan. St. Louis, MO: Concordia Publishing House, 1961.

_________. *Lectures on Romans*. Vol. 25 of *Luther's Works*. Edited by Hilton C. Oswald. St. Louis, MO: Concordia Publishing House, 1972.

Malik, Alexander J. "Confessing Christ in the Islamic Context." In Sugirtharajah, *Asian Faces of Jesus*, 75–84.

Maloney, George A. *The Cosmic Christ: From Paul to Teilhard*. New York: Sheed and Ward, 1968.

Mann, Jeff. "Binding the God." In Evans and Healey, *Queer and Catholic*, 61–72.

Marcus, Eric. *Making Gay History: The Half-Century Fight for Lesbian and Gay Rights*. New York: Harper, 2002.

Martin, Bernard. *John Newton: A Biography*. Melbourne: William Heinemann, 1950.

Masequesmay, Gina, and Sean Metzger, eds. *Embodying Asian/American Sexualities*. Lanham, MD: Lexington Books, 2009.

Matzner, Andrew. *'O Au No Keia: Voices From Hawai'i's Mahu and Transgender Communities*. Bloomington, IN: Xlibris Corporation, 2001.

May, Gerald G. *Addiction and Grace: Love and Spirituality in the Healing of Addictions*. New York: HarperOne, 1988.

May, Larry, and Stacey Hoffman, eds. *Collective Responsibility: Five Decades of Debate in Theoretical and Applied Ethics*. Lanham, MD: Roman and Littlefield Publishers, 1991.

McFague, Sallie. *Models of God: Theology for a Ecological, Nuclear Age*. Philadelphia, PA: Fortress Press, 1987.

_________. *The Body of God: An Ecological Theology*. Minneapolis, MN: Fortress Press, 1993.

McFarland, Ian A. *In Adam's Fall: A Meditation on the Christian Doctrine of Original Sin*. Malden, MA: Wiley-Blackwell, 2010.

McLaughlin, Eleanor. "Feminist Christologies: Re-Dressing the Tradition." In Stevens, *Reconstructing the Christ Symbol*, 118–49.

McMinn, Mark R. *Sin and Grace in Christian Counseling: An Integrative Paradigm*. Downers Grove, IL: IVP Academic, 2008.

McNally, Terrence. *Corpus Christi: A Play*. New York: Grove Press, 1998.

McNeill, John J. *Freedom, Glorious Freedom: The Spiritual Journey to the Fullness of Life for Gays, Lesbians, and Everybody Else*. Boston: Beacon Press, 1995.

Mecca, Tommi Avicolli, ed. *Smash the Church, Smash the State!: The Early Years of Gay Liberation*. San Francisco: City Lights Books, 2009.

Meem, Deborah T., Michelle A. Gibson, and Jonathan F. Alexander, eds. *Finding Out: An Introduction to LGBT Studies*. Los Angeles: SAGE Publications, 2010.

Mellema, Gregory F. *Collective Responsibility*. Amsterdam, Netherlands: Rodopi, 1997.

Menninger, Karl. *Whatever Became of Sin?* New York: Bantam Books, 1973.

Mercadante, Linda A. *Victims and Sinners: Spiritual Roots of Addiction and Recovery*. Louisville, KY: Westminster John Knox Press, 1996.

Metropolitan Community Church Transgender Ministries. *MCC TRANSFormative Church Ministry Program*. Available at mcctm@mccchurch.net.

Michaelson, Jay. *God vs. Gay?: The Religious Case for Equality*. Boston: Beacon Press, 2011.

Migliore, Daniel L. "Commanding Grace: Karl Barth's Theological Ethics." In Migliore, ed., *Commanding Grace*, 1–25.

__________, ed. *Commanding Grace: Studies in Karl Barth's Ethics*. Grand Rapids, MI: William B. Eerdmans Publishing, 2010.

Miller, Neil. *Out of the Past: Gay and Lesbian History: From 1869 to the Present*. Revised edition. New York: Alyson Books, 2006.

Minns, Denis. *Irenaeus: An Introduction*. London: T&T Clark International, 2010.

Mohammed, Ovey N. "Jesus and Krishna." In Sugirtharajah, *Asian Faces of Jesus*, 9–24.

Mollenkott, Virginia Ramey. *Sensuous Spirituality: Out from Fundamentalism*. New York: Crossroad, 1992.

__________. *Omnigender: A Trans-Religious Approach*. Cleveland, OH: Pilgrim Press, 2001.

Mollenkott, Virginia Ramey, and Vanessa Sheridan. *Transgender Journeys*. Cleveland, OH: Pilgrim Press, 2003.

Montefiore, H.W. "Jesus, The Revelation of God." In Pittenger, *Christ for Us Today*, 101–16.

Moon, Dawne. *God, Sex, and Politics: Homosexuality and Everyday Theologies*. Chicago: University of Chicago Press, 2004.

Moore, Gareth. *A Question of Truth: Christianity and Homosexuality*. London, UK: Continuum, 2003.

Moxnes, Halvor. *Putting Jesus in His Place: A Radical Vision of Household and Kingdom*. Louisville, KY: Westminster John Knox Press, 2003.

Murphy, Jeffrie G. *Punishment and Rehabilitation*. 3rd edition. Belmont, CA: Wadsworth Publishing, 1995.

Nelson, Derek R. *What's Wrong with Sin?: Sin in Individual and Social Perspective from Schleiermacher to Theologies of Liberation*. London: T&T Clark, 2009.

Nelson, James B. "Where Are We?: Seven Sinful Problems and Seven Virtuous Possibilities." In Ellison and Douglas, *Sexuality and the Sacred*, 95–104.

Nelson, James B., and Sandra P. Longfellow, eds. *Sexuality and the Sacred: Sources for Theological Reflection*. Louisville, KY: Westminster/John Knox Press, 1994.

Newton, John. "Amazing Grace." 1779.

Niebuhr, Reinhold. *The Nature and Destiny of Man: A Christian Interpretation*. New York: Charles Scribner's Sons, 1941.

Nimmons, David. *The Soul Beneath the Skin: The Unseen Hearts and Habits of Gay Men*. New York: St. Martin's Griffin, 2002.

Ormerod, Neil. *Creation, Grace, and Redemption*. Maryknoll, NY: Orbis Books, 2007.

Osborn, Eric. *Irenaeus of Lyons*. Cambridge, UK: Cambridge University Press, 2001.

Pagels, Elaine. *Adam, Eve, and the Serpent: Sex and Politics in Early Christianity*. New York: Vintage Books, 1988.

Palmer, Timothy, and Debra W. Haffner. *A Time to Seek: Study Guide on Sexual and Gender Diversity*. Available at http://www.religiousinstitute.org/sites/default/files/study_guides/timetoseek-final.pdf. Accessed on December 11, 2011.

Park, Andrew Sung. *The Wounded Heart of God: The Asian Concept of Han and the Christian Doctrine of Sin*. Nashville, TN: Abingdon Press, 1993.

Park, Pauline. "An Interview with Pauline Park." In Masequesmay and Metzger, *Embodying Asian/American Sexualities*, 105–13.

Paris, Jenell Williams. *The End of Sexual Identity: Why Sex Is Too Important to Define Who We Are*. Downers Grove, IL: IVP Books, 2011.

Perry, Troy. *The Lord Is My Shepherd and He Knows I'm Gay*. Los Angeles: Nash Publishing, 1972.

Peterson, Thomas V. "Gay Men's Spiritual Experience in the Leather Community." In Thumma and Gray, *Gay Religion*, 337–50.

Philo. *On Abraham*. In Philo, *The Works of Philo*, 411–34.

_________. *The Works of Philo*. Edited and translated by C.D. Yonge. New updated edition. Peabody, MA: Hendrickson Publishers, Inc., 1993.

Pinn, Anthony B., and Dwight N. Hopkins, eds. *Loving the Body: Black Religious Studies and the Erotic*. New York: Palgrave Macmillan, 2004.

Pittenger, Norman, ed. *Christ for Us Today*. London: SCM Press, 1968.

Plantinga, Cornelius. *Not the Way It's Supposed to Be: A Breviary of Sin*. Grand Rapids, MI: William B. Eerdmans Publishing, 1995.

Plaskow, Judith. *Sex, Sin and Grace: Women's Experience and the Theologies of Reinhold Niebuhr and Paul Tillich*. Washington, DC: University Press of America, 1980.

Portman, John. *A History of Sin: Its Evolution to Today and Beyond*. Lanham, MD: Rowman and Littlefield Publishers, 2007.

Prabhu, Anjali. *Hybridity: Limits, Transformations, Prospects*. Albany, NY: State University of New York Press, 2007.

Quinn, Philip L., and Charles Taliaferro, eds. *A Companion to Philosophy of Religion*. Malden, MA: Blackwell Publishing, 1997.

Ratti, Rakesh, ed. *A Lotus of Another Color: An Unfolding of the South Asian Gay and Lesbian Experience*. Boston: Alyson Publications, 1993.

Recinos, Harold J., and Hugo Magallanes, eds. *Jesus in the Hispanic Community: Images of Christ from Theology to Popular Religion*. Louisville, KY: Westminster John Knox Press, 2009.

Rees, Geoffrey. *The Romance of Innocent Sexuality*. Eugene, OR: Cascade Books, 2011.

Reynolds, Thomas E. *Vulnerable Communion: A Theology of Disability and Hospitality*. Grand Rapids, MI: Brazos Press, 2008.

Richardson, Alan, and John Bowden, eds. *The Westminster Dictionary of Christian Theology*. Philadelphia, PA: The Westminster Press, 1983.

Robertson, Alexander, and James Donaldson, eds. *Ante-Nicene Fathers*. 10 vols. Reprint ed. Peabody, MA: Hendrickson Publishers, 2004.

Roden, Frederick Roden, ed. *Jewish/Christian/Queer: Crossroads and Identities*. Farnham, UK: Ashgate, 2009.

Rogers, Eugene F. "The Spirit Rests on the Son Paraphysically." In Jensen, *The Lord and Giver of Life*, 87–95.

_________, ed. *Theology and Sexuality: Classic and Contemporary Readings*. Oxford, UK: Blackwell Publishers, 2002.

Rudy, Kathy. *Sex and the Church: Gender, Homosexuality, and the Transformation of Christian Ethics*. Boston: Beacon Press, 1997.

Ruether, Rosemary Radford. *Gaia and God: An Ecofeminist Theology of Earth Healing*. New York: HarperOne, 1992.

_________. *Integrating Ecofeminism, Globalization, and World Religions*. Lanham, MD: Rowman and Littlefield Publishers, 2005.

_________. *Sexism and God-Talk: Toward a Feminist Theology*. Boston: Beacon Press, 1983.

_________. *Women Healing Earth: Third World Women on Ecology, Feminism, and Religion*. Maryknoll, NY: Orbis Books, 1996.

Russell, Norman. *Fellow Workers with God: Orthodox Thinking on Theosis*. Crestwood, NY: St. Vladimir's Seminary Press, 2009.

_________. *The Doctrine of Deification in the Greek Patristic Tradition*. Oxford, UK: Oxford University Press, 2004.

Saiving Goldstein, Valerie. "The Human Situation: A Feminine View." *Journal of Religion* 40, no. 2 (April 1960): 100–12.

Samartha, Stanley J. "The Cross and the Rainbow: Christ in a Multireligious Culture." In Sugirtharajah, *Asian Faces of Jesus*, 104–23.

Sanders, E.P. "Sin, Sinners (NT)." In Freedman, *Anchor Yale Bible Dictionary*, 6:40–47.

Schaff, Philip, ed. *Nicene and Post-Nicene Fathers*. First series. 14 vols. Reprint ed. Peabody, MA: Hendrickson Publishers, 2004.

_________. *The Creeds of Christendom: With a History and Critical Notes*. 6th edition. Grand Rapids, MI: Baker Books, 2007.

_________. *The Greek and Latin Creeds*. Volume 2 of Schaff, *The Creeds of Christendom*.

Schaff, Philip, and Henry Wace, eds. *Nicene and Post-Nicene Fathers*. Second series. 14 vols. Reprint ed. Peabody, MA: Hendrickson Publishers, 2004.

Schmiechen, Peter. *Saving Power: Theories of Atonement and Forms of the Church*. Grand Rapids, MI: William B. Eerdmans Publishing, 2005.

Schneider, Laurel C. "Promiscuous Incarnation." In Kamitsuka, *The Embrace of Eros*, 231–46.

_________. "What If It Is a Choice?: Some Implications of the Homosexuality Debates for Theology." In Ellison and Douglas, *Sexuality and the Sacred*, 197–204.

_________. "What Race Is Your Sex?" In Harvey, Case, and Gorsline, *Disrupting White Supremacy from Within*, 142–62.

Schreiter, Robert J., ed. *Faces of Jesus in Africa*. Maryknoll, NY: Orbis Books, 1991.

Schwager, Raymund. *Must There Be Scapegoats?: Violence and Redemption in the Bible*. Translated by Maria L. Assad. San Francisco: Harper and Row, 1987.

Sedgwick, Eve Kosofsky. *Epistemology of the Closet*. Updated edition. Berkeley, CA: University of California Press, 2008.

Sheldrake, Philip. *Befriending Our Desires*. London: Darton, Longman, and Todd, 2001.

Sheridan, Vanessa. *Crossing Over: Liberating the Transgendered Christian*. Cleveland, OH: Pilgrim Press, 2001.

Shore-Goss, Robert E. "Gay and Lesbian Theologies." In Floyd-Thomas and Pinn, *Liberation Theologies in the United States*, 181–208.

Shrake, Eunai. "Homosexuality and Korean Immigrant Protestant Churches." In Masequesmay and Metzger, *Embodying Asian/American Sexualities*, 145–56.

Shuster, Marguerite. *The Fall and Sin: What We Have Become as Sinners*. Grand Rapids, MI: William B. Eerdmans Publishing, 2004.

Siker, Jeffrey S., ed. *Homosexuality and Religion: An Encyclopedia*. Westport, CT: Greenwood Press, 2007.

Sittler, Joseph. *Evocations of Grace: Writings on Ecology, Theology, and Ethics*. Grand Rapids, MI: William B. Eerdmans Publishing, 2000.

Smedes, Lewis B. *Shame and Grace: Healing the Shame We Don't Deserve*. New York: HarperSanFrancisco, 1993.

Smith, Christine M. "Sin and Evil in Feminist Thought." *Theology Today* 50, no. 2 (July 1993): 208–19.

Smith, David L. *With Willful Intent: A Theology of Sin*. Wheaton, IL: BridgePoint Books, 1993.

Smith, Morton. *Clement of Alexandria and a Secret Gospel of Mark*. Cambridge, MA: Harvard University Press, 1973.

_________. *The Secret Gospel: The Discovery and Interpretation of the Secret Gospel According to Mark*. Middletown, CA: Dawn Horse Press, 1982.

Sneed, Roger A. *Representations of Homosexuality: Black Liberation Theology and Cultural Criticism*. New York: Palgrave Macmillan, 2010.

Sölle, Dorothee. *Thinking About God: An Introduction to Theology*. Harrisburg, PA: Trinity Press International, 1990.

Spencer, Daniel T. *Gay and Gaia: Ethics, Ecology, and the Erotic*. Cleveland, OH: Pilgrim Press, 1996.

Spong, John Shelby. *The Sins of Scripture: Exposing the Bible's Texts of Hate to Reveal the God of Love*. New York: HarperOne, 2005.

Sprinkle, Stephen V. *Unfinished Lives: Reviving the Memories of LGBTQ Hate Crimes Victims*. Eugene, OR: Resource Publications, 2011.

Steenberg, M.C. *Irenaeus on Creation: The Cosmic Christ and the Saga of Redemption*. Leiden, Netherlands: Brill, 2008.

Steinberg, Leo. *The Sexuality of Christ in Renaissance Art and in Modern Oblivion*. 2nd edition. Chicago: University of Chicago Press, 1996.

Stevens, Maryanne, ed. *Reconstructing the Christ Symbol: Essays in Feminist*

Christology. New York: Paulist Press, 1993.

Stinton, Diane B. *Jesus of Africa: Voices of Contemporary African Christology*. Maryknoll, NY: Orbis Books, 2004.

Stone, Ken, ed. *Queer Commentary and the Hebrew Bible*. Cleveland, OH: Pilgrim Press, 2001.

Streufert, Mary J., ed. *Transformative Lutheran Theologies: Feminist, Womanist, and Mujerista Perspectives*. Minneapolis, MN: Fortress Press, 2010.

Stuart, Elizabeth. *Gay and Lesbian Theologies: Repetitions with Critical Difference*. Aldershot, UK: Ashgate, 2003.

__________. *Just Good Friends: Towards a Lesbian and Gay Theology of Relationships*. London: Mowbray, 1995.

__________. "Salvation." In Stuart, Braunston, Edwards, McMahon, and Morrison, *Religion Is a Queer Thing*, 86–95.

Stuart, Elizabeth, Andy Braunston, Malcolm Edwards, John McMahon, and Tim Morrison, eds. *Religion Is a Queer Thing: A Guide to the Christian Faith for Lesbian, Gay, Bisexual and Transgendered People*. Cleveland, OH: Pilgrim Press, 1997.

Suchocki, Marjorie Hewitt. *The Fall to Violence: Original Sin in Relational Theology*. New York: Continuum, 1994.

Sugirtharajah, R.S., ed. *Asian Faces of Jesus*. Maryknoll, NY: Orbis Books, 1993.

Swidler, Arlene, ed. *Homosexuality and World Religions*. Valley Forge, PA: Trinity Press International, 1993.

"*Symbolum Quicunque*: The Athanasian Creed." In Schaff, *The Greek and Latin Creeds*, 66–71.

Tanis, Justin. *Trans-Gendered: Theology, Ministry, and Communities of Faith*. Cleveland, OH: Pilgrim Press, 2003.

Tashman, Brian. "Robertson: God Will Destroy America for Marriage Equality" (June 27, 2011). Available at http://www.rightwingwatch.org/content/robertson-god-will-destroy-america-marriage-equality. Accessed on December 11, 2011.

Taylor, Barbara Brown. *Speaking of Sin: The Lost Language of Salvation*. Lanham, MD: Cowley Publications, 2000.

Terrell, JoAnne Marie. *Power in the Blood?: The Cross in the African American Experience*. Maryknoll, NY: Orbis Books, 1998.

Thistlethwaite, Susan Brooks. *Dreaming of Eden: American Religion and Politics in a Wired World*. New York: Palgrave Macmillan, 2010.

__________. *Sex, Race, and God: Christian Feminism in Black and White*. New York: Crossroad, 1989.

Thomson, Oliver. *A History of Sin*. Edinburgh: Canongate Press, 1993.

Thumma, Scott, and Edward R. Gray, eds. *Gay Religion*. Walnut Creek, CA: AltaMira Press, 2005.

Townes, Emilie M., ed. *A Troubling in My Soul: Womanist Perspectives on Evil and Suffering*. Maryknoll, NY: Orbis Books, 1993.

__________. *Womanist Ethics and the Cultural Production of Evil*. New York: Palgrave Macmillan, 2006.

Tran, Diep Khac, Bryan, and Rhode, eds. "Transgender/Transsexual Roundtable." In Eng and Hom, *Q&A*, 227–43.

Tran, William. "GAM4GWM." In Kumashiro, *Troubling Intersections of Race and Sexuality*, 81–82.

Trible, Phyllis. *Texts of Terror: Literary-Feminist Readings of Biblical Narratives*. Philadelphia: Fortress Press, 1984.

Uyeda, Ann Yuri. "All at Once, All Together: One Asian American Lesbian's Account of the 1989 Asian Pacific Lesbian Network Retreat." In Lim-Hing, *The Very Inside*, 109–21.

Verbrugge, Verlyn D., ed. *New International Dictionary of New Testament Theology*. Abridged edition. Grand Rapids, MI: Zondervan, 2000.

Villafañe, Eldin. *Beyond Cheap Grace: A Call to Radical Discipleship, Incarnation and Justice*. Grand Rapids, MI: William B. Eerdmans Publishing, 2006.

Walker, Jon. *Costly Grace: A Contemporary View of Dietrich Bonhoeffer's* The Cost of Discipleship. Abilene, TX: Leafwood Publishers, 2010.

Warner, Michael. *The Trouble with Normal: Sex, Politics, and the Ethics of Queer Life*. Cambridge, MA: Harvard University Press, 1999.

Wat, Eric C. "Preserving the Paradox: Stories From a *Gay-Loh*." In Leong, *Asian American Sexualities*, 71–80.

_________. *The Making of a Gay Asian Community: An Oral History of Pre-AIDS Los Angeles*. Lanham, MD: Rowman and Littlefield Publishers, 2002.

Webb, William J. *Slaves, Women and Homosexuals: Exploring the Hermeneutics of Cultural Analysis*. Downers Grove, IL: InterVarsity Press, 2001.

Weiss, Robert. *Cruise Control: Understanding Sex Addiction in Gay Men*. Los Angeles, CA: Alyson Books, 2005.

West, Traci C. "A Space for Faith, Sexual Desire, and Ethical Black Ministerial Practices." In Pinn and Hopkins, *Loving the Body*, 31–50.

_________. *Disruptive Christian Ethics: When Racism and Women's Lives Matter*. Louisville, KY: Westminster John Knox Press, 2006.

White, Mel. *Stranger at the Gate: To Be Gay and Christian in America*. New York: Plume, 1994.

Wilchins, Riki. *Queer Theory, Gender Theory: An Instant Primer*. Los Angeles: Alyson Books, 2004.

Wilcox, Melissa M. "Queer Theory and the Study of Religion." In Boisvert and Johnson, *Queer Religion*, 2:227–51.

Wiley, Tatha. *Original Sin: Origins, Developments, Contemporary Meanings*. New York: Paulist Press, 2002.

Williams, Delores S. "Sin, Nature, and Black Women's Bodies." In Adams, *Ecofeminism and the Sacred*, 24–29.

Williams, Robert. *Just as I Am: A Practical Guide to Being Out, Proud and Christian*. New York: HarperPerennial, 1992.

Wilson, Nancy. *Our Tribe: Queer Folks, God, Jesus, and the Bible*. New York: HarperSanFrancisco, 1995.

Wimberly, Edward P. *Moving from Shame to Self-Worth: Preaching and Pastoral Care*. Nashville, TN: Abingdon Press, 1999.

Wood, Robert W. *Christ and the Homosexual (Some Observations)*. New York: Vantage Press, 1960.

Yagi, Seiichi. "Christ and Buddha." In Sugirtharajah, *Asian Faces of Jesus*, 25–45.

Yancey, Philip. *What's So Amazing About Grace?* Grand Rapids, MI: Zondervan, 1997.

Yip, Lai Shan. "Listening to the Passion of Catholic *nu-tongzhi*: Developing a Catholic Lesbian Feminist Theology in Hong Kong." In Boisvert and Johnson, Queer Religion, 2:63–80.

Yoshikawa, Yoko. "The Heat Is on *Miss Saigon* Coalition: Organizing Across Race and Sexuality." In Eng and Hom, *Q&A*, 41–56.

Yoshino, Kenji. *Covering: The Hidden Assault on Our Civil Rights*. New York: Random House, 2006.

Zahl, Paul F.M. *Grace in Practice: A Theology of Everyday Life*. Grand Rapids, MI: William B. Eerdmans Publishing, 2007.

Index

M

N

O

P

Q

R

S

About the Author

Patrick S. Cheng is the Assistant Professor of Historical and Systematic Theology at the Episcopal Divinity School in Cambridge, Massachusetts. He is the author of *From Sin to Amazing Grace: Discovering the Queer Christ* (Seabury, 2012) and *Radical Love: An Introduction to Queer Theology* (Seabury, 2011). He has contributed chapters to the second edition of *Sexuality and the Sacred* (WJK, 2010) and *The Queer Bible Commentary* (SCM, 2006), and his articles have appeared in a number of peer-reviewed journals, including *CrossCurrents*, *Spiritus*, *Journal of Feminist Studies in Religion*, and *Semeia*. Dr. Cheng holds a Ph.D., M.Phil., and M.A. from Union Theological Seminary in New York, a J.D. from Harvard Law School, and a B.A. from Yale College. He writes for the *Huffington Post* and is an ordained minister with the Metropolitan Community Churches. For more information about Dr. Cheng, see http://www.patrickcheng.net.